D1563514

COMMONSENSE
COASTAL
NAVIGATION

Also by Hewitt Schlereth

COMMONSENSE CELESTIAL NAVIGATION

COMMONSENSE SAILBOAT BUYING

COMMONSENSE

COASTAL

NAVIGATION

—·—

HEWITT SCHLERETH

W·W·NORTON & COMPANY
New York · London

Library of Congress Cataloging in Publication Data

Schlereth, Hewitt.
    Commonsense coastal navigation.

    Bibliography: p.
    Includes index.
    1. Coastwise navigation. I. Title.
VK559.S34 1982   623.89'2   81–38407
ISBN 0–393–03224–8   AACR2

W. W. Norton & Company, Inc. 500 Fifth Avenue, New York, N.Y. 10110
W. W. Norton & Company Ltd. 37 Great Russell Street, London WC1B 3NV

Book design by Jacques Chazaud

1 2 3 4 5 6 7 8 9 0

To
Life on the Water

The days passed happily with me wherever my ship sailed.
JOSHUA SLOCUM

The greatest hazard to navigation is a bored navigator.
ANONYMOUS

Contents

———————

Preface

—— —— ——

This book has two sources.

The first came about during the years I worked as a yacht broker and discovered that most buyers were quite new to boating and were unaware of some very basic facts about life on the water. I found, for example, that in addition to showing my customers how to operate engines, winches, and stoves, I needed to give them a flash course in the rules of the road. From this need developed the basic content of the first chapter of each part of the book.

The second impetus came in the form of a request from the members of a local yacht club that I give them a course in piloting—a term commonly used for what I prefer to call coastal navigation: navigation using shore objects as reference.

This group was composed about equally of people who had bought boats from me, had kept their boats at my yard, and had studied celestial with me following the publication of my first book. In any case, the group consisted primarily of professionals and independent businessmen, people who were quite accustomed to using their own minds to reason from first principles and who would, therefore, prefer to be shown rather than told navigation.

With this in mind and also aware that the equipment on the boats of these individuals ranged from basic through very sophisticated, I decided to stick to the basics applicable to all navigation, to try to elucidate the fact that navigation is two things: (1) a dead reckoning track, or DR, and (2) methods of checking up on this DR. Since I knew from practice that high-precision measurements are not generally achievable in small boats, I decided to stick to the methods of checking the DR that I had found most appropriate as navigator in my own and other people's boats. Accordingly I began a series of eight two-hour sessions with this group by showing them the tide table contained in Part I, Chapter 9 and explaining the fundamental mechanics underlying its usefulness.

The reaction of the group to this added a lot to my constant belief that people prefer to understand things, not to do them by rote. It is really more fun and, finally, on that day when the radar, Loran, Omega, Omni, ADF, Satnav, and all the other marvels decide to pack it in, you'll still get there by keeping the DR and a good lookout.

Old Log Inn
Rowayton, Connecticut
June 30, 1981

COMMONSENSE

COASTAL

NAVIGATION

Introduction

The Minnow and the Whale

In the deep ocean a whale has as much freedom of move-
ment as a minnow. As whale and minnow approach
shore, however, there soon comes a time when the whale's
freedom begins to be restricted. His need for precise navigation becomes acute as the bottom angles toward the surface, but the minnow can swim practically onto the beach
in perfect safety. As a coastwise navigator the minnow
effectively works in a bigger sea than the whale; there are
more places he can safely go, and so fewer places he can get
into trouble.

Navigationally, a relationship like that of the whale and
the minnow exists between the needs of a ship and a yacht.
What is a hazard to a ship may be no hazard at all to a small
boat. At the entrance to Long Island Sound, for example,
there is a buoy marking Valiant Rock. Well, Valiant Rock is
some twenty feet under water at mean low tide so for most
yachts the buoy doesn't need to be there. For a loaded
tanker it is another matter altogether.

Small boats are also more maneuverable than ships and so can approach hazards more closely because they can dodge at the last moment. A sailboat suddenly coming upon a rock awash a few hundred feet ahead can alter course and get away. A tanker might need a mile or more to make such a maneuver and so precise knowledge of her position at all times is critical.

This point was impressed on me very strongly near the end of the Marblehead–Halifax race of 1973. I was navigator on *Calypso*, a forty-three-foot yawl and we were running east for the turning-mark into Halifax harbor. We were going eight knots under chute in a very heavy fog that had been with us since Cape Sable. From the helm you could just see the lookout standing in the bow pulpit.

Finding the buoy that marked the turn north into Halifax harbor and the finish was obviously very important and somewhat difficult under the circumstances, but I didn't expect any undue difficulty because we had been successfully running along the sequence of buoys leading to our turning-mark and finding them as the time came up on my stopwatch. Well, the time for this buoy came up and I stuck my head out of the companionway and asked if anyone saw the mark. A few minutes passed, the fog swirled around, and nobody said a word. Then the lookout said, "There it is—to port." Seconds later, the helmsman confirmed the sighting. I, however, did not see the buoy. "What color was it?" I asked. Both lookout and helmsman said it was black. Since the Canadian buoyage system is similar to that in the United States, this was the correct color for the inbound side of the channel into Halifax and a rough confirmation that the two men had seen the buoy even though I had not. It was entirely possible that I had missed it in the fog and early morning light.

Nevertheless, after giving the course and time to the finish, I went below and sat down to watch the depthfinder. Now, the channel into Halifax at this buoy is fifty-nine fathoms deep, but just to the left (west) of the course up the channel the depth is twenty-two fathoms and there is a set of rocks called The Sisters. Sure enough, the depthfinder showed nearly sixty fathoms and I began to relax a little. That's when the depthfinder went to twenty fathoms! As I leaped for the companionway, I heard the lookout yell "rocks" and felt the boat lurch as the helmsman jibed her all standing.

As I got to the cockpit, the rocks were in sight to leeward, the boat stalled with wind abeam and spinnaker plastered the mast and fore-rigging. Main and mizzen were swiftly sheeted home and we beat our way out of there, just lugging the spinnaker.

Here's the point: If a ship had made this mistake and turned inside the buoy, she'd have been doomed at the turn—no way to stop her in time. We, however, minnow-like, were able to dodge at the last instant and escape again to sea.

The above is not meant to suggest that small boats can be navigated carelessly; quite the contrary. In the race we were conning our boat about as well as we could, given the circumstances and equipment available and appropriate to a yacht of our type. The point is that the instruments and methods of navigation appropriate to small boats do not permit decimal-point precision, but this is offset to a huge degree by the fact that both the margin for error and the ability to correct it is greater.

Since navigation of ships in coastal waters is quite a critical matter, the space and equipment devoted to it are normally quite extensive. There are large compasses which can give the course to one-half degree; highly accurate speed-and-distance instruments; radar, sonar; Omega; and two or more officers whose sole job is the navigation of the ship and who work at a large chart table upon which any chart can be spread without folding. Naturally, this is proper and appropriate for a ship that needs careful, accurate, and continual conning in what are to her confining coastal waters.

But what about us, the minnows, in our boats that are forty feet or less in length? There simply isn't room for the stuff a ship can carry, nor the money, nor anyone, as a rule, who can spend full-time navigating.

Well, first of all, remember that due to scale a small boat sails in a wider sea and is more agile than a ship. Navigating need not be the continual, concentrated thing it is on a ship. Simpler and somewhat rougher methods can be adopted which, with an alert helmsman, will keep the boat out of trouble. Furthermore, since most of us sail shorthanded with small and often very young crews, it makes sense to adopt methods that will enable a large part of the navigating to be done from the cockpit, since more than likely the skipper is also helmsman, navigator, and deck ape.

This book, then, is a compilation of methods and techniques that I have learned and used over the years, have worked well for me, and seem appropriate to the piloting of small boats where a large part of the work must be carried on in the cockpit in the midst of other concerns.

The book is divided into three parts to make the job of learning easier and also to put the text into line with the natural progression of a new boatman's requirements: first one has to learn to get around during the day, then at night, then in fog. Come to think of it, there are some few parts of the world where fog is not of active concern to boatmen— so that particular body of knowledge can be ignored by the lucky fellows who have fogless boating. Even they will have moments of limited visibility on rainy days and nights.

The methods and techniques discussed in this book are based on the consideration that the skipper is usually both navigator and helmsman, and consequently his ability to spend time with charts and tables is limited. So we concentrate here on the things that can be done from the helm by observation of shore, water, and sky and by use of simple instruments that can be carried in a pocket. In using this book bear in mind that the *principles* of these methods are not different from those used to navigate ships. Rather, the utilization of the principles is carried out with different, fewer, and less precise *instruments*. If this should cause concern, consider that the Polynesians make long oceanic voyages among their islands without any instruments—not even a compass. Much can be learned by knowing what to look *for* and what to look *at* in the natural world around you. It is one of the great pleasures of being on the water.

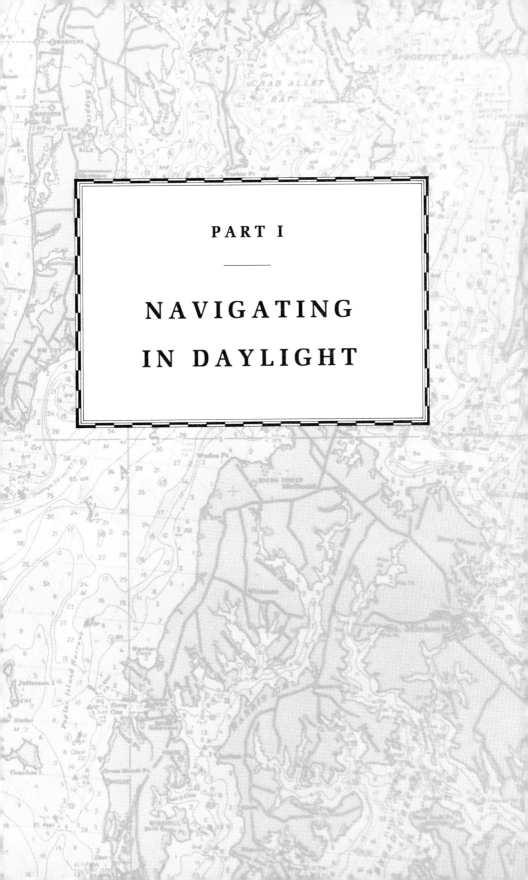

PART I

NAVIGATING
IN DAYLIGHT

1

Rules
of the Road

If you are new to boating and have just bought your first boat, before you do anything you are going to want to get out on the water in it and try it out. Being human, you are not going to want to plunge into the mysteries of the nautical road map—the chart—or delve into books like this one. That can come later, when you want to roam farther afield than your immediate area. First you want to go boating and get the feel of your new toy.

To do this safely and without embarrassment about all you need to know at first are a few simple conventions which are called the rules of the road. You may be surprised—and then delighted—to find out that nautical rules are similar to those that apply on the streets around your house. Before we get to the rules, though, we've got to discuss the road.

Briefly, a nautical road is called a channel and is the fairway of relatively deep water that leads into and out of harbors, which in densely populated areas are boat parking lots. Just as cars are not parked in the middle of a freeway, boats don't anchor in the channel.

To help you stay in the channel the sides are marked by a system of buoys—red buoys on one side and black buoys on the other. The convention here is that red buoys are on the right side of the channel if you are going into a harbor. The time-honored way of remembering this is the three R's—Red Right Returning (to harbor). So when you are coming into port, you keep the red buoys to your right; when you are leaving, you keep them on your left (except in British or Bermudan waters, where the colors are reversed!). A sharp turn or corner in a channel will often be marked by a buoy with horizontal red and black bands; the color of the top band indicates whether it is to be treated as a red or black buoy. If you get into the habit of looking as far ahead of your boat as you can, you will usually be able to see the pattern and establish the fairway.

Once you are underway in the channel, go slowly, but not so slowly that the boat is unresponsive. You will get along fine if you apply the rules you know for driving: drive on the right side of the channel. If you come to an intersection with another channel, the guy on your right has the right-of-way. Be very careful, though. If you are the guy on the right, the other fellow may misjudge your relative velocities or may simply be fuzzy about who has the right-of-way.

Once you are clear of the harbor and have set sail (or opened the throttle a bit), you are in a freer and less restricted environment. Open water, unlike a road, can be traveled freely in any direction. Here the direction from A to B is not "go up the road and turn left." It's "point the bow at B and go directly there."

Even in open water, however, there will be other boats, so conventions must be observed to prevent collisions. Here are some possible situations:

1. You and another boat are on converging courses.

If you are under sail, the boat on starboard tack has the right-of-way. If you are both on the same tack, the boat to leeward has the right-of-way. Under power, the guy on the right has the right-of-way. A sailboat under power, by the way, is considered to be a powerboat.

You may have heard that a sailboat has the right-of-way over a power boat and this is true. But in any crossing situation vigilance is only commonsense. A lot of boats have autopilots and the watchkeeper may have been lulled to sleep by the sun, the fresh air, or other distractions.

If you have to give way to another boat, make your turn a definite one and *cross well astern* of him. Never try to cross ahead of someone unless you can pass well ahead.

2. You are overtaking someone—that is, you are coming up on him from a position aft of his beam.

This is an easy one to remember because it is absolutely flat: the overtaking boat must keep clear. You may pass to either side (well clear), but you must keep clear. This applies even if you are a sailboat under sail and are coming up on a power vessel.

3. You and another boat are approaching pretty much head-on.

The natural thing is for each person to turn to his right. You may, however, pass on either side. The main thing whenever you do make a maneuver is to make it well in advance and to make it definite so that your intention is clear to the other vessel.

4. The other vessel is a commercial vessel (ship, tug, tanker, fisherman).

The official rules of the road have recently been changed to make it unlawful for small boats to hinder vessels in a channel when the channel is the only place the larger vessel can navigate. My personal rule has always been to stay out of the way of moving steel objects that are one thousand times bigger than I am. I would like to recommend this rule to you, unofficial as it is. Besides, the people in charge of commercial vessels are engaged in earning a living under the pressure of a schedule; you're just out having fun, presumably, with time and space to spare.

5. Whenever you are out on the water, it is expected that you will keep a good lookout and that if you are the boat with the right-of-way, you will make no sudden, last-minute moves which will make it difficult for the other guy to allow you your rights. No "after you, Alphonse" stuff. Give the other guy time to maneuver to clear you. If you think he's going to cut it too close or is waiting too long, give him a lot of quick blasts with your horn or yell to wake him up. At this point you are obligated by the rules to continue on your course—with caution. But if he doesn't respond, maneuver to get clear.

Looking and thinking sufficiently far ahead of yourself should keep you out of this kind of situation. But if it comes down to the last instant and collision is imminent, try to lessen the blow by reversing or sheering away; and, for heaven's sake, don't let anybody try to fend off. Your boat can take a tremendous amount of abuse that human arms, legs, and hands cannot.

I hope it is clear that in this chapter I have not attempted to give any more than the most basic, rule-of-thumb concepts in an attempt to help you begin boating with some idea of the conventions that apply to boats and ships underway on the water.

The general principles underlying the rules can be stated briefly this way: (1) the guy on the right has the right-of-way, (2) the guy who got there first has the right-of-way—for example, the boat you're overtaking got there first, (3) the vessel least free to maneuver has the right-of-way. In the early days of steam sail was given the right-of-way, since sailing ships are much more difficult to maneuver than powered vessels of the same size. Full cognizance of this should leave no doubt about what to do when you meet a tug, ship, or commercial fishing boat. Finally (4) no one has the right-of-way *through* someone else. The right-of-way vessel is expected to hold course and speed but *not* to the point of impact.

Please note that the method of marking channels discussed here is unique to the United States. The chart is always your best guide to the system of buoyage (channel marking) in use.

Although it is really beyond the intent of this chapter, you should know there are four official rules of the road for waters: International, Inland, Great Lakes, and Western Rivers. During the present revision and conversion to metric measurements, the last two are being pretty much subsumed into the Inland rules.

Most of this is not of pressing concern to yachtsmen, but I might mention two points: (1) In certain rivers and on parts of the intracoastal waterway power boats going downstream have right-of-way over boats heading upstream. (2) By the end of this year, sound signals will be required in crossing situations. Unless I miss my guess, this rule will, like the one about marine toilets, perhaps be more honored in the breach than the observance. So I have not included the signals in this book.

Since official rules are often written in a stiff and legalistic manner, I would recommend a useful alternative, *The New Boatman's Manual*, by Carl D. Lane (W. W. Norton & Company).

The official rules are contained in three pamphlets named as follows:

Rules of the Road—International—Inland (CG–169)
Rules of the Road—Western Rivers (CG–184)
Rules of the Road—Great Lakes (CG–172)

Copies are available from: United States Coast Guard/ CAS = 2/81/ 400 7th Street, SW/ Washington, D.C. 20590.

2

The Chart

About the only thing that is as fascinating to look at as a catalog, in my opinion, is a chart. I don't think I have ever looked at any chart and not learned something, sometimes something surprising. This was brought home to me only recently when I happened to find a large scale chart of the harbor of Mamaroneck, New York. Now, I have lived in and around Mamaroneck for almost thirty years and must have been in and out of the harbor at least five hundred times. Yet as I browsed about this chart, I discovered a tidewater creek that I had never known about. Called Otter Creek, it runs off from the right of the main channel, through the back lots of a plush residential area, practically up to the main drag through town, U.S. Route 1, the historic Boston Post Road. Someday soon I am going to get into a kayak and go up this creek with the flooding tide. I fully expect to see an otter, too.

If you would like to test the truth of this thesis and also

start to learn to use the basic tool of coastal navigation, let me suggest that you get a large scale chart of the area or harbor that you know well from your normal boating activities and, some convenient evening, spread it out on the dining room table or the floor. (Don't be surprised when the kids, the cats, and the dogs want to get in on the exercise also.)

To get the right chart you will need to consult a chart catalog. There are four of them that cover the United States, one each for the Atlantic and Gulf Coasts, Pacific Coast, Alaska, and the Great Lakes. These catalogs are free and can be had by writing to: Distribution Service (C44), National Ocean Survey, Riverdale, Maryland 20840.

The catalogs are very simply set up. The entire coastline of the area covered by the catalog is shown. Superimposed upon it in the appropriate places are the borders of the charts available with the number of that chart in a corner (see figure 2.1). The relative scales of the charts are quite obvious from the catalog and the terminology is simple: the smaller the scale, the larger the area the entire chart covers. Scale is also expressed mathematically and the scale of each chart in the catalog is printed in a list alongside the respective coastline. Scale is expressed as a ratio between the unreal (the chart) and the real world that it represents. A scale written as 1:40,000 means that one unit on the chart stands for 40,000 units on the particular part of the surface of the earth that it portrays. If you are mathematically inclined, you can distinguish small and large scale by considering the scale ratio to be a fraction. The fraction 1/40,000, is a smaller number than 1/10,000, and so, relative to the latter, it indicates a small scale chart.

If you are new to chart reading, you will also find very helpful a booklet referred to as Chart No. 1 and titled *Nautical Chart Symbols and Abbreviations*. With this at hand you can settle down to several enjoyable evenings in which

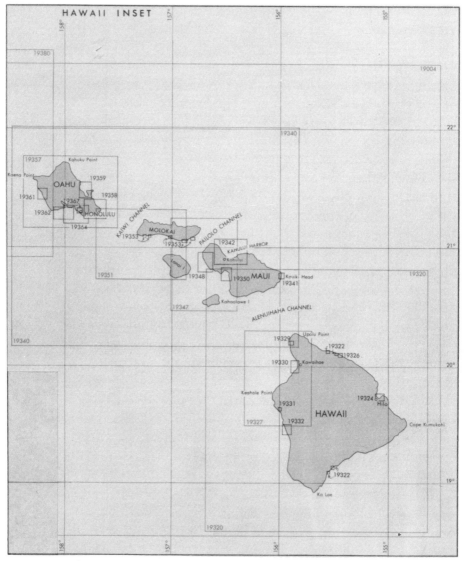

Figure 2.1 Chart catalog page showing charts available for Hawaii.

you will be, almost unconsciously, learning to relate what you are familiar with in the real world to its representation on the surface of a sheet of paper.

After you have familiarized yourself at home with this first chart, take it down to your boat some evening while there is still light, sit at the helm, and look from the chart to the reality around you. The chart shows things as they would be seen from vertically overhead, but you see them horizontally from the surface of a plane. A certain adaption has to be made in your head in order for you to relate these two different views to each other.

If you find you are enjoying this sort of thing, why don't you fold the chart up into a convenient size and, next time you leave port, put it next to you on the cockpit seat and refer to it as you travel down the channel and into your normal cruising grounds. Who knows, you may discover another Otter Creek.

Once you have gotten used to the chart world of the area most familiar to you, get a smaller scale chart, say one that covers your area plus thirty or forty miles in one direction or the other. In the range of latitudes covered by the United States, this will usually be one with a scale of 1:80,000. This is a convenient scale because the chart at this scale covers about the distance you can cruise in a day in a moderate-sized boat. Again, the easy way is to familiarize yourself with this chart in the comfort of your home. You should find this interesting because there will be a much greater variety of buoys than simple cans (black) and nuns (red)—buoys with bells, gongs, whistles, and lights; lighthouses on hills and islands; rocks and reefs; sunken wrecks; and unexploded mines. A far from humdrum world, right there in your backyard. And if this doesn't get your imagination revved up, go out and buy Chart No. 4190—Samoa Islands.

Now that you are familiar with the chart covering a day's cruising distance from your home base, sit down some

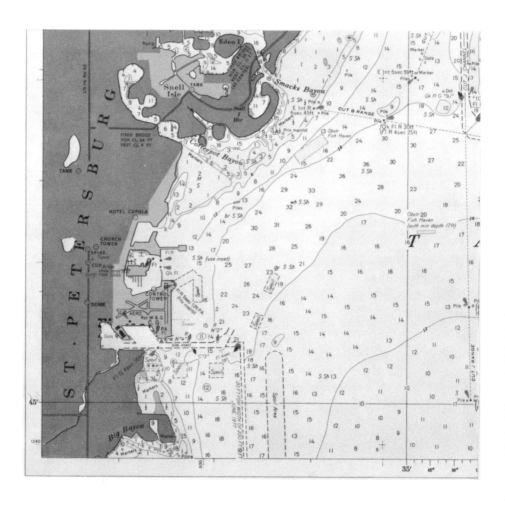

Figure 2.2 St. Petersburg, Florida, detail. Scale 1:40,000. One mile is the distance from the latitude line marked 45' to the first horizontal mark above it on the left margin.

34

Figure 2.3 St. Petersburg, Florida. Scale 1:20,000. Here the scale is laid out in the lower right corner and shown as well in the right margin from 27° 46′ to 27° 46′30″.

evening at home and plan a day-long trip to somewhere. This might well be a place you are already used to going without a chart. This time, however, do it with the chart. Pick out a convenient buoy near the exit of your port and a buoy near the entrance to the harbor of your destination. Draw a line between them. You may find a common yardstick useful for this. You will certainly find it useful as your trips get more ambitious and you need to draw longer lines. Having drawn the course line, you need to know two things: the direction to the destination and the distance to the destination.

To determine the direction, you have several choices. One is to use the compass roses that are printed on the chart. They are circular affairs in violet ink and one circle is printed inside the other. The inner ring is the magnetic compass rose (figures 2.4–2.5). The outer (true) rose is marked with a star at the major compass point—north—and subdivided clockwise into one-degree increments from 0° (north), to 90° (E), 180° (S), 270° (W) and 360°, which is 0° (north again). In most parts of the world the inner ring is a little askew to the outer ring, which gives true directions based on the latitude and longitude convention. The amount that the inner (magnetic) ring varies from the outer (true) ring is called the variation and is caused by the fact that the point on the earth which attracts the magnet in the compass is not at the geographic North Pole. The amount of this variation changes as you move about the earth; each chart you use has the variation incorporated on it in the two roses. The variation also changes with time and this rate of change is printed at the common center of the roses. By convention, variation is termed east or west, depending upon whether the magnetic compass is out of alignment with the true direction due to a clockwise or counterclockwise twist. If the magnetic rose is shifted clockwise relative to the true, the variation is termed easterly; if the inner rose is shifted counterclockwise, the variation is westerly.

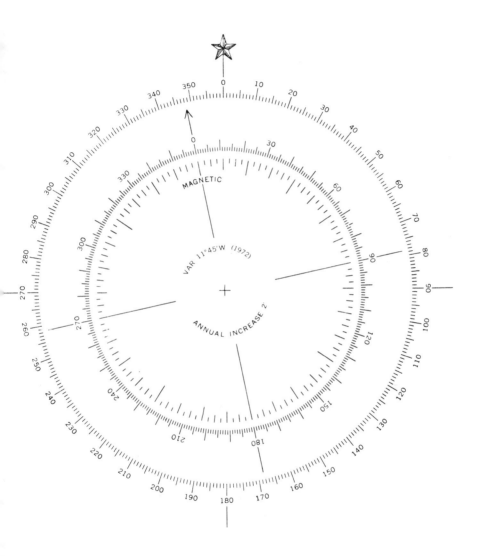

Figure 2.4 True and magnetic compass roses. Inner rose (magnetic) is turned counterclockwise (toward west) showing a variation of almost 12° west.

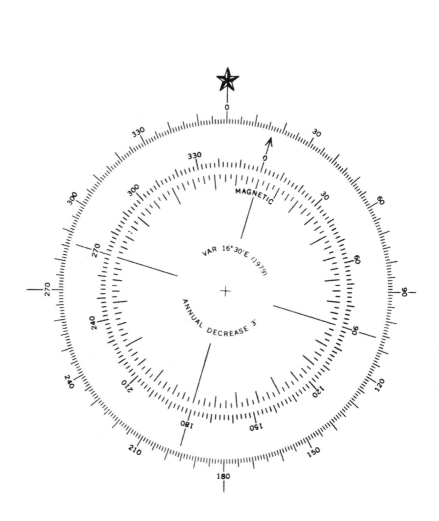

***Figure* 2.5** True and magnetic compass roses. Inner rose (magnetic) is twisted clockwise (toward east) showing a variation of over 16° east.

Since your boat is probably equipped with a magnetic compass, what you need to know is the magnetic direction in which your course line runs. The traditional way to do this is to take a pair of parallel rules and place one edge on your course line and then "walk" them over to the magnetic (inner) rose until one edge runs through the center of the rose. Then look along the edge to read the number where edge and rose intersect. This is the magnetic or compass direction of the destination.

Now parallel rules are easy enough to use if you can spread the chart out completely, but it often happens in a small boat that the chart must be folded and because of the innate perversity of things, the roses are usually on the other side of the chart. To navigate from the helm it is practically a necessity to fold the chart, so you need a way to determine the course without the compass rose or parallel rules. What I suggest is a portable compass rose, which is a circular protractor with a string (figure 2.6). Place it on the chart with the center on the course line and then by eye line it up so that 0° points in the direction of true north (straight toward the top edge on most charts by long-standing convention). If a line of longitude crosses your course line, put the center of the protractor there and 0° right on the line of longitude. If this is not practical, just align it by eye. I have found that most people can do this to within a degree or two with very little practice. For coastwise, daylight sailing, this is close enough. Stretch the string out over your course line.

Your course is read at the point where the edge of the protractor and the string intersect. Since you have aligned the protractor with true north, the course indicated by the protractor is the true, not the magnetic, course. To find the compass course remember that west variation means the magnetic direction is counterclockwise so many degrees relative to the true, and east variation means the compass direction is clockwise some number of degrees relative to

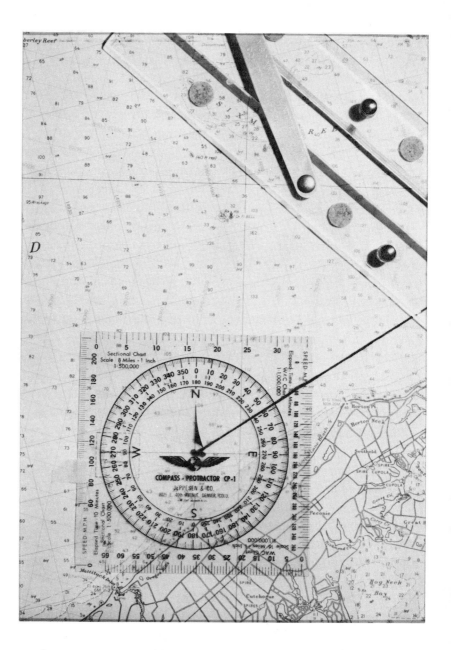

Figure 2.6 A portable compass rose.

the true direction. Turn the protractor, either actually or mentally, the number of degrees printed in the middle of the rose. That number is your compass course. I think you can see that if you use this method, you won't have to memorize rules. What you are in effect doing is recreating the relationship between true and magnetic which is given on the printed roses. It is also a graphic illustration of the fact that there is only one course to be sailed, but there are two ways to measure it—i.e., true and magnetic directions are not two different courses, but two ways of measuring or stating the same course.

Now you also need to know the length of your course line or the distance between your starting point and destination. The distance scale is printed at the sides of the chart and is usually scaled in minutes (represented by ') between lines of latitude. One minute between lines of latitude on the surface of the earth is one nautical mile—6,080 feet. There are minutes at the top of the chart, too, but these are minutes between lines of longitude and, except at the equator, are less than one nautical mile since longitude lines get closer together as they approach the poles. Latitude lines are evenly spaced north to south so distance must always be measured at the side of the chart between the latitude lines, never at the top or bottom.

Again, because of the nature of things, the right or left side of the chart may not always be available, so you may find it useful before setting out to find out how many miles your hand can span and use this as a rough guide to find out how far you have come along the track. Also before setting out you can measure the distance with a pair of dividers and write it down. Dividers, however, have sharp points and are painful to stow in a pocket. If the handspan trick seems a little too rough and ready, take an ordinary pencil and, starting at the eraser end, cut marks into the wood every mile. You may find it useful to do this for the several scales you normally use—a different color for each scale. If there are many scales, mark the scale on the pencil. This way when you set off on your trip you will have a quick and ready way to see how far you are along toward your destination as time passes without having to leave the helm.

For your first attempts at coastal navigation I hope you will set out only in fair weather and keep the initial distances short—say, no more than three hours running. As you gain experience, however, the voyages are going to get longer. Eventually rain or spray will get onto the chart. To protect the chart, try keeping it folded in a plastic envelope of convenient size. This way you can flip it over to see either side. Mark the course on it before you set out and write the distance and direction on the line on each half of the chart for easy reference during the day. When setting up the course on the chart, go along the line carefully by eye to make sure that you haven't put the course across or near a shoal or rock. If you have, choose an intermediate mark, and proceed thence to your objective. Also make note of any buoys that lie close to your intended track, as they are a good check of your distance run and the accuracy of your steering.

On my last boat—which was quite cramped, the main cabin headroom being only four feet—I found it useful to cut out, from the Small Craft series of charts, the large scale charts of the harbors I might be visiting and put them in acetate in a three-ring binder, two charts per page. This binder I could keep stowed under the deck in the cockpit and the acetate protected the charts from spray and rain. Over the years the binder got pretty rusty and tattered, but the charts stayed in very good shape.

So far I have assumed, if you are a sailor, that you would be able to sail your courses directly, without having to tack. How to do this will be taken up in Chapter 8.

Should it happen that you need to divert from your planned course and enter another harbor, the course to steer can be determined by putting the protractor down on the chart at your approximate position, aligning it north to south, stretching the string out to determine the course, and then cranking in the variation by actually or mentally twisting the protractor in the appropriate direction—clockwise for east variation, counterclockwise for west variation.

CHAPTER

3

The Compass

The marine compass for small boats has been developed to such a state today that Christopher Columbus would probably have paid a fortune if he could have had one, so basic is a good compass to all navigation. This instrument is so important that it is probably a good idea to have some kind of notion of how it is made.

Basically the magnetic compass is a bundle of magnetized steel needles which are fastened to the underneath side of an aluminum disc. On top of this disc is painted the compass rose—today usually in numerical degrees with only the four cardinal points (N, S, E, W) designated by the appropriate letter. In the center of this disc a jeweled bearing is placed and the bearing rides on a pin which is housed in a cagelike device of two concentric rings called gimballs. The outer gimball is attached to the inside of a clear plastic sphere in such a way that no matter how the sphere is tilted, the compass disc remains level. At the forward edge of the outer gimball ring is located a vertical reference pin called the lubber line, and the needles are arranged in such a way that when the lubber line is pointed at magnetic north, the N on the disc and the lubber line coincide.

To help dampen the oscillations of the compass disc caused by the various motions of a boat underway, the clear plastic sphere is filled with a mixture of alcohol and water about the consistency of vodka, although the alcohol in question is methyl, not grain (and therefore should not be made into a martini, even under desperate circumstances). This plastic sphere is enclosed in a plastic case which contains a light for use at night and compensating magnets which are used to tune out influences other than variation which may reveal themselves in the form of an additional deviation of the compass card to the east (clockwise) or west (counterclockwise).

Anyway, the compass is such a basic and important navigation tool that you should have a good one. For boats up to about thirty feet I like the models which have a card (disc) with about a four-inch apparent diameter. I tend to prefer the bracket-mounted type because it can be put away when you are not underway and thus, unlike one permanently mounted in a bulkhead, is not exposed unnecessarily to the sun. The sun causes expansion and contraction of the dampening fluid so that eventually the seals break and the fluid leaks out. Also, a bracket-mounted compass can be lifted out of its bracket and, handheld, can do double duty as a handbearing compass.

The rule of thumb in choosing a compass is to select one as large as the space will allow since larger compasses tend to be steadier. The so-called five-degree card (figure 3.1) has been found easy on the eyes and most conducive to accurate steering.

Boats larger than thirty feet can be steered a little more steadily and so can benefit from a large compass. Five-inch compasses are the norm today for quite large boats (up to forty-five feet), but I can tell you that the extra distance

Figure 3.1 Five-inch compass. This may be set in pedestal of sailboat or flush-mounted in front of wheel on a powerboat.

between the degree markings of a six-inch compass are a joy to glasses-wearing types past forty.

If you are buying a compass or want to check the one that came with your boat, do it this way:

—Hold it out at arm's length and aim it at some reference point across the street or across the store. Note the reading at the lubber line. Move your arm quickly to one side or the other and re-aim the compass at the reference point. The card should settle down quickly. As this is a relative test, you will need to do it to several different compasses to see which one seems best to you.

—Repeat this test, only this time move your arm up or down instead of to the side.

Once you have selected the compass, mount it at a comfortable height for viewing when you are seated, but consider what is around before you do. A radio in close vicinity is very likely to affect a compass. It is often tempting to mount the compass in the bridge deck of a sailboat, since then it can be on the centerline and equally visible from either side of the cockpit. If your boat has an inboard engine, though, this position will be too close to it; the compass will be mightily attracted to all that iron. This attraction would rotate the card out of line and, much as the location of the magnetic pole gives rise to variation, would cause an additional disparity called deviation.

Once you have mounted the compass in your boat, a process called *compensation* should be carried out to remove the errors known as deviations. Like variation, deviation is a clockwise or counterclockwise twist induced in compasses by ferrous objects, such as an engine, in the vicinity of the compass. Deviation can also be caused by electricity passing through a wire, since this creates a magnetic field around the wire. You might say that deviation is the variation caused by the boat and what is on the boat and the way those things are distributed around the boat in relation to the compass. It is desirable to get rid of this deviation so that the compass will be affected only by the local variation. This way the compass will be in agreement with the magnetic rose on whatever chart is being used. The reason that you don't want to eliminate the variation of the compass is that then it would be accurate for only a small area and since the variation changes as you move from place to place, you would have to recompensate your compass constantly.

Although compensating a compass is quite easy in theory, it requires a certain amount of practice to do fluently since a large number of minutiae must be mentally juggled. So it's probably not an appropriate topic for a book such as this, which aims primarily to help relative beginners get out on the water and enjoy their boats.

Any yachtsman, however, should be able to tell if his

compass needs compensating so that he can call in a profes-
sional to do the work. Checking the compass to find out if
deviation is present can easily be done by means of the
tables of the bearings of the sun, which are included in this
chapter.

The tables give, by date and latitude, the true direction
in which to look to see the sun rise. If you know this direction (bearing), it is relatively simple to look at your compass
to see if the direction shown agrees tolerably with the direction given in the table.

The only tricky thing about this table is that the dates
proceed *counterclockwise* around the page, beginning in
the upper left with January 1. The tables are good for any
year and are valid for either north or south latitudes, since
the sun rises at the same point of the compass in latitudes
which are numerically the same. Whether those latitudes
are north or south of the equator does not matter.

Here's how to use the tables to check your compass. Say
you are out on the water at sunrise on August 2 in latitude
24°N. Table 3.1 shows the sun's true bearing to be 70°. Let's
further say that the chart for your particular area shows the
variation to be 15° west. Use the following format:

Date: August 2
Latitude: 24°N

Sun's true bearing:	70°
Variation $\begin{array}{c}+W\\-E\end{array}$	+15°
Sun's magnetic bearing at rising:	85°

Having determined that the magnetic direction to look
to see the sun is 85°, sight across the compass and determine if this is indeed the direction in which it lies. If you
cannot detect a difference by eye, your compass is probably
all right, but you should also do further checks by putting
the boat on headings of north, south, east and west and

Date	0°–11° N & S Rise	12°–19° N & S Rise	20°–24° N & S Rise	25°–29° N & S Rise	30°–33° N & S Rise	34°–35° N & S Rise	36°–37° N & S Rise	38°–39° N & S Rise	40°–41° N & S Rise	Date
Jan. 2	113°	114°	115°	116°	117°	118°	119°	120°	121°	11
10	112°	113°	114°	115°	116°	117°	118°	119°	120°	3 Dec.
16	111°	112°	113°	114°	115°	116°	117°	117°	118°	27
21	110°	111°	112°	113°	114°	115°	115°	116°	117°	22
25	109°	110°	111°	112°	113°	113°	114°	115°	116°	17
29	108°	109°	110°	111°	112°	112°	112°	113°	114°	14
Feb. 2	107°	108°	109°	110°	110°	111°	111°	112°	113°	10
5	106°	107°	108°	108°	109°	110°	110°	111°	111°	6
9	105°	106°	107°	107°	108°	108°	108°	109°	110°	3 Nov.
12	104°	105°	105°	106°	107°	107°	108°	108°	109°	31
15	103°	104°	104°	105°	106°	106°	106°	107°	107°	28
18	102°	103°	103°	104°	104°	105°	105°	106°	106°	25
20	101°	102°	102°	103°	103°	103°	104°	104°	105°	22
23	100°	101°	101°	101°	102°	102°	103°	103°	103°	19
26	99°	100°	100°	100°	101°	101°	101°	102°	102°	17
Mar. 1	98°	98°	99°	99°	100°	100°	100°	100°	101°	14
3	97°	97°	98°	98°	98°	99°	99°	99°	99°	11
6	96°	96°	97°	97°	97°	97°	98°	98°	98°	9
8	95°	95°	96°	96°	96°	96°	96°	96°	97°	6
11	94°	94°	94°	95°	95°	95°	95°	95°	95°	4
13	93°	93°	93°	93°	94°	94°	94°	94°	94°	1 Oct.
16	92°	92°	92°	92°	92°	92°	93°	93°	93°	28
18	91°	91°	91°	91°	91°	91°	91°	91°	91°	26
21	90°	90°	90°	90°	90°	90°	90°	90°	90°	23
23	89°	89°	89°	89°	89°	89°	89°	89°	89°	21
26	88°	88°	88°	88°	88°	88°	88°	87°	87°	18
28	87°	87°	87°	87°	86°	86°	86°	86°	86°	16
31	86°	86°	86°	85°	85°	85°	85°	85°	85°	13
Apr. 3	85°	85°	84°	84°	84°	84°	84°	84°	83°	10
5	84°	84°	83°	83°	83°	83°	82°	82°	82°	8
8	83°	83°	82°	82°	82°	81°	81°	81°	81°	5
11	82°	82°	81°	81°	80°	80°	80°	80°	79°	2 Sept.
13	81°	80°	80°	80°	79°	79°	79°	78°	78°	30
16	80°	79°	79°	79°	78°	78°	77°	77°	77°	28
19	79°	78°	78°	77°	77°	77°	76°	76°	75°	25
22	78°	77°	77°	76°	76°	75°	75°	74°	74°	22
25	77°	76°	76°	75°	74°	74°	74°	73°	73°	19
28	76°	75°	75°	74°	73°	73°	72°	72°	71°	16
May 1	75°	74°	73°	73°	72°	72°	71°	71°	70°	12
5	74°	73°	72°	72°	71°	70°	70°	69°	69°	9
8	73°	72°	71°	70°	70°	69°	69°	68°	67°	5
12	72°	71°	70°	69°	68°	68°	67°	67°	66°	2 Aug.
16	71°	70°	69°	68°	67°	67°	66°	65°	64°	28
21	70°	69°	68°	67°	66°	65°	65°	64°	63°	24
26	69°	68°	67°	66°	65°	64°	63°	63°	62°	19
June 1	68°	67°	66°	65°	63°	63°	62°	61°	60°	12
10	67°	66°	64°	63°	62°	62°	61°	60°	59°	3 July

Table 3.1 **True bearings of the sun**

In using these tables it is not necessary to be too finicky about interpolation. The difference in bearings is never more than 2°, so just take the nearest date to the one you want.

Remember that the dates go up on the right-hand side and note that the bottom and top lines cover the interval June 10 through July 3 and December 11 through January 2, respectively.

	Latitudes										
	42°–43° N & S	44°–45° N & S	46°–47° N & S	48°–49° N & S	50° N & S	51° N & S	52° N & S	53° N & S	54° N & S	55° N & S	
Date	Rise	Rise	Rise	Rise	Rise	Rise	Rise	Rise	Rise	Rise	Da
Jan. 2	122°	124°	125°	127°	127°	128°	129°	130°	132°	133°	11
10	121°	122°	123°	125°	126°	127°	127°	129°	130°	131°	3 D
16	119°	120°	122°	123°	124°	125°	126°	127°	128°	129°	27
21	118°	119°	120°	121°	122°	123°	124°	125°	126°	127°	22
25	116°	117°	119°	120°	120°	121°	122°	123°	124°	125°	17
29	115°	116°	117°	118°	119°	119°	120°	121°	122°	123°	14
Feb. 2	114°	114°	115°	116°	117°	118°	118°	119°	120°	121°	10
5	112°	113°	114°	115°	115°	116°	116°	117°	118°	119°	6
9	111°	111°	112°	113°	114°	114°	115°	115°	116°	117°	3 N
12	109°	110°	111°	112°	112°	113°	113°	114°	114°	115°	31
15	108°	109°	109°	110°	110°	111°	111°	112°	113°	113°	28
18	107°	107°	108°	108°	109°	109°	110°	110°	111°	111°	25
20	105°	106°	106°	107°	107°	108°	108°	108°	109°	109°	22
23	104°	104°	105°	105°	106°	106°	106°	107°	107°	108°	19
26	102°	103°	103°	104°	104°	104°	105°	105°	105°	105°	17
Mar. 1	101°	101°	102°	102°	103°	103°	103°	103°	104°	104°	14
3	100°	100°	100°	101°	101°	101°	101°	102°	102°	102°	11
6	98°	99°	99°	99°	99°	100°	100°	100°	100°	101°	9
8	97°	97°	97°	98°	98°	98°	98°	98°	99°	99°	6
11	95°	96°	96°	96°	96°	96°	97°	97°	97°	97°	4
13	94°	94°	94°	95°	95°	95°	95°	95°	95°	95°	1 O
16	93°	93°	93°	93°	93°	93°	93°	93°	93°	93°	28
18	91°	91°	91°	92°	92°	92°	92°	92°	92°	92°	26
21	90°	90°	90°	90°	90°	90°	90°	90°	90°	90°	23
23	89°	89°	89°	88°	88°	88°	88°	88°	88°	88°	21
26	87°	87°	87°	87°	87°	87°	87°	87°	87°	86°	18
28	86°	86°	86°	85°	85°	85°	85°	85°	85°	85°	16
31	85°	84°	84°	84°	84°	84°	84°	83°	83°	83°	13
Apr. 3	83°	83°	83°	82°	82°	82°	82°	82°	81°	81°	10
5	82°	82°	81°	81°	81°	80°	80°	80°	80°	80°	8
8	80°	80°	80°	79°	79°	79°	79°	78°	78°	78°	5
11	79°	79°	78°	78°	78°	77°	77°	77°	76°	76°	2 Se
13	78°	77°	77°	76°	76°	76°	75°	75°	75°	74°	30
16	76°	76°	75°	75°	74°	74°	74°	73°	73°	72°	28
19	75°	74°	74°	73°	73°	72°	72°	72°	71°	71°	25
22	73°	73°	72°	72°	71°	71°	70°	70°	69°	69°	22
25	72°	71°	71°	70°	70°	69°	69°	68°	68°	67°	19
28	71°	70°	69°	68°	68°	67°	67°	66°	66°	65°	16
May 1	69°	69°	68°	67°	66°	66°	65°	65°	64°	63°	12
5	68°	67°	66°	65°	65°	64°	63°	63°	62°	61°	9
8	66°	66°	65°	64°	63°	62°	62°	61°	60°	59°	5
12	65°	64°	63°	62°	61°	61°	60°	59°	58°	57°	2 Au
16	64°	63°	61°	60°	60°	59°	58°	57°	56°	55°	28
21	62°	61°	60°	59°	58°	57°	56°	55°	54°	53°	24
26	61°	60°	58°	57°	56°	55°	54°	53°	52°	51°	19
June 1	59°	58°	57°	55°	54°	53°	53°	51°	50°	49°	12
10	58°	56°	55°	53°	53°	52°	51°	50°	48°	47°	3 Ju

Table 3.1 **True bearings of the sun (*cont.*)**

In using these tables it is not necessary to be too finicky about interpolation. The difference in bearings is never more than 2°, so just take the nearest date to the one you want.

Remember that the dates go up on the right-hand side and note that the bottom and top lines cover the interval June 10 *through* July 3 and December 11 *through* January 2, respectively.

looking again. Not only will this completely check the compass, it will also illustrate very aptly that the *boat turns around the compass* and not vice versa. Since the bearing of the sun does not change dramatically in the first five minutes or so after rising (the moment when its lower edge rests on the horizon), you should have time to do a complete round. Should you want to use this method at or near sunset, the sun's magnetic bearing at sunset is found by subtracting the magnetic bearing at sunrise from 360°. Should there be a difference of five degrees or more between the bearing calculated from the table and the one actually observed, call in a compass adjuster.

4

Speed, Time,
and Distance

One of the essentials to proper navigation is knowledge of your speed through the water. Knowing this, the elapsed time from the start of your trip, and the compass heading you have steered, enables you to calculate the distance you have run along your planned course line, and so determine approximately where you are. A position determined in this manner is called the dead-reckoning position and is the basis of all navigation. The dead-reckoning position is commonly abbreviated and called simply the DR. It may help you to fix it in your mind at this point by calling it the DDR for Distance *and* Direction Run. The subject of the DR will be taken up again in the next chapter. Right now, let's discuss some methods of determining how fast your boat is going through the water. We've already discussed the other component of the DR—direction—in Chapters 2 and 3.

You probably already know that electronic instruments are available to tell you both your speed through the water and the distance traveled. These instruments are commonly called a knotmeter and log. The knotmeter corresponds to the speedometer in your car, but instead of measuring speed in statute miles per hour (one statute or land mile equals 5,280 feet), it measures speed in nautical miles per hour or knots. One knot is a speed of one nautical mile per hour (one nautical mile equals 6,080 feet or one minute of arc along a great circle on the surface of the earth). The log is equivalent to the odometer in your car except that it is normally set to read in nautical, not statute, miles.

Electronic instruments are very seductive and they certainly dress up a boat, but they do have their disadvantages. One is cost. By the time a good knotmeter and log are purchased and installed, you will be out the best part of one thousand dollars. The most serious disadvantage of these instruments is that they are rather delicate and a humid environment eventually raises havoc with them. My experience has been that electronic devices work fine for two or three years, but then begin to get faulty and require lots of expensive maintenance. A racing sailboat probably needs these instruments, but most cruising boats, I feel, are better without them. There are other methods of determining your speed, which are not vulnerable to wet and humidity. I think even racing navigators should know these as a back-up in the event that the knotmeter or log packs it in during a race. However, if you do have or want these instruments, you will need to calibrate them, so let's look at ways of doing that first.

Table 4.1 is a reproduction of Table 19 from the *American Practical Navigator,* published by the U.S. Hydrographic Center and referred to as NVPUB (navigation publication) #9 or *Bowditch* after its original author, Nathaniel Bowditch. I have included the first two pages of the table which cover speeds up to sixteen knots, since this is a book for *cruising* boatmen.

This table can be used in two ways: first to determine

Speed, Time, and Distance

Min-utes	Speed in knots																Min-utes
	0.5	1.0	1.5	2.0	2.5	3.0	3.5	4.0	4.5	5.0	5.5	6.0	6.5	7.0	7.5	8.0	
	Miles	*Miles*	*Miles*	*Miles*	*Miles*	*Miles*	*Miles*	*Miles*	*Miles*	*Miles*	*Miles*	*Miles*	*Miles*	*Miles*	*Miles*	*Miles*	
1	0.0	0.0	0.0	0.0	0.0	0.0	0.1	0.1	0.1	0.1	0.1	0.1	0.1	0.1	0.1	0.1	1
2	0.0	0.0	0.0	0.1	0.1	0.1	0.1	0.1	0.2	0.2	0.2	0.2	0.2	0.2	0.2	0.3	2
3	0.0	0.0	0.1	0.1	0.1	0.2	0.2	0.2	0.2	0.2	0.3	0.3	0.3	0.4	0.4	0.4	3
4	0.0	0.1	0.1	0.1	0.2	0.2	0.2	0.3	0.3	0.3	0.4	0.4	0.4	0.5	0.5	0.5	4
5	0.0	0.1	0.1	0.2	0.2	0.2	0.3	0.3	0.4	0.4	0.5	0.5	0.5	0.6	0.6	0.7	5
6	0.0	0.1	0.2	0.2	0.2	0.3	0.4	0.4	0.4	0.5	0.6	0.6	0.6	0.7	0.8	0.8	6
7	0.1	0.1	0.2	0.2	0.3	0.4	0.4	0.5	0.5	0.6	0.6	0.7	0.8	0.8	0.9	0.9	7
8	0.1	0.1	0.2	0.3	0.3	0.4	0.5	0.5	0.6	0.7	0.7	0.8	0.9	0.9	1.0	1.1	8
9	0.1	0.2	0.2	0.3	0.4	0.4	0.5	0.6	0.7	0.8	0.8	0.9	1.0	1.0	1.1	1.2	9
10	0.1	0.2	0.2	0.3	0.4	0.5	0.6	0.7	0.8	0.8	0.9	1.0	1.1	1.2	1.2	1.3	10
11	0.1	0.2	0.3	0.4	0.5	0.6	0.6	0.7	0.8	0.9	1.0	1.1	1.2	1.3	1.4	1.5	11
12	0.1	0.2	0.3	0.4	0.5	0.6	0.7	0.8	0.9	1.0	1.1	1.2	1.3	1.4	1.5	1.6	12
13	0.1	0.2	0.3	0.4	0.5	0.6	0.8	0.9	1.0	1.1	1.2	1.3	1.4	1.5	1.6	1.7	13
14	0.1	0.2	0.4	0.5	0.6	0.7	0.8	0.9	1.0	1.2	1.3	1.4	1.5	1.6	1.8	1.9	14
15	0.1	0.2	0.4	0.5	0.6	0.8	0.9	1.0	1.1	1.2	1.4	1.5	1.6	1.8	1.9	2.0	15
16	0.1	0.3	0.4	0.5	0.7	0.8	0.9	1.1	1.2	1.3	1.5	1.6	1.7	1.9	2.0	2.1	16
17	0.1	0.3	0.4	0.6	0.7	0.8	1.0	1.1	1.3	1.4	1.6	1.7	1.8	2.0	2.1	2.3	17
18	0.2	0.3	0.4	0.6	0.8	0.9	1.0	1.2	1.4	1.5	1.6	1.8	2.0	2.1	2.2	2.4	18
19	0.2	0.3	0.5	0.6	0.8	1.0	1.1	1.3	1.4	1.6	1.7	1.9	2.1	2.2	2.4	2.5	19
20	0.2	0.3	0.5	0.7	0.8	1.0	1.2	1.3	1.5	1.7	1.8	2.0	2.2	2.3	2.5	2.7	20
21	0.2	0.4	0.5	0.7	0.9	1.0	1.2	1.4	1.6	1.8	1.9	2.1	2.3	2.4	2.6	2.8	21
22	0.2	0.4	0.6	0.7	0.9	1.1	1.3	1.5	1.6	1.8	2.0	2.2	2.4	2.6	2.8	2.9	22
23	0.2	0.4	0.6	0.8	1.0	1.2	1.3	1.5	1.7	1.9	2.1	2.3	2.5	2.7	2.9	3.1	23
24	0.2	0.4	0.6	0.8	1.0	1.2	1.4	1.6	1.8	2.0	2.2	2.4	2.6	2.8	3.0	3.2	24
25	0.2	0.4	0.6	0.8	1.0	1.2	1.5	1.7	1.9	2.1	2.3	2.5	2.7	2.9	3.1	3.3	25
26	0.2	0.4	0.6	0.9	1.1	1.3	1.5	1.7	2.0	2.2	2.4	2.6	2.8	3.0	3.2	3.5	26
27	0.2	0.4	0.7	0.9	1.1	1.4	1.6	1.8	2.0	2.2	2.5	2.7	2.9	3.2	3.4	3.6	27
28	0.2	0.5	0.7	0.9	1.2	1.4	1.6	1.9	2.1	2.3	2.6	2.8	3.0	3.3	3.5	3.7	28
29	0.2	0.5	0.7	1.0	1.2	1.4	1.7	1.9	2.2	2.4	2.7	2.9	3.1	3.4	3.6	3.9	29
30	0.2	0.5	0.8	1.0	1.2	1.5	1.8	2.0	2.2	2.5	2.8	3.0	3.2	3.5	3.8	4.0	30
31	0.3	0.5	0.8	1.0	1.3	1.6	1.8	2.1	2.3	2.6	2.8	3.1	3.4	3.6	3.9	4.1	31
32	0.3	0.5	0.8	1.1	1.3	1.6	1.9	2.1	2.4	2.7	2.9	3.2	3.5	3.7	4.0	4.3	32
33	0.3	0.6	0.8	1.1	1.4	1.6	1.9	2.2	2.5	2.8	3.0	3.3	3.6	3.8	4.1	4.4	33
34	0.3	0.6	0.8	1.1	1.4	1.7	2.0	2.3	2.6	2.8	3.1	3.4	3.7	4.0	4.2	4.5	34
35	0.3	0.6	0.9	1.2	1.5	1.8	2.0	2.3	2.6	2.9	3.2	3.5	3.8	4.1	4.4	4.7	35
36	0.3	0.6	0.9	1.2	1.5	1.8	2.1	2.4	2.7	3.0	3.3	3.6	3.9	4.2	4.5	4.8	36
37	0.3	0.6	0.9	1.2	1.5	1.8	2.2	2.5	2.8	3.1	3.4	3.7	4.0	4.3	4.6	4.9	37
38	0.3	0.6	1.0	1.3	1.6	1.9	2.2	2.5	2.8	3.2	3.5	3.8	4.1	4.4	4.8	5.1	38
39	0.3	0.6	1.0	1.3	1.6	2.0	2.3	2.6	2.9	3.2	3.6	3.9	4.2	4.6	4.9	5.2	39
40	0.3	0.7	1.0	1.3	1.7	2.0	2.3	2.7	3.0	3.3	3.7	4.0	4.3	4.7	5.0	5.3	40
41	0.3	0.7	1.0	1.4	1.7	2.0	2.4	2.7	3.1	3.4	3.8	4.1	4.4	4.8	5.1	5.5	41
42	0.4	0.7	1.0	1.4	1.8	2.1	2.4	2.8	3.2	3.5	3.8	4.2	4.6	4.9	5.2	5.6	42
43	0.4	0.7	1.1	1.4	1.8	2.2	2.5	2.9	3.2	3.6	3.9	4.3	4.7	5.0	5.4	5.7	43
44	0.4	0.7	1.1	1.5	1.8	2.2	2.6	2.9	3.3	3.7	4.0	4.4	4.8	5.1	5.5	5.9	44
45	0.4	0.8	1.1	1.5	1.9	2.2	2.6	3.0	3.4	3.8	4.1	4.5	4.9	5.2	5.6	6.0	45
46	0.4	0.8	1.2	1.5	1.9	2.3	2.7	3.1	3.4	3.8	4.2	4.6	5.0	5.4	5.8	6.1	46
47	0.4	0.8	1.2	1.6	2.0	2.4	2.7	3.1	3.5	3.9	4.3	4.7	5.1	5.5	5.9	6.3	47
48	0.4	0.8	1.2	1.6	2.0	2.4	2.8	3.2	3.6	4.0	4.4	4.8	5.2	5.6	6.0	6.4	48
49	0.4	0.8	1.2	1.6	2.0	2.4	2.9	3.3	3.7	4.1	4.5	4.9	5.3	5.7	6.1	6.5	49
50	0.4	0.8	1.2	1.7	2.1	2.5	2.9	3.3	3.8	4.2	4.6	5.0	5.4	5.8	6.2	6.7	50
51	0.4	0.8	1.3	1.7	2.1	2.6	3.0	3.4	3.8	4.2	4.7	5.1	5.5	6.0	6.4	6.8	51
52	0.4	0.9	1.3	1.7	2.2	2.6	3.0	3.5	3.9	4.3	4.8	5.2	5.6	6.1	6.5	6.9	52
53	0.4	0.9	1.3	1.8	2.2	2.6	3.1	3.5	4.0	4.4	4.9	5.3	5.7	6.2	6.6	7.1	53
54	0.4	0.9	1.4	1.8	2.2	2.7	3.2	3.6	4.0	4.5	5.0	5.4	5.8	6.3	6.8	7.2	54
55	0.5	0.9	1.4	1.8	2.3	2.8	3.2	3.7	4.1	4.6	5.0	5.5	6.0	6.4	6.9	7.3	55
56	0.5	0.9	1.4	1.9	2.3	2.8	3.3	3.7	4.2	4.7	5.1	5.6	6.1	6.5	7.0	7.5	56
57	0.5	1.0	1.4	1.9	2.4	2.8	3.3	3.8	4.3	4.8	5.2	5.7	6.2	6.6	7.1	7.6	57
58	0.5	1.0	1.4	1.9	2.4	2.9	3.4	3.9	4.4	4.8	5.3	5.8	6.3	6.8	7.2	7.7	58
59	0.5	1.0	1.5	2.0	2.5	3.0	3.4	3.9	4.4	4.9	5.4	5.9	6.4	6.9	7.4	7.9	59
60	0.5	1.0	1.5	2.0	2.5	3.0	3.5	4.0	4.5	5.0	5.5	6.0	6.5	7.0	7.5	8.0	60

54

Speed, Time, and Distance

Min-utes	Speed in knots																	Min-utes
	8.5	9.0	9.5	10.0	10.5	11.0	11.5	12.0	12.5	13.0	13.5	14.0	14.5	15.0	15.5	16.0	
	Miles	Miles	Miles	Miles	Miles	Miles	Miles	Miles	Miles	Miles	Miles	Miles	Miles	Miles	Miles	Miles	
1	0.1	0.2	0.2	0.2	0.2	0.2	0.2	0.2	0.2	0.2	0.2	0.2	0.2	0.2	0.3	0.3	1
2	0.3	0.3	0.3	0.3	0.4	0.4	0.4	0.4	0.4	0.4	0.4	0.5	0.5	0.5	0.5	0.5	2
3	0.4	0.4	0.5	0.5	0.5	0.6	0.6	0.6	0.6	0.6	0.7	0.7	0.7	0.8	0.8	0.8	3
4	0.6	0.6	0.6	0.7	0.7	0.7	0.8	0.8	0.8	0.9	0.9	1.0	1.0	1.0	1.0	1.1	4
5	0.7	0.8	0.8	0.8	0.9	0.9	1.0	1.0	1.0	1.1	1.1	1.2	1.2	1.2	1.3	1.3	5
6	0.8	0.9	1.0	1.0	1.0	1.1	1.2	1.2	1.2	1.3	1.4	1.4	1.4	1.5	1.6	1.6	6
7	1.0	1.0	1.1	1.2	1.2	1.3	1.3	1.4	1.5	1.5	1.6	1.6	1.7	1.8	1.8	1.9	7
8	1.1	1.2	1.3	1.3	1.4	1.5	1.5	1.6	1.7	1.7	1.8	1.9	1.9	2.0	2.1	2.1	8
9	1.3	1.4	1.4	1.5	1.6	1.6	1.7	1.8	1.9	2.0	2.0	2.1	2.2	2.2	2.3	2.4	9
10	1.4	1.5	1.6	1.7	1.8	1.8	1.9	2.0	2.1	2.2	2.2	2.3	2.4	2.5	2.6	2.7	10
11	1.6	1.6	1.7	1.8	1.9	2.0	2.1	2.2	2.3	2.4	2.5	2.6	2.7	2.8	2.8	2.9	11
12	1.7	1.8	1.9	2.0	2.1	2.2	2.3	2.4	2.5	2.6	2.7	2.8	2.9	3.0	3.1	3.2	12
13	1.8	2.0	2.1	2.2	2.3	2.4	2.5	2.6	2.7	2.8	2.9	3.0	3.1	3.2	3.4	3.5	13
14	2.0	2.1	2.2	2.3	2.4	2.6	2.7	2.8	2.9	3.0	3.2	3.3	3.4	3.5	3.6	3.7	14
15	2.1	2.2	2.4	2.5	2.6	2.8	2.9	3.0	3.1	3.2	3.4	3.5	3.6	3.8	3.9	4.0	15
16	2.3	2.4	2.5	2.7	2.8	2.9	3.1	3.2	3.3	3.5	3.6	3.7	3.9	4.0	4.1	4.3	16
17	2.4	2.6	2.7	2.8	3.0	3.1	3.3	3.4	3.5	3.7	3.8	4.0	4.1	4.2	4.4	4.5	17
18	2.6	2.7	2.8	3.0	3.2	3.3	3.4	3.6	3.8	3.9	4.0	4.2	4.4	4.5	4.6	4.8	18
19	2.7	2.8	3.0	3.2	3.3	3.5	3.6	3.8	4.0	4.1	4.3	4.4	4.6	4.8	4.9	5.1	19
20	2.8	3.0	3.2	3.3	3.5	3.7	3.8	4.0	4.2	4.3	4.5	4.7	4.8	5.0	5.2	5.3	20
21	3.0	3.2	3.3	3.5	3.7	3.8	4.0	4.2	4.4	4.6	4.7	4.9	5.1	5.2	5.4	5.6	21
22	3.1	3.3	3.5	3.7	3.8	4.0	4.2	4.4	4.6	4.8	5.0	5.1	5.3	5.5	5.7	5.9	22
23	3.3	3.4	3.6	3.8	4.0	4.2	4.4	4.6	4.8	5.0	5.2	5.4	5.6	5.8	5.9	6.1	23
24	3.4	3.6	3.8	4.0	4.2	4.4	4.6	4.8	5.0	5.2	5.4	5.6	5.8	6.0	6.2	6.4	24
25	3.5	3.8	4.0	4.2	4.4	4.6	4.8	5.0	5.2	5.4	5.6	5.8	6.0	6.2	6.5	6.7	25
26	3.7	3.9	4.1	4.3	4.6	4.8	5.0	5.2	5.4	5.6	5.8	6.1	6.3	6.5	6.7	6.9	26
27	3.8	4.0	4.3	4.5	4.7	5.0	5.2	5.4	5.6	5.8	6.1	6.3	6.5	6.8	7.0	7.2	27
28	4.0	4.2	4.4	4.7	4.9	5.1	5.4	5.6	5.8	6.1	6.3	6.5	6.8	7.0	7.2	7.5	28
29	4.1	4.4	4.6	4.8	5.1	5.3	5.6	5.8	6.0	6.3	6.5	6.8	7.0	7.2	7.5	7.7	29
30	4.2	4.5	4.8	5.0	5.2	5.5	5.8	6.0	6.2	6.5	6.8	7.0	7.2	7.5	7.8	8.0	30
31	4.4	4.6	4.9	5.2	5.4	5.7	5.9	6.2	6.5	6.7	7.0	7.2	7.5	7.8	8.0	8.3	31
32	4.5	4.8	5.1	5.3	5.6	5.9	6.1	6.4	6.7	6.9	7.2	7.5	7.7	8.0	8.3	8.5	32
33	4.7	5.0	5.2	5.5	5.8	6.0	6.3	6.6	6.9	7.2	7.4	7.7	8.0	8.2	8.5	8.8	33
34	4.8	5.1	5.4	5.7	6.0	6.2	6.5	6.8	7.1	7.4	7.6	7.9	8.2	8.5	8.8	9.1	34
35	5.0	5.2	5.5	5.8	6.1	6.4	6.7	7.0	7.3	7.6	7.9	8.2	8.5	8.8	9.0	9.3	35
36	5.1	5.4	5.7	6.0	6.3	6.6	6.9	7.2	7.5	7.8	8.1	8.4	8.7	9.0	9.3	9.6	36
37	5.2	5.6	5.9	6.2	6.5	6.8	7.1	7.4	7.7	8.0	8.3	8.6	8.9	9.2	9.6	9.9	37
38	5.4	5.7	6.0	6.3	6.6	7.0	7.3	7.6	7.9	8.2	8.6	8.9	9.2	9.5	9.8	10.1	38
39	5.5	5.8	6.2	6.5	6.8	7.2	7.5	7.8	8.1	8.4	8.8	9.1	9.4	9.8	10.1	10.4	39
40	5.7	6.0	6.3	6.7	7.0	7.3	7.7	8.0	8.3	8.7	9.0	9.3	9.7	10.0	10.3	10.7	40
41	5.8	6.2	6.5	6.8	7.2	7.5	7.9	8.2	8.5	8.9	9.2	9.6	9.9	10.2	10.6	10.9	41
42	6.0	6.3	6.6	7.0	7.4	7.7	8.0	8.4	8.8	9.1	9.4	9.8	10.2	10.5	10.8	11.2	42
43	6.1	6.4	6.8	7.2	7.5	7.9	8.2	8.6	9.0	9.3	9.7	10.0	10.4	10.8	11.1	11.5	43
44	6.2	6.6	7.0	7.3	7.7	8.1	8.4	8.8	9.2	9.5	9.9	10.3	10.6	11.0	11.4	11.7	44
45	6.4	6.8	7.1	7.5	7.9	8.2	8.6	9.0	9.4	9.8	10.1	10.5	10.9	11.2	11.6	12.0	45
46	6.5	6.9	7.3	7.7	8.0	8.4	8.8	9.2	9.6	10.0	10.4	10.7	11.1	11.5	11.9	12.3	46
47	6.7	7.0	7.4	7.8	8.2	8.6	9.0	9.4	9.8	10.2	10.6	11.0	11.4	11.8	12.1	12.5	47
48	6.8	7.2	7.6	8.0	8.4	8.8	9.2	9.6	10.0	10.4	10.8	11.2	11.6	12.0	12.4	12.8	48
49	6.9	7.4	7.8	8.2	8.6	9.0	9.4	9.8	10.2	10.6	11.0	11.4	11.8	12.2	12.7	13.1	49
50	7.1	7.5	7.9	8.3	8.8	9.2	9.6	10.0	10.4	10.8	11.2	11.7	12.1	12.5	12.9	13.3	50
51	7.2	7.6	8.1	8.5	8.9	9.4	9.8	10.2	10.6	11.0	11.5	11.9	12.3	12.8	13.2	13.6	51
52	7.4	7.8	8.2	8.7	9.1	9.5	10.0	10.4	10.8	11.3	11.7	12.1	12.6	13.0	13.4	13.9	52
53	7.5	8.0	8.4	8.8	9.3	9.7	10.2	10.6	11.0	11.5	11.9	12.4	12.8	13.3	13.7	14.1	53
54	7.6	8.1	8.6	9.0	9.4	9.9	10.4	10.8	11.2	11.7	12.2	12.6	13.0	13.5	14.0	14.4	54
55	7.8	8.2	8.7	9.2	9.6	10.1	10.5	11.0	11.5	11.9	12.4	12.8	13.3	13.8	14.2	14.7	55
56	7.9	8.4	8.9	9.3	9.8	10.3	10.7	11.2	11.7	12.1	12.6	13.1	13.5	14.0	14.5	14.9	56
57	8.1	8.6	9.0	9.5	10.0	10.4	10.9	11.4	11.9	12.4	12.8	13.3	13.8	14.2	14.7	15.2	57
58	8.2	8.7	9.2	9.7	10.2	10.6	11.1	11.6	12.1	12.6	13.0	13.5	14.0	14.5	15.0	15.5	58
59	8.4	8.8	9.3	9.8	10.3	10.8	11.3	11.8	12.3	12.8	13.3	13.8	14.3	14.8	15.2	15.7	59
60	8.5	9.0	9.5	10.0	10.5	11.0	11.5	12.0	12.5	13.0	13.5	14.0	14.5	15.0	15.5	16.0	60

Table 4.1 Computation of speed using time and distance.

your speed and then to determine the distance run in a given time at that speed.

To determine speed:

1. From the chart pick out two buoys and measure the distance between thenm.

2. Make a run from one buoy to the other and time the run with a stopwatch.

3. Find the time of the run in the left or right column headed *Minutes.*

4. Look along the row left or right until you find the distance run.

5. The speed in knots is at the top of the column in which you find the distance.

6. Make the same run in the opposite direction and repeat steps 3 through 5.

7. Average the speeds. This tends to cancel effects of any current.

8. Continue on and set the knotmeter to the speed determined at step 7, following instructions in the knotmeter manual.

9. If you also have a log, make a note of the reading at the beginning of the first run and at the end of the record run. Calibrate in accordance with the instruction manual for the instrument.

Example:

It takes 16 minutes and 30 seconds to travel .9 miles. From the table, the speed is 3.5 knots.

If you want to interpolate, you can call it 17 minutes and find the speed between .8 and 1.0 on the 17-minute line to be 3.25 knots.

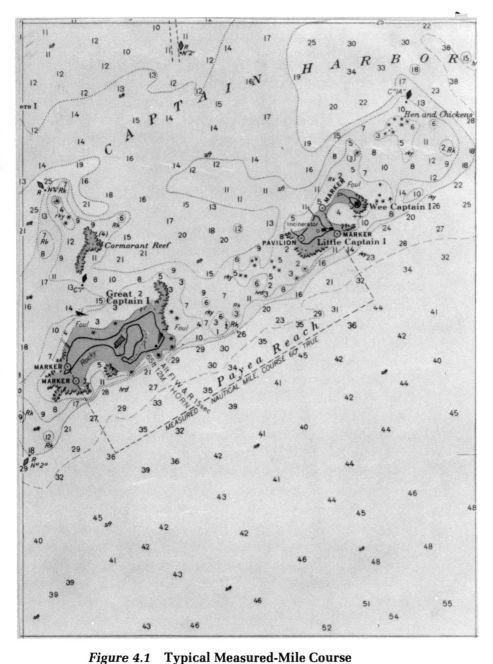

Figure 4.1   Typical Measured-Mile Course

Course to remain at right angle to terminal markers is shown as
dashed line. Boats with tachometers can run the course at various
engine RPM settings and make a table equating speed and RPM—
very useful, especially in fog or if your electronics go haywire.

In many cruising areas there exist what are called "measured-mile" ranges (see figure 4.1). These usually consist of two stakes or other objects lined up behind each other at each end of a carefully measured distance of one mile and a course to steer that will keep you parallel to the measured distance. To use, get yourself on course and speed and start your stopwatch as the two stakes or whatever come in line. Run until the ranges at the other end of the course are in line. Stop the watch. Note the time. Repeat, running the mile in the other direction. Look up the speeds in table 4.2 (Table 18, also from Bowditch) and average them.

As you can see, Table 4.2 only goes up to thirteen minutes (twelve minutes sixty seconds), so if it takes you, say, fifteen minutes to run the mile, halve the time (seven minutes thirty seconds), look up that speed and divide that speed in half. Thus, seven minutes thirty seconds equals 8 knots; your speed was 4 knots.

You can also use Table 4.1 for a measured mile. Just look along the time line 'til you come to the distance of one mile. Look to the top of the column for your speed. In the example above, fifteen minutes is four knots by Table 4.1.

Now, obviously, Table 4.1 can also be used to determine your speed while traveling in one direction. If your course shows that you are going to be passing fairly close to two buoys, time your run between them, measure the distance between them on the chart and look up the speed in the table. This, of course, is going to give you your speed over the bottom; since the buoys are anchored and you are going one way, any effect from a current will not be canceled.

In the event that you don't have instruments to calibrate and don't want to keep referring to tables, there are other methods which don't require leaving the helm or bringing a table up. The neatest is based on estimating the length of the bow wave your boat is making.

It is a fact of nature that a wave in the water moves at a

Sec.						Minutes							Sec.
	1	2	3	4	5	6	7	8	9	10	11	12	

Sec.	1 Knots	2 Knots	3 Knots	4 Knots	5 Knots	6 Knots	7 Knots	8 Knots	9 Knots	10 Knots	11 Knots	12 Knots	Sec.
0	60. 000	30. 000	20. 000	15. 000	12. 000	10. 000	8. 571	7. 500	6. 667	6. 000	5. 455	5. 000	0
1	59. 016	29. 752	19. 890	14. 938	11. 960	9. 972	8. 551	7. 484	6. 654	5. 990	5. 446	4. 993	1
2	58. 065	29. 508	19. 780	14. 876	11. 921	9. 945	8. 531	7. 469	6. 642	5. 980	5. 438	4. 986	2
3	57. 143	29. 268	19. 672	14. 815	11. 881	9. 917	8. 511	7. 453	6. 630	5. 970	5. 430	4. 979	3
4	56. 250	29. 032	19. 565	14. 754	11. 842	9. 890	8. 491	7. 438	6. 618	5. 960	5. 422	4. 972	4
5	55. 385	28. 800	19. 459	14. 694	11. 803	9. 863	8. 471	7. 423	6. 606	5. 950	5. 414	4. 966	5
6	54. 545	28. 571	19. 355	14. 634	11. 765	9. 836	8. 451	7. 407	6. 593	5. 941	5. 405	4. 959	6
7	53. 731	28. 346	19. 251	14. 575	11. 726	9. 809	8. 431	7. 392	6. 581	5. 931	5. 397	4. 952	7
8	52. 941	28. 125	19. 149	14. 516	11. 688	9. 783	8. 411	7. 377	6. 569	5. 921	5. 389	4. 945	8
9	52. 174	27. 907	19. 048	14. 458	11. 650	9. 756	8. 392	7. 362	6. 557	5. 911	5. 381	4. 938	9
10	51. 429	27. 692	18. 947	14. 400	11. 613	9. 730	8. 372	7. 347	6. 545	5. 902	5. 373	4. 932	10
11	50. 704	27. 481	18. 848	14. 343	11. 576	9. 704	8. 353	7. 332	6. 534	5. 892	5. 365	4. 925	11
12	50. 000	27. 273	18. 750	14. 286	11. 538	9. 677	8. 333	7. 317	6. 522	5. 882	5. 357	4. 918	12
13	49. 315	27. 068	18. 653	14. 229	11. 502	9. 651	8. 314	7. 302	6. 510	5. 873	5. 349	4. 911	13
14	48. 649	26. 866	18. 557	14. 173	11. 465	9. 626	8. 295	7. 287	6. 498	5. 863	5. 341	4. 905	14
15	48. 000	26. 667	18. 462	14. 118	11. 429	9. 600	8. 276	7. 273	6. 486	5. 854	5. 333	4. 898	15
16	47. 368	26. 471	18. 367	14. 062	11. 392	9. 574	8. 257	7. 258	6. 475	5. 844	5. 325	4. 891	16
17	46. 753	26. 277	18. 274	14. 008	11. 356	9. 549	8. 238	7. 243	6. 463	5. 835	5. 318	4. 885	17
18	46. 154	26. 087	18. 182	13. 953	11. 321	9. 524	8. 219	7. 229	6. 452	5. 825	5. 310	4. 878	18
19	45. 570	25. 899	18. 090	13. 900	11. 285	9. 499	8. 200	7. 214	6. 440	5. 816	5. 302	4. 871	19
20	45. 000	25. 714	18. 000	13. 846	11. 250	9. 474	8. 182	7. 200	6. 429	5. 806	5. 294	4. 865	20
21	44. 444	25. 532	17. 910	13. 793	11. 215	9. 449	8. 163	7. 186	6. 417	5. 797	5. 286	4. 858	21
22	43. 902	25. 352	17. 822	13. 740	11. 180	9. 424	8. 145	7. 171	6. 406	5. 788	5. 279	4. 852	22
23	43. 373	25. 175	17. 734	13. 688	11. 146	9. 399	8. 126	7. 157	6. 394	5. 778	5. 271	4. 845	23
24	42. 857	25. 000	17. 647	13. 636	11. 111	9. 375	8. 108	7. 143	6. 383	5. 769	5. 263	4. 839	24
25	42. 353	24. 828	17. 561	13. 585	11. 077	9. 351	8. 090	7. 129	6. 372	5. 760	5. 255	4. 832	25
26	41. 860	24. 658	17. 476	13. 534	11. 043	9. 326	8. 072	7. 115	6. 360	5. 751	5. 248	4. 826	26
27	41. 379	24. 490	17. 391	13. 483	11. 009	9. 302	8. 054	7. 101	6. 349	5. 742	5. 240	4. 819	27
28	40. 909	24. 324	17. 308	13. 433	10. 976	9. 278	8. 036	7. 087	6. 338	5. 732	5. 233	4. 813	28
29	40. 449	24. 161	17. 225	13. 383	10. 942	9. 254	8. 018	7. 073	6. 327	5. 723	5. 225	4. 806	29
30	40. 000	24. 000	17. 143	13. 333	10. 909	9. 231	8. 000	7. 059	6. 316	5. 714	5. 217	4. 800	30
31	39. 560	23. 841	17. 062	13. 284	10. 876	9. 207	7. 982	7. 045	6. 305	5. 705	5. 210	4. 794	31
32	39. 130	23. 684	16. 981	13. 235	10. 843	9. 184	7. 965	7. 031	6. 294	5. 696	5. 202	4. 787	32
33	38. 710	23. 529	16. 901	13. 187	10. 811	9. 160	7. 947	7. 018	6. 283	5. 687	5. 195	4. 781	33
34	38. 298	23. 377	16. 822	13. 139	10. 778	9. 137	7. 930	7. 004	6. 272	5. 678	5. 187	4. 775	34
35	37. 895	23. 226	16. 744	13. 091	10. 746	9. 114	7. 912	6. 990	6. 261	5. 669	5. 180	4. 768	35
36	37. 500	23. 077	16. 667	13. 043	10. 714	9. 091	7. 895	6. 977	6. 250	5. 660	5. 172	4. 762	36
37	37. 113	22. 930	16. 590	12. 996	10. 682	9. 068	7. 877	6. 963	6. 239	5. 651	5. 165	4. 756	37
38	36. 735	22. 785	16. 514	12. 950	10. 651	9. 045	7. 860	6. 950	6. 228	5. 643	5. 158	4. 749	38
39	36. 364	22. 642	16. 438	12. 903	10. 619	9. 023	7. 843	6. 936	6. 218	5. 634	5. 150	4. 743	39
40	36. 000	22. 500	16. 364	12. 857	10. 588	9. 000	7. 826	6. 923	6. 207	5. 625	5. 143	4. 737	40
41	35. 644	22. 360	16. 290	12. 811	10. 557	8. 978	7. 809	6. 910	6. 196	5. 616	5. 136	4. 731	41
42	35. 294	22. 222	16. 216	12. 766	10. 526	8. 955	7. 792	6. 897	6. 186	5. 607	5. 128	4. 724	42
43	34. 951	22. 086	16. 143	12. 721	10. 496	8. 933	7. 775	6. 883	6. 175	5. 599	5. 121	4. 718	43
44	34. 615	21. 951	16. 071	12. 676	10. 465	8. 911	7. 759	6. 870	6. 164	5. 590	5. 114	4. 712	44
45	34. 286	21. 818	16. 000	12. 632	10. 435	8. 889	7. 742	6. 857	6. 154	5. 581	5. 106	4. 706	45
46	33. 962	21. 687	15. 929	12. 587	10. 405	8. 867	7. 725	6. 844	6. 143	5. 573	5. 099	4. 700	46
47	33. 645	21. 557	15. 859	12. 544	10. 375	8. 845	7. 709	6. 831	6. 133	5. 564	5. 092	4. 694	47
48	33. 333	21. 429	15. 789	12. 500	10. 345	8. 824	7. 692	6. 818	6. 122	5. 556	5. 085	4. 688	48
49	33. 028	21. 302	15. 721	12. 457	10. 315	8. 802	7. 676	6. 805	6. 112	5. 547	5. 078	4. 681	49
50	32. 727	21. 176	15. 652	12. 414	10. 286	8. 780	7. 660	6. 792	6. 102	5. 538	5. 070	4. 675	50
51	32. 432	21. 053	15. 584	12. 371	10. 256	8. 759	7. 643	6. 780	6. 091	5. 530	5. 063	4. 669	51
52	32. 143	20. 930	15. 517	12. 329	10. 227	8. 738	7. 627	6. 767	6. 081	5. 521	5. 056	4. 663	52
53	31. 858	20. 809	15. 451	12. 287	10. 198	8. 717	7. 611	6. 754	6. 071	5. 513	5. 049	4. 657	53
54	31. 579	20. 690	15. 385	12. 245	10. 169	8. 696	7. 595	6. 742	6. 061	5. 505	5. 042	4. 651	54
55	31. 304	20. 571	15. 319	12. 203	10. 141	8. 675	7. 579	6. 729	6. 050	5. 496	5. 035	4. 645	55
56	31. 034	20. 455	15. 254	12. 162	10. 112	8. 654	7. 563	6. 716	6. 040	5. 488	5. 028	4. 639	56
57	30. 769	20. 339	15. 190	12. 121	10. 084	8. 633	7. 547	6. 704	6. 030	5. 479	5. 021	4. 633	57
58	30. 508	20. 225	15. 126	12. 081	10. 056	8. 612	7. 531	6. 691	6. 020	5. 471	5. 014	4. 627	58
59	30. 252	20. 112	15. 063	12. 040	10. 028	8. 592	7. 516	6. 679	6. 010	5. 463	5. 007	4. 621	59
60	30. 000	20. 000	15. 000	12. 000	10. 000	8. 571	7. 500	6. 667	6. 000	5. 455	5. 000	4. 615	60
Sec.	1	2	3	4	5	6	7	8	9	10	11	12	Sec.

Speed Table for Measured Mile

Table 4.2 **Speed Table for Measured Mile.**

59

speed in knots equal to about one and one-third times the square root of its length in feet. In case you don't remember, the square root of a number is that number which, when multiplied by itself, gives the original number. The square root of 4 is 2 ($2 \times 2 = 4$); the square root of 9 is 3 ($3 \times 3 = 9$); the square root of 16 is 4 ($4 \times 4 = 16$), etc.

Now, as your boat moves through the water, the bow pushes the water away and starts a wave. Depending upon the speed of the boat, another wave pops up behind the bow wave. The distance between these two is the wavelength of the bow wave; wavelengths are measured from crest to crest. If you estimate the distance between these two waves, take the square root of that distance, and add one-third of that square root, you will have a good approximation of your speed. Naturally, this method only works well in reasonably smooth water; but for the sake of an example or two, assume that you are traveling out of a harbor in which the speed limit is 3 knots. You look at the two bow waves, one aft of the other, and estimate the distance between them to be four feet. The square root of 4 is 2 and ⅓ of 2 is about .7, so you are doing about 2.7 knots and are complying with the harbor regulations. If you are sailing in really light weather and your waves are only six inches apart, you would be doing about 1 knot, just "ghosting" along. (Square root of .5 feet = .7 plus ⅓ of .7 = .933 or .9 knots.) At the other extreme, say you are booming along on a reach, well heeled over, and the second wave is all the way aft. In other words, the boat is sailing along with her bow on one wave, her stern on the other and a great hollow between. If this were a forty-footer, the distance between the wave crests might be as much as thirty-six feet; square root of 36 is 6, plus ⅓ of 6, or 2; you find that the boat is doing about 8 knots. This is what is termed her *hull speed*—i.e., thirty-six feet is about the largest wave she can generate; she can't go any faster unless she climbs out on top of the wave, and to do that she would need a flat bottom and a lot of power.

Despite the above, there are occasions when light sailboats running in heavy seas before very strong winds can exceed hull speed. This is due to the fact that the force of gravity is added to the power of the sail when such a boat is running downhill on the forward slope of a large wave. It has been said that Cal 40s (which are quite light and have relatively flat bottoms) have approached speeds of twenty-five knots in these conditions. But, of course, this is racing and I doubt that any cruising sailor would have the desire (or the crew) to push his boat to this extreme.

To get back to the subject at hand, the three questions of interest to the pilot of a small boat are: How fast am I going? How long will it take me to get to my destination? How far have I gone? The answers to these three questions are contained in a very basic algebraic equation which we all know: speed multiplied by time equals distance. In conventional symbols: $S \times T = D$*

Let's take the questions one at a time and use the formula on each.

How fast?

Here we want to find S, using algebra, so the equation becomes: $S = \dfrac{D}{T}$

The only tricky thing in using this equation is keeping the units consistent. The above equation will give you speed in knots *if* time is expressed in hours and distance in nautical miles. For example: You time a run between two buoys. The time is 1 hour 20 minutes; the distance between the buoys is 7.3 nautical miles.

---

* A handy method of remembering the formulas for getting distance, time, or speed is to remember just one: $\dfrac{D}{T \times S}$. Just cover the information desired and what remains is the formula that yields that information. For example, to get distance, cover D and what remains is $T \times S$ (time multiplied by speed); to get time, cover T and what remains is distance divided by speed, etc.

$$S = \frac{D}{T}$$

$$S = \frac{7.3}{1.33}$$ (1 hour 20 minutes = 1⅓ hours)

$$S = 5.49 \text{ knots}$$

If you take the time in minutes, you multiply the right side of the equation by 60, since there are 60 minutes in an hour:

$$S = \frac{D}{T} \times 60$$

The above example would then be:

$$S = \frac{7.3}{80} \times 60$$

$$S = 5.48 \text{ knots}$$

The small difference in answers is due to the fact that 80 minutes is a more accurate representation of time than 1.33 hours.

If you take the time in seconds, as you might in a fast power boat, the formula is:

$$S = \frac{D}{T} \times 3600$$

since there are 3600 seconds in an hour. Using the previous example again:

$$S = \frac{7.3}{4800} \times 3600$$

$$S = 5.47 \text{ knots}$$

For all practical purposes, our speed is 5.5 knots and it is speed *over the bottom,* since our distance was between two buoys. For speed through the water you would use as reference something floating free in the water and figure what part of a nautical mile is represented by the length of your boat. Say you have a thirty-footer and as the bow passes a floating milk carton, you start your stopwatch. As the carton passes the stern, you stop the watch and read one second.

First, what part of a nautical mile is 30 feet? Well, there are 6080 feet in a nautical mile, so:

$$\frac{30}{6080} = .00493 \text{ nautical miles}$$

Now put this into the formula.

$$S = \frac{.00493}{1} \times 3600$$
$$S = 17.76 \text{ knots}$$

How long?

Once you know your speed, the time to cover a given distance is given by the equations:

$$\text{Time (in hours)} = \frac{D}{S}$$
$$\text{Time (in minutes)} = \frac{D}{S} \times 60$$
$$\text{Time (in seconds)} = \frac{D}{S} \times 3600$$

There are several less cumbersome methods than using the above formulas. Here are two of my favorites; and I like them because you can do them in your head. (1) To find the time (in minutes) required to cover one mile at a given speed, divide 60 by the speed. Example: if you are going 15 knots, you will cover a mile in 4 minutes. Then, if you have, say, 8 miles to go, you know it's going to take 32 minutes to get there. (2) Another quick way to determine about how long it is going to take you to cover a given distance is called the "six-minute rule" and is based on the fact that six minutes is one-tenth of an hour. Thus, if you take one-tenth of your speed in knots, that number is the amount of miles you will travel in six minutes. For example, if you are going 12 knots, which is 12 nautical miles an hour, in one-tenth of an hour, or 6 minutes, you will go 1.2 nautical miles. If you are going 5 knots, in 6 minutes you will go .5 or one-half nautical mile.

Suppose you are going 3 knots and are 2 miles from your port; how long will it take to get there? Well, using the six-minute rule, in 6 minutes you will go .3 miles. To go 2 miles you will need to cover about 7 times .3 of a mile. Six minutes (the time needed to go .3 nautical miles) times 7 is 42, so you are about 42 minutes from your objective.

How far?

The distance you have run along your course is calculated from the basic formula as originally stated and is so much a part of everyday life as to be scarcely worth mentioning:

When time is in hours: $S \times T = D,$

$$\text{When time is in minutes: } \frac{S \times T}{60} = D,$$

$$\text{When time is in seconds: } \frac{S \times T}{3600} = D,$$

These formulas lend themselves to easy solution by calculator, but calculators are vulnerable to water and there are other methods of doing speed, time, and distance problems. One of my favorites is to use a cheap, six-inch, plastic slide rule.

Figure 4.2 is a close-up of such a slide rule. In using it I use only the top two scales because it obviates the possibilities of running off the scale. Instead of A & B as the names of the scales, I use the A (top) scale for time and the B scale represents speed and/or distance. The solution is graphic and represents pretty much the way you would express the problem to yourself in English. For instance, assume you have timed a run between two buoys 1.8 miles apart at 11 minutes and 30 seconds. The formulation, in English, of this situation would be: If I went 1.8 miles in 11.5 minutes, how many miles would I go in 60 minutes? Stated mathematically this is:

$$\frac{11.5 \text{ minutes}}{1.8 \text{ miles}} = \frac{60 \text{ minutes}}{X \text{ miles}}$$

Read aloud or mentally, the above says 11.5 minutes is to 1.8 miles as 60 minutes is to what (unknown) number of miles. You set it up on the slide rule just like that. Time is the top scale, so find 11.5 and put 1.8 under it; the hairline on the clear plastic slide is there to help you line up the numbers.

With this done, look along the time scale to 6; and underneath the 6 is the distance you will go in one hour and therefore your speed in knots, since, by definition, the distance you go in one hour is your speed: 9.4 nautical miles or 9.4 knots.

Now that you know your speed, suppose you want to know how long it will take you to reach your objective, which is, say, 7 nautical miles away. Here is the relationship.

$$\frac{60 \text{ minutes}}{9.4 \text{ miles}} = \frac{X \text{ minutes}}{7 \text{ miles}}$$

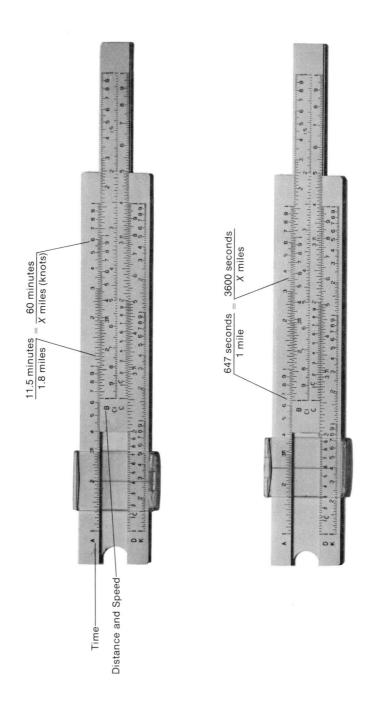

$$\frac{11.5 \text{ minutes}}{1.8 \text{ miles}} = \frac{60 \text{ minutes}}{X \text{ miles (knots)}}$$

$$\frac{647 \text{ seconds}}{1 \text{ mile}} = \frac{3600 \text{ seconds}}{X \text{ miles}}$$

Time

Distance and Speed

Figure 4.2 The slide rule may be used to calculate time, speed, and distance.

Leave the rule as is, 9.4 under 6, and look along the distance scale for 7. Above it is the time, in minutes, to travel 7 miles—a little less than 45 minutes.

You will notice that the slide rule does not tell you whether the 45 is 4.5 or .45 or 450, etc., but this is no problem, since commonsense indicates that if it takes an hour to go 9 miles, it is going to take a major part of the hour to go 7.

Also, note that your times are in the same units. Thus, if you use minutes on the left ratio, the answer is going to be in minutes or, as in the first example, you must use minutes on both sides of the equation.

Now, suppose you do the measured mile in 10 minutes and 47 seconds.

Well, 10 minutes is 600 seconds; 1 hour is 3600 seconds, so the problem is this:

$$\frac{647 \text{ seconds}}{1 \text{ mile}} = \frac{3600 \text{ seconds}}{X \text{ miles}}$$

Answer: 5.5 knots

The nice thing about a plastic slide rule is that it works beautifully when wet and a small one is easy to pocket. If you want to be able to read the scale easier or work to greater precision, get a ten-inch rule and keep it in the winch-handle alcove or just inside the companionway within easy reach.

Suppose you are sailing along in a thirty foot boat and you spot a branch or a paper cup or some other thing floating in the water close ahead of you. You note the moment that it passes your bow and count the seconds until it passes the sterm. Say it was 3 seconds. How fast are you going? Basically, the question boils down to: If I went 30 feet in 3 seconds, how far will I go in 3600 seconds (1 hour)? What you need to do first is to find out what part 30 feet is of a

nautical mile, then you can use the procedure already discussed to solve the problem on the slide rule. Here we go:

$$\frac{30 \text{ feet}}{6080 \text{ feet (1 nautical mile)}} = \frac{X \text{ (\% of 1 nautical mile)}}{1 \text{ (nautical mile)}}$$

Put 30 over 6080 (61 on the small rule) and look over
the 1 on the S–D scale for the number. This is the percentage of a nautical mile represented by 30 feet. Don't worry
about decimals, just take the number, 49. Once you have
done this for your boat, you won't have to do it again,
because it will always be the same. Okay, now set it up as
you did in the earlier case—time over distance, distance
being the percentage of a nautical mile represented by your
thirty-foot boat:

$$\frac{3 \text{ seconds}}{49 \text{ (some \% of a nautical mile)}} = \frac{3600 \text{ seconds}}{X \text{ nautical miles}}$$

Answer = 5.9. It should be very obvious to you, since
you are there, whether this is .59 or 59 or 5.9 knots, which
is why you don't have to worry whether your boat is .49,
.049 or .0049 of a nautical mile. In this case, the answer is
5.9 knots and is easy to reconcile: if you go 30 feet in 3
seconds, you are going 10 feet per second; in 3600 seconds,
then, you would go 36,000 feet, or just a little under 6 nautical miles (3600 divided by 6080) in 1 hour.

In this example an object floating on the water was
used, so the answer is your speed through the water, since
an object floating on the water is subject to the same tidal
current, or lack of it, as you are. If you had used a buoy or
lobster pot or something else anchored to the bottom, the
answer would have been your speed over the bottom.

This about exhausts the subject of speed, time, and dis-

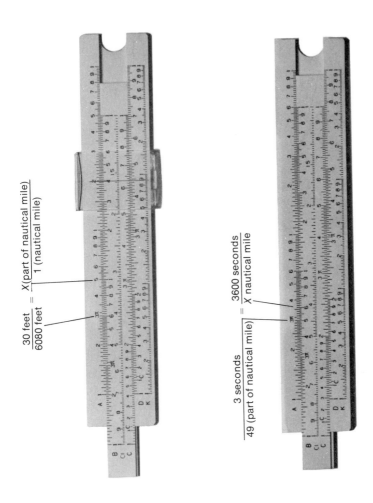

$$\frac{30 \text{ feet}}{6080 \text{ feet}} = \frac{X(\text{part of nautical mile})}{1 \text{ (nautical mile)}}$$

$$\frac{3 \text{ seconds}}{49 \text{ (part of nautical mile)}} = \frac{3600 \text{ seconds}}{X \text{ nautical mile}}$$

Figure 4.3 A slide rule used to calculate speed through the water.

tance. I hope I have shown you that there are several simple ways to extract the information needed, ways that are not only cheap and adequate for the needs of small boats, but also inherently more reliable than gadgets.

5

Dead Reckoning

So far most of this section of the book has been devoted to ways of determining course and distance run along a course. The reason is that these two factors are the components of the DR, or dead-reckoning, position. Very simply your DR position is where you would be if your course had been steered accurately and your distance run along the course line were known accurately. That is all it is, your position reckoned solely on the basis of the course steered and distance traveled through the water. In plotting a DR position on the chart no account is taken of or allowances made for tidal currents, leeway, or head or following seas. You make these adjustments later.

Looked at one way the DR is your position given no disturbing influences at all. To keep a DR you simply keep a record of course steered and distance traveled along that course. From time to time you mark this position on the chart, either mentally or with a pencil, and as opportunity allows you check the DR position by means of other techniques. Basically navigation boils down to keeping the DR and using whatever other information comes to hand to confirm or deny the validity of the DR. The DR is the basis, the backbone, of navigation because without it you have no reference point against which to weigh the validity of your other information. Let's take an example:

Suppose you had been sailing north for two hours from a buoy at the entrance to your home port. You have been doing about five knots, so you should be ten miles north of the buoy according to your DR. You have on board an electronic position finder, which you turn on. For some reason this device gives you two position fixes that are, respectively, one mile due east and one mile due west of the DR position. Which is correct? (See figure 5.1).

Well, suppose that the wind were from the northwest and the tide from the west. This would mean that the tide was pushing you toward position B (east), and, since you were hard on the wind on port tack, you would have been making leeway to the east also. Clearly, you are much more likely to be at point B than point A. But without the DR you would have had no way of chosing between the two positions.

The above example is not entirely fanciful. Electronic instruments are temperamental and too great a reliance on them or any other single instrument or technique can only lead to one thing—becoming LOST.

Look at it this way: there are only two variables in the DR—distance and direction. How far you have gone is dependent upon your speed and at the speeds we're talking about you can't get very far off in the space of a few hours. Direction is dependent on the accuracy with which the course has been steered. Generally courses get steered accurately because although you may wander a bit to one side or the other, the wanderings tend to average out to the base course. Therefore if you keep a record of courses steered and speeds run, you can't get lost. You may be a little to one

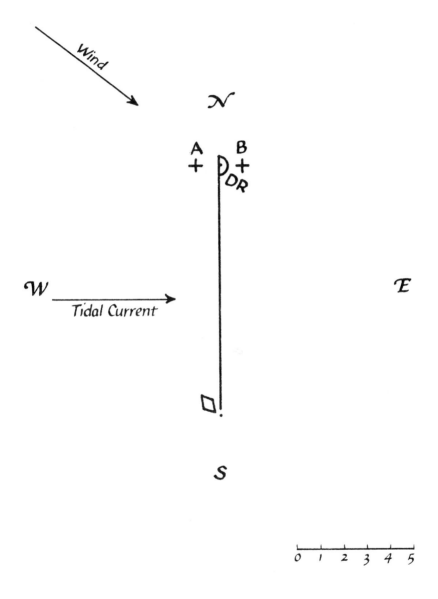

Figure 5.1 Use of the DR to select the more likely of two electronically determined positions.

side or the other of the DR, or a little farther ahead or behind it, but you're not lost. The DR is the sine qua non of navigation and it astonishes me that most texts do not stress this fact.

If you are ever in a situation in which the DR cannot be reconciled with a position determined by other means, stick with the DR until you can positively and satisfactorily confirm or deny its validity.

In a racing boat it is fairly common practice for some member of the group on watch to make a record every half-hour of the course steered and the distance run. This is normally written down in a notebook called the *log*. Periodically the navigator will look over this record and plot the DR position so that all interested parties (i.e., everybody on board) can see how far the boat has gone and, most important, how far to the turning-mark or the end of the race. As the navigator is able to determine the precise position of the boat by other means, he stops one DR track and begins another at the newly determined position (fix).

In a cruising boat this amount of detailed record keeping will probably not be possible, but a note should be made of the starting time and any distinct change of course should be written down (logged) in some manner. Then as needed a DR position can be worked out against which to check positions (fixes) derived by the methods described in the remainder of this book.

In coastal cruising checking the DR usually means nothing more than keeping track of the big items as they roll by—things like cities, islands, headlands, power stations, prominent lighthouses, etc. It's that easy and pleasant.

DR Navigation—Day

You set out for a day's leisurely cruising from Annapolis—down the bay and then back to port by sunset. After clearing Bell 2, you decide to check your tachometer to see if the speed table is still correct by running the measured mile. You head across the bay steering 100° by the compass until you sight the white and orange buoy marking the north end of the measured-mile course. Then you come right to 190° magnetic, which parallels the course, and as you get the two shore markers in line, you start your stopwatch. The time for the run is ten minutes fifteen seconds, which is a shade under the six knots you got at these RPM when you made up the table. Could be the bottom's getting foul or there could be a little current against you, so you advance the throttle a bit and go to a heading of 200° for black Bell 73 off Poplar Island. The time is 10:00 A.M.

On the chart, which is 1:80,000 scale, the latitude lines are drawn in at ten minutes (ten nautical miles) intervals, which is very handy. Since your course is nearly perpendicular to them, they give you a quick and easy distance scale. At six knots, the distance between each set represents a running time of little over an hour and one-half.

—At 10:20 you look to your right and see a lighthouse, the Thomas Point Shoal (checks with DR).

—At 11:30 you see the light tower at Bloody Point Bar ahead to the left (checks with DR).

—At 12:30 you sight the light tower off Poplar Island dead ahead. This means you're to the left of your desired track at about point A, so you come right 10° and

—at 1:30 you round Bell 71 and head back up the Bay for home and dinner.

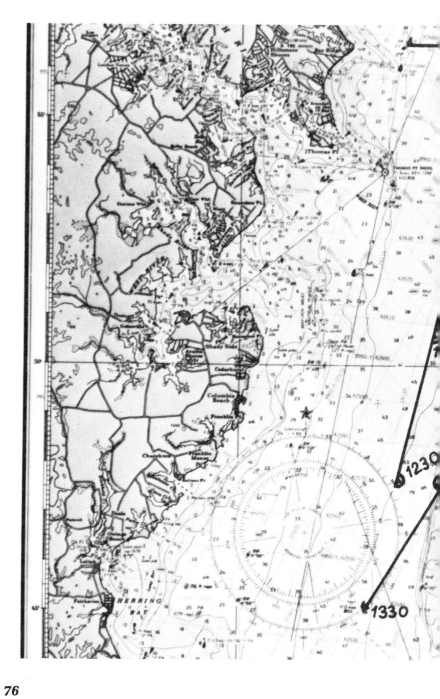

Figure 5.2
A leisurely trip with no trouble,
regularly checking the DR.

CHAPTER

6

—————

Bearings

When I was a kid sailing around in dinky boats without compasses or charts or anything in the way of conventional navigation tools, I used to have a fantasy about lighthouses. Wouldn't it be nice, I thought, if this or that lighthouse could have threads radiating out around it like the spokes on a wheel. Each would be a different color and would be marked every so many feet with the distance away from the lighthouse. That way after a while I could very easily tell where I was—say, on the magenta thread three miles out—and could convert this to my distance from home and dinner.

As I grew up and learned about compasses and trigonometry, I found out that such a threadlike system did in fact exist, only the threads were invisible and imaginary although highly practical.

If you have two circular protractors, get them out some evening and align them with any edge of the table so that both 0° (north) marks are perpendicular to the closer edge of the table. Now imagine that one protractor represents a compass at a lighthouse and the other the compass on your boat. Cruise your boat around in the vicinity of the lighthouse, keeping the compass aligned correctly north, and stop now and then. When you stop, lay a straightedge or yardstick across the centers of both protractors and read the numbers. Depending upon which side of the protractors you read, the number on one will be the same as on the other or will differ by 180°. This is the principle of what is called a bearing. As you pass by a point on shore and look across your compass at it, imagine that the point on shore is the lubber line and note which mark of the compass is pointed at it. This is the bearing from you to the onshore point.

From the experiment with the protractors, you know that your bearing from the onshore point is just the opposite of (or 180° from) your compass reading. If there were a compass rose marked around the lighthouse or other point, you could very quickly draw a line through the correct number (bearing) and know that you were somewhere on that line. Your compass has selected the imaginary thread.

As a matter of fact you can either use your protractor or prepare the chart in advance by buying clear, stick-on compass roses and applying them to the chart while including the variation by twisting the rose the proper number of degrees to the west or east. If you are keeping the chart in a clear plastic envelope, you can use a china-marking pen to draw the bearings.

If there is another lighthouse or buoy in sight, you can take the bearing of this, draw the line, and, since you must be where the lines cross, fix your position approximately. The degree of precision depends upon two things: (1) the accuracy with which you can take the bearing, which, in turn, depends a lot on the state of the sea and the amount of motion to the boat; (2) the angle at which the bearing lines cross (figures 6.1 and 6.2).

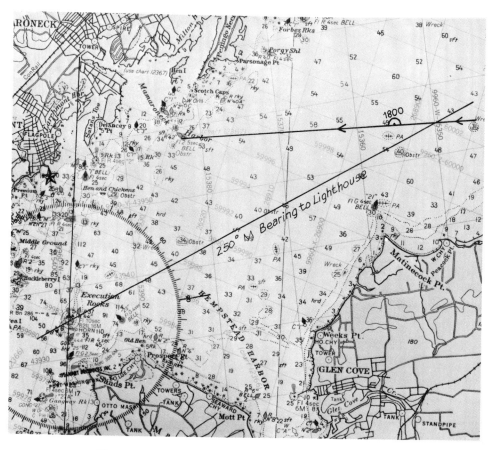

Figure 6.1 At 1800 hours depthfinder reads 55′. Looking along bearing to lighthouse indicates boat is probably to left of track, probably about where bearing crosses 54′ on chart.

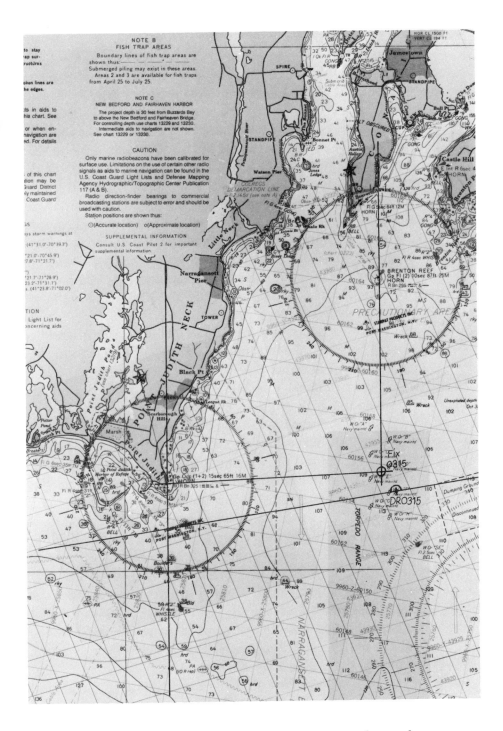

Figure 6.2 Fix with bearing lines crossing at an angle nearly ideal (90°).

As I indicated in an earlier chapter, if your steering compass is bracket-mounted, you can use it to take bearings. This may get awkward, however, especially at night when you will need a longish cord in order to have light, so you may want to get a separate, handheld compass for this purpose. Such handbearing compasses are available in many sizes and prices. The tests to use on such compasses are the same as the ones given in Chapter 3. The main thing I think you should do with a handbearing compass is mount its hanging bracket under cover, but within easy reach. That way you will use it. As you will see in later chapters, there are several additional uses for the handbearing compass.

Another use of the bearing is to determine whether or not you are likely to collide with another boat. The basic principle is: if you are on a collision course with another boat, a bearing taken at intervals on the other boat will not change. Look at figure 6.3.

Here two boats, one going north and the other west, are approaching each other at right angles. The bearing from A to B is approximately 45°; the bearing from B to A is about 225°. A little while later A takes another bearing and, as near as he can tell, it is unchanged. A has also been watching the shore behind B and has observed that B is moving westward against the background. If A is moving much faster than B, B would appear to stand stationary, or move backward, against the background (A^3–B^2) and the bearing would widen. This is a situation in which A may pass well ahead of B but since B is the vessel with the right-of-way, A must exercise caution and good judgment to be sure that she crosses well ahead. If the bearing narrowed and B moved west against the background, it would indicate that B was pulling ahead of A and, thus, A would cross astern, which is the proper and safe way.

Now in the event that the bearing changes and indicates that you are going to pass ahead or astern of another boat, don't forget that much depends upon the rate of

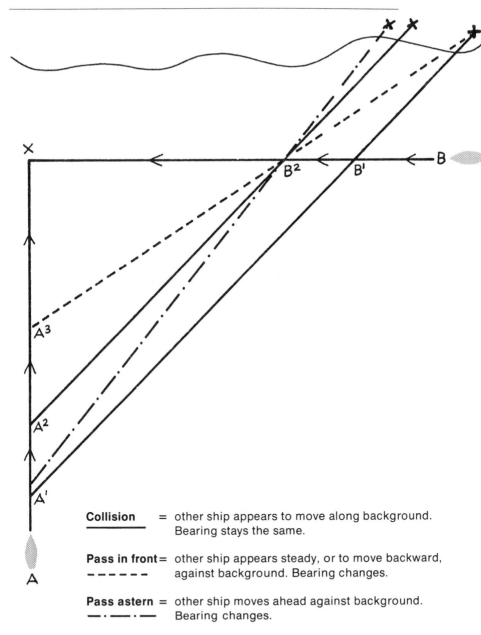

Collision = other ship appears to move along background.
Bearing stays the same.

Pass in front = other ship appears steady, or to move backward,
against background. Bearing changes.

Pass astern = other ship moves ahead against background.
Bearing changes.

Figure 6.3 Use the bearing to determine if you are on a collision
course with another vessel. Remember to exercise extreme caution if it appears that you are going to pass in front of another
boat.

change of the bearing. Remember the limitations with which you are working on a small boat in a seaway. If the bearing seems to be changing, but only slowly, assume it to be steady. If the other fellow has the right-of-way, change course to pass astern—well astern—and remember to make your change distinct enough to be noted by the other vessel.

While we are on this subject, it seems like a good time to go into the other rule of the road for two sailboats which are under sail and meet in a crossing situation.

If both boats are on the same tack, the vessel to windward keeps out of the way of the boat to leeward. Thus in figure 6.3 if the wind had been blowing from the northeast, boat A would have been the privileged vessel (having the right-of-way)—just the reverse of the situation when both boats are under power.

This rule comes to us from the days of the square-riggers which unlike modern sloops were very difficult to tack. In the situation of figure 6.3 it would be much easier and safer for the windward vessel B to bear-off a little and cross A astern. She could probably do this just by steering, without having to handle the sheets at all.

Suppose you were out walking one day on your way to do some shopping and as you started to cross the street to the store, you saw that work was going on in the street and there was a trench in the direct line from you to the entrance of the store. Instead of crossing the street where you originally planned, you might walk on a bit and cross where you had a line to the entrance unobstructed by the trench. In doing this you would have unconsciously applied the principle of the danger bearing: in the first instance the bearing from you to the entryway of the store would take you into a hazard—the ditch—so you don't approach on that bearing. You wait until you have a bearing that does not cross a hazard and then proceed.

Figure 6.4 shows an analogous situation on the water. There are two peninsulas and the one to the east has a light-

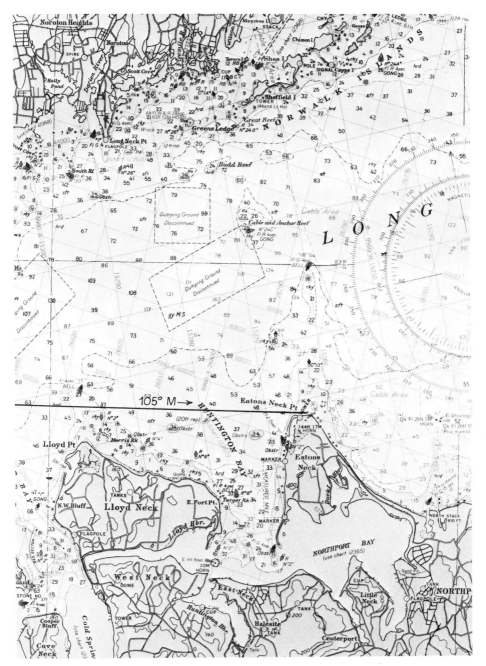

Figure 6.4 For a boat approaching Eatons Neck Point from the west, any bearing to the lighthouse less than 105° magnetic is a danger bearing.

house. Approaching from the west in order to avoid the rocks and shoals off Lloyd Point, you would need to be very careful if the bearing to the lighthouse were 105° magnetic or less. If you like, you can imagine the bearing lines from the lighthouse to be lanes or paths. This makes it very clear that if you try to approach Eatons Neck (the eastern peninsula) on lane 82°, you will put your boat aground in the mud and sand of Lloyd Point.

It is also useful to remember that we are talking here about the *bearing* and not the *heading* of the boat. If you were heading on an easterly course, the boat's head (bow) might be pointed a number of degrees higher than the danger bearing, but because of leeway and/or current the boat's course through the water might be such that you could be coming at the lighthouse on one of the dangerous paths. So if you are trying to get by a point or other obstruction, it is important to take a bearing and not rely solely on the boat's heading as shown by the steering compass. One night during a race I was trying to skin this very point and nearly put us aground because I didn't make sufficient allowance for the difference between the bearing and the heading of the boat. Best thing, if cruising, is to give yourself a generous margin (say 10°) for error.

Figure 6.5 shows another use of the danger bearing. Approaching again from the west, it is interesting to note that you cannot get to northward of the island simply by steering between red buoy # 10G1 and black buoy # 15. The direct line between them runs right across the bricks. Instead, you must plot a danger bearing and not approach the black buoy on any bearing less than 78°.

In using the danger bearing keep in mind that if the danger is to the right of you, safety lies in keeping it to the right. Therefore, the safe bearings are those that are numerically *greater* than the danger bearing. This is because of the fact that as something moves to your right (relatively), it moves clockwise on the face of the compass and the num-

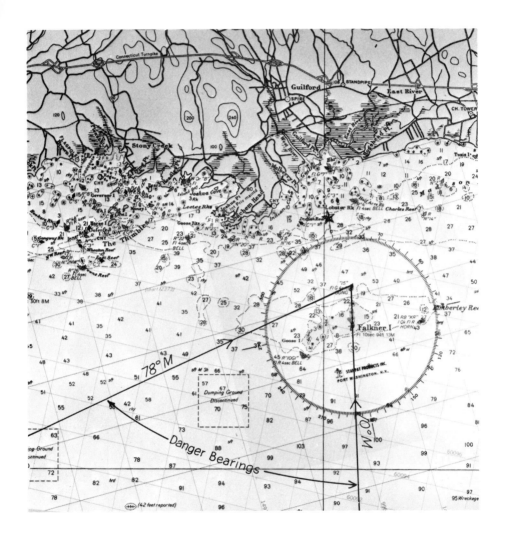

Figure 6.5 An approach to the buoy on courses less than 78 °
magnetic may lead onto rocks.

bers increase as you go clockwise around the compass ring. Similarly, if the danger is to your left, the safe bearings will be *less* than the danger bearing.

This discussion has reminded me of another principle of navigation: when you are looking at a chart and planning a course, it is more important to note where you *can not* go than to try to remember where you can go since, for small boats, there are generally more of the latter than the former. Thus in planning the approach to Falkner Island, it is far easier to remember the danger bearing upon which you can not approach than to remember all the other bearings, upon which you can approach.

CHAPTER

7

Distance Off

W e have seen that it is useful to be able to take a bearing on a known object on shore or a buoy in the water for purposes of locating, or fixing, your position. To get a fix with bearings alone requires at least two bearings. However, one bearing will provide a fix if you can determine your distance from the object on which you have the bearing. Even in the absence of a bearing it is often very useful to know, say, how far off the beach (or rocks) you are so that a glance at the chart will tell you if you are likely to clear any dangers that might be ahead. There are many ways of estimating the distance you are away from something, some of which are very accurate and some of which (my favorites) belong to the quick and easy school of navigation. I'll start with the easiest and work along to the more difficult and precise methods.

1. Most of us do our sailing in populated areas, so there are often houses and buildings along the shore. Well, if you can see the line where shore and water meet, you are about

three miles offshore. If you can just count the windows (if they are normal-sized and you are not shortsighted), you are about two miles away from the house or building whose windows you are counting. If you can make out the windows clearly or count the trees, you are within a mile.

2. This second method is one I read about in a book by Harold Gatty, who navigated for the aviator, Wiley Post. The technique is so simple that it entranced me then and still does.

Say there is a house on shore and you want to find out how far away it is. Hold your forefinger up with the back of your hand toward your face. Close your left eye and, using your right eye, line your finger up with the right edge of the house. Now close your right eye and open your left eye. Your finger will appear to have moved to the right of the house. Estimate how many house-lengths your finger appears to have moved. Let's say it was 15 house-lengths. Now estimate the width of the house. Say it looks like a pretty normal house to you and the houses you are used to are 60 feet wide. Well, 15 times 60 feet is 900 feet, the distance your finger appeared to move. Multiply this number by 10 and you have your distance off shore—9,000 feet—or one and one-half nautical miles.

For the reason this works, see figure 7.1. Basically it depends on the fact that the ratio between the space separating the eyes of an average human and the length of his outstretched arm is about one to ten.

3. A classic way to find distance off is by what is called bow and beam bearings. You take note of the time and speed when an object bears 45° on one side of the bow or the other—that is, when the relative angle between your heading and the bearing to the object is 45°. When the object is abeam (90° relative to your bearing), again note the time. From the elapsed time and speed, calculate the distance you have traveled through the water. That distance is equal to the distance you were away from the object at the time it

G is "guesstimated" distance
X is distance off
2.5 inches is distance between eyes
26 inches is length of arm

$$\frac{X}{26 \text{ inches}} = \frac{6}{2.5 \text{ inches}}$$

$$2.5\,X = 26\,G$$

$$X = \frac{26\,G}{2.5}$$

$$X = 10.4\,G$$

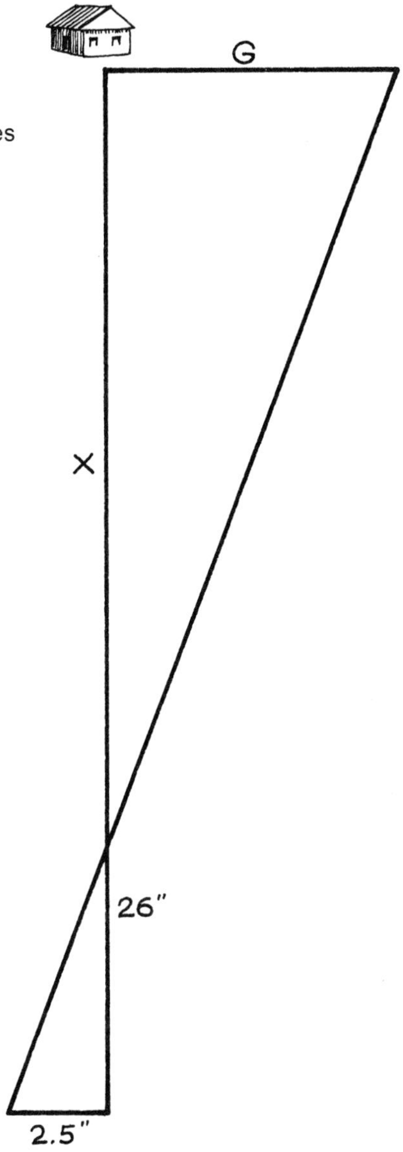

G

X

26"

2.5"

Figure 7.1 Schematic explanation of how you can estimate your distance off shore by using your out-stretched arm.

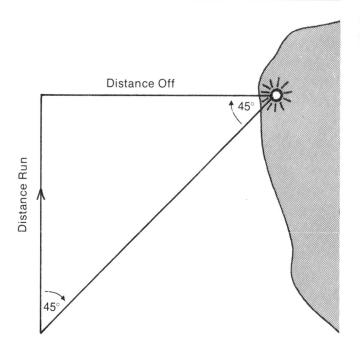

Distance Off

Distance Run

45°

45°

Figure 7.2 Bow and beam bearings used to estimate distance off.

came abeam. Figure 7.2 shows diagramatically why this works.

4. If you have a depthfinder or hand leadline on board, you can find your distance off by a bearing and knowledge of the depth of water. Look along the bearing line until you come to the indicated depth. You are about where the depth and the line coincide. It is a good idea to look farther along the bearing line, as it might happen that you are near a trench which has nearly the same depths on each side. This has occasionally happened to me and is another instance in which the DR is invaluable in helping to sort out the most likely position.

None of these useful, quick methods is as reliable as a fix obtained by two, or preferably more, bearings on known objects with good, broad crossing angles. Further, when using these or any other methods, don't ever forget to see how the positions or distances obtained square with the DR. It is an essential check.

Basically, of course, the navigator is always checking the validity of the DR by whatever means are available and appropriate. Thus, he may check the DR position for distance off by bow and beam bearings, and, additionally, check the distance off by trying to count the windows on a house ashore or by taking a bearing and a sounding of the depth. Having through these means pretty well fixed his position, he may than go on to see how well his calculated speed through the water squares with the time and distance run from his last fix.

I don't think there is any need to belabor this next point. Maybe it is best to just point out that the need for crosschecks varies inversely with the visibility. It is least needed during daylight in clear weather when just looking around can give a good estimate of the position and most needed at night in fog when the navigator is restricted to the basics of DR and a good lookout.

8

The Magic Number—Sixty

If you mark out an angle of one degree on a sheet of paper and imagine that the two lines forming the sides of that angle are extended sixty miles, then the distance between the two lines is one mile. This simple fact is very useful in practical navigation.

For instance, suppose you are running along a coastline and see your next landmark, a lighthouse, three miles ahead. Let's say that for one reason or another you feel it is advisable to pass one mile offshore of this lighthouse. Without looking at the chart, how many degrees should you alter course? Well, if the lighthouse were sixty miles away, you would have to alter course one degree, since at sixty miles one degree would cover a distance of one mile. Since you are only three miles away, each degree only covers one-twentieth of a mile, so you will have to change your course twenty degrees to seaward in order to pass the light one mile offshore.

This particular technique is very useful at night due to

the fact that lighthouses are highly visible at night in clear weather. Suppose you had just picked up the light of a lighthouse whose range of visibility was thirty miles. At thirty miles, one degree covers a span of one-half mile. To pass, say, five miles offshore of the light in this case, therefore, you would have to change course ten degrees. Simply divide the magic number, sixty, by the distance, thirty, and multiply the result by the number of miles off you wish to pass the light ($60 \div 30 = 2$; $2 \times 5 = 10°$).

Another use of the magic number is to roughly determine the relative length of time to stay on each tack when you want to average, or make good, a given course.

Say your boat is able to tack in one hundred degrees (the difference between the headings you are able to steer on each tack while going to windward) and that on one tack your track is thirty degrees to the right of your desired course, and on the other tack seventy degrees to the left of course. Now if you sailed sixty miles on one tack, you would end up thirty miles to the right of your course. Roughly, then, you can reason it out this way (see figure 8.1): If I go sixty miles on the tack to the right, I'll be thirty miles from the desired course line; therefore, my tacks should be in the ratio of two to one, twice as long on the tack away from the course as on the one back to it. Similar thinking leads to a ratio of sixty to seventy on the other tack—longer on the tack to the line than on the one away. Obviously, this last is not a good tactic. You are effectively spending more time sailing away from your objective than toward it. So when sailing upwind, spend most of your time on the tack closest to the desired course line (called the rhumb line).

It is interesting to note that a strict triginometric solution of this example gives the ratio of 1.879 to 1 for the case in which the track is 30° to one side of the rhumb. Since leeway is not considered, nor the effects of waves and helmsmanship, I don't think it appropriate to worry about a

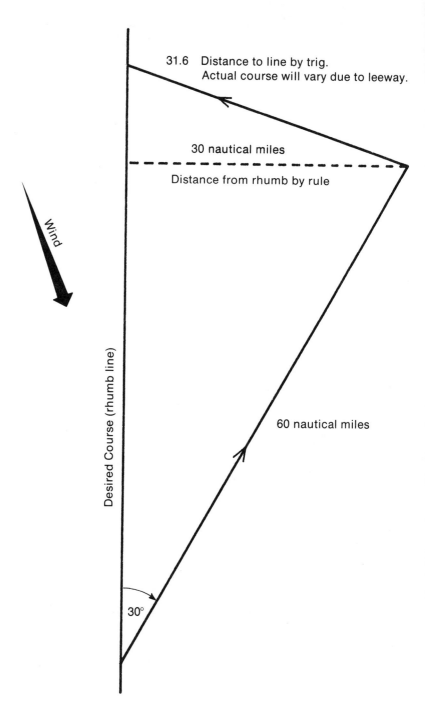

Figure 8.1 Tacking upwind and determining ratio of time on each tack.

strict mathematical approach; but I am including a table so that you can see that simply dividing sixty by the angle off the rhumb line will put you very much in the ball park.

The number in body of table is the ratio of time on tack closest to desired course and time on tack farthest from desired course. If your boat, for example, tacks through 100° and 30° is the closest you can come to desired course, stay on closest tack 1.9 times as long as other tack—19 minutes to 10 minutes, 28 minutes to 15 minutes, etc.

		Tacking Angle			
		80°	90°	100°	110°
	10°	5.4	5.7	5.8	5.7
Angle between Desired Course and Closest Tack	20°	2.5	2.7	2.9	2.9
	30°	1.5	1.7	1.9	2.0
	40°	1.0	1.2	1.3	1.5
	50°	—	—	1.0	1.1
	60°	—	—	—	—

Table 8.1   **Tacking upwind.**

9

Tides
and Currents

Tides

As we all probably know by now, the rise and fall of the waters on which many of us cruise are caused by the gravitational attraction of the sun and the moon on the water. When the gravitational forces of the sun and moon are in phase and working together at the times of a new and the full moon, the tides go through what is called their *spring* range. Then the high tides are highest and low tides are lowest. In other words, the range of the tide is greatest.

The range when the tide is least is when the moon is half-full, because then the gravity of the moon and sun are working against each other and the effective force acting on the water is less. When the range of the tides is least, they are called *neap* tides. During the neap tides, high tide is lower than spring high tide and low tide is higher than spring low tide. In our area (Larchmont, New York) for example, the difference between high and low water during the spring range is nine feet; during the neap range, the difference is six feet.

Note that spring, as used here, has nothing to do with the season of the year. Since there are generally one full and one new moon each month, there are two days during which the tides reach their highest and lowest and two days in which they are in their neap range. Other days they obviously oscillate between these two ranges, depending upon where the moon is in its phases between full (or new) and one-half. The average of these ranges is called the mean tide range and this mean tidal range is the reference most often used for the depth data given on most charts. This means, for example, if you are looking at a chart and it is full moon, or nearly so, the actual depths of the water at low tide will be less than shown on the chart. Likewise, on the days of a half moon, the depth of the water is greater than shown on the chart.

Most places in the world have two high tides daily, and here the tides are said to be semidiurnal. Those that have only one are said to be diurnal. Then there are places in the world that have one or the other depending upon the phase of the moon. Some places have really eccentric tides, such as the double high tide of Southampton, England and the double low of Hoek Van Holland in the Netherlands.

Now, the moon takes about twenty-four hours and forty-eight minutes to circle the earth; and, for numerous reasons, when there is a high tide on your side of the earth, there is also another high tide directly opposite you on the other side of the earth. This tide will reach you in twelve hours and twenty-four minutes after your present high tide and, in the meantime, low tide will occur. The sequence of tides, then, for places having the normal two high tides per day (semidiurnal) is this:

> high tide
> low tide
> high tide
> low tide

Since this complete cycle takes twenty-four hours and forty-eight minutes, the timing cycle looks like this:

high tide

six hours twelve minutes

low tide

six hours twelve minutes

high tide

six hours twelve minutes

low tide

six hours twelve minutes

high tide

Thus, if you know the time of high tide, you can figure the approximate time of the following low by adding six hours, twelve minutes, or the time of the next high by adding twelve hours, twenty-four minutes.

For places where the tide sequence is one high and one low per day (diurnal), this is the pattern:

high tide

twelve hours twenty-four minutes

low tide

twelve hours twenty-four minutes

high tide

Various agencies of the maritime nations publish annual tables which predict the times of high and low tides and direction and velocity of tidal currents. In the United States these tables are published by the National Oceanic and Atmospheric Administration (NOAA). Both the tide table and the tidal current tables list daily predictions for what are called *reference stations* in the main body of the table and then provide a further list in the back which gives the factors to be applied to the reference in order to come up with the predictions for other places (usually in the same geographical area as the base station).

Tables 9.1 through 9.3 show samples of the NOAA tables and give examples of their use. About the only tricky thing in these tables is that they use standard time for the meridian printed on each page; if you're on some form of daylight saving, you will have to add an hour to the times shown in the table.

If these tables have a flaw, it is that the *precision* with which the data is given (time to the minute, heights to the tenth of a foot) can seduce you into an erroneous conclusion of its *accuracy*. These tables are produced from mathematical models by computers, so naturally they use very precise units. Judgment and commonsense, however, say the data is probably correct to within an hour in time and a foot or so vertically.

Another Way

One of the things I have tried to do in the books I have written is to make each as complete within itself as is reasonably possible. This alleviates as much as possible the frustration a reader must feel when he finds after reading a book that he has to buy any number of other books in order to put into practice what he has read. It is also in keeping with the idea that you can do a lot by knowing what to look for in the world around you.

With this in mind, in addition to showing you how to use the tide tables published both privately and by the government of the United States and other countries, I am including in this chapter a perpetual tide table which I found in the 1936 edition of *The American Practical Navigator*. This is the book I mentioned earlier, which is commonly referred to as *Bowditch*, for its original author,

NEWPORT, R.I., 1979

TIMES AND HEIGHTS OF HIGH AND LOW WATERS

APRIL

DAY	TIME h.m.	HT. ft.	DAY	TIME h.m.	HT. ft.
1 SU	0420	-0.3	16 M	0332	-0.4
	1052	3.3		1024	3.2
	1620	-0.1		1537	-0.3
	2316	3.6		2245	3.7
2 M	0505	0.0	17 TU	0420	-0.3
	1144	3.0		1118	3.1
	1702	0.2		1628	-0.2
				2339	3.6
3 TU	0011	3.3	18 W	0513	-0.2
	0552	0.3		1215	3.0
	1239	2.8		1726	0.0
	1752	0.4			
4 W	0107	3.0	19 TH	0041	3.5
	0651	0.6		0615	-0.1
	1339	2.7		1318	3.1
	1856	0.6		1835	0.1
5 TH	0207	2.9	20 F	0146	3.5
	0811	0.7		0724	0.0
	1439	2.7		1424	3.3
	2024	0.7		1953	0.0
6 F	0305	2.9	21 SA	0251	3.5
	0933	0.6		0839	-0.1
	1533	2.8		1523	3.6
	2149	0.6		2114	-0.1
7 SA	0357	3.0	22 SU	0352	3.7
	1021	0.5		0946	-0.3
	1623	3.0		1621	3.9
	2240	0.4		2226	-0.4
8 SU	0447	3.1	23 M	0447	3.8
	1052	0.3		1044	-0.5
	1709	3.3		1714	4.2
	2314	0.2		2325	-0.6
9 M	0531	3.3	24 TU	0540	4.0
	1124	0.1		1135	-0.7
	1751	3.5		1804	4.5
	2348	0.0			
10 TU	0613	3.4	25 W	0017	-0.8
	1154	-0.1		0630	4.0
	1833	3.7		1222	-0.8
				1852	4.6
11 W	0022	-0.2	26 TH	0104	-0.9
	0654	3.5		0718	4.0
	1226	-0.3		1307	-0.8
	1912	3.9		1939	4.6
12 TH	0055	-0.4	27 F	0149	-0.8
	0734	3.5		0804	3.9
	1259	-0.4		1348	-0.7
	1951	3.9		2026	4.5
13 F	0132	-0.5	28 SA	0231	-0.7
	0813	3.5		0850	3.7
	1337	-0.4		1427	-0.5
	2031	4.0		2111	4.3
14 SA	0209	-0.5	29 SU	0313	-0.4
	0855	3.4		0937	3.5
	1413	-0.5		1508	-0.2
	2113	3.9		2158	4.0
15 SU	0250	-0.5	30 M	0350	-0.2
	0937	3.3		1025	3.3
	1455	-0.4		1545	0.0
	2156	3.8		2246	3.6

MAY

DAY	TIME h.m.	HT. ft.	DAY	TIME h.m.	HT. ft.
1 TU	0430	0.1	16 W	0411	-0.4
	1115	3.0		1102	3.4
	1627	0.3		1620	-0.2
	2336	3.3		2323	3.9
2 W	0509	0.3	17 TH	0504	-0.3
	1208	2.9		1200	3.4
	1712	0.5		1720	0.0
3 TH	0028	3.0	18 F	0023	3.7
	0555	0.5		0603	-0.1
	1305	2.8		1301	3.5
	1808	0.7		1829	0.1
4 F	0127	2.9	19 SA	0126	3.6
	0650	0.6		0709	-0.1
	1400	2.8		1404	3.6
	1914	0.8		1947	0.1
5 SA	0223	2.8	20 SU	0230	3.6
	0751	0.6		0818	-0.1
	1456	2.9		1504	3.8
	2032	0.8		2109	0.0
6 SU	0317	2.9	21 M	0330	3.6
	0849	0.5		0925	-0.2
	1547	3.1		1600	4.1
	2138	0.6		2220	-0.2
7 M	0407	3.0	22 TU	0426	3.7
	0941	0.4		1023	-0.3
	1634	3.4		1653	4.3
	2226	0.4		2316	-0.3
8 TU	0455	3.1	23 W	0519	3.7
	1026	0.2		1114	-0.4
	1717	3.6		1743	4.5
	2308	0.1			
9 W	0538	3.3	24 TH	0007	-0.5
	1106	0.0		0609	3.8
	1759	3.9		1159	-0.4
	2349	-0.1		1830	4.6
10 TH	0622	3.4	25 F	0052	-0.5
	1148	-0.2		0657	3.8
	1841	4.1		1243	-0.4
				1916	4.6
11 F	0030	-0.3	26 SA	0133	-0.5
	0705	3.5		0742	3.7
	1229	-0.4		1322	-0.3
	1923	4.2		2002	4.4
12 SA	0110	-0.5	27 SU	0211	-0.4
	0748	3.6		0828	3.6
	1310	-0.5		1401	-0.2
	2006	4.3		2047	4.2
13 SU	0152	-0.6	28 M	0247	-0.2
	0831	3.6		0912	3.5
	1352	-0.5		1439	0.0
	2050	4.3		2130	4.0
14 M	0234	-0.6	29 TU	0323	0.0
	0919	3.5		0958	3.3
	1438	-0.4		1516	0.2
	2137	4.2		2216	3.7
15 TU	0321	-0.5	30 W	0357	0.1
	1008	3.5		1046	3.2
	1525	-0.3		1556	0.4
	2228	4.0		2302	3.4
			31 TH	0433	0.3
				1134	3.0
				1638	0.6
				2352	3.2

JUNE

DAY	TIME h.m.	HT. ft.	DAY	TIME h.m.	HT. ft.
1 F	0513	0.4	16 SA	0006	3.9
	1227	3.0		0550	-0.2
	1728	0.7		1243	3.8
				1823	0.1
2 SA	0044	3.2	17 SU	0106	3.7
	0558	0.5		0650	-0.1
	1321	3.0		1343	3.9
	1823	0.8		1938	0.2
3 SU	0138	2.9	18 M	0208	3.6
	0650	0.5		0755	0.0
	1414	3.1		1441	4.0
	1927	0.8		2059	0.1
4 M	0232	2.9	19 TU	0307	3.5
	0745	0.5		0859	0.0
	1505	3.2		1539	4.1
	2031	0.7		2210	0.1
5 TU	0325	2.9	20 W	0403	3.5
	0840	0.4		0959	0.0
	1555	3.5		1632	4.3
	2133	0.5		2308	0.0
6 W	0415	3.1	21 TH	0458	3.5
	0931	0.2		1052	-0.1
	1642	3.7		1723	4.4
	2227	0.3			
7 TH	0504	3.2	22 F	0001	-0.1
	1023	0.0		0546	3.5
	1727	4.0		1140	-0.1
	2316	0.0		1809	4.4
8 F	0551	3.4	23 SA	0042	-0.1
	1111	-0.2		0633	3.6
	1812	4.3		1222	-0.1
				1856	4.4
9 SA	0002	-0.3	24 SU	0118	-0.1
	0636	3.6		0719	3.6
	1159	-0.4		1300	-0.1
	1857	4.5		1940	4.3
10 SU	0048	-0.5	25 M	0151	-0.1
	0723	3.7		0804	3.6
	1246	-0.5		1337	0.0
	1943	4.6		2023	4.2
11 M	0136	-0.6	26 TU	0223	0.0
	0811	3.8		0848	3.5
	1336	-0.5		1414	0.2
	2031	4.6		2105	4.0
12 TU	0222	-0.6	27 W	0254	0.1
	0900	3.8		0932	3.4
	1425	-0.5		1450	0.4
	2119	4.5		2148	3.8
13 W	0310	-0.6	28 TH	0326	0.2
	0951	3.8		1017	3.3
	1518	-0.4		1529	0.4
	2212	4.4		2230	3.5
14 TH	0401	-0.5	29 F	0358	0.2
	1046	3.8		1101	3.2
	1612	-0.2		1609	0.5
	2307	4.1		2315	3.3
15 F	0454	-0.4	30 SA	0436	0.3
	1142	3.8		1150	3.2
	1713	0.0		1651	0.7

TIME MERIDIAN 75° W. 0000 IS MIDNIGHT. 1200 IS NOON.
HEIGHTS ARE REFERRED TO MEAN LOW WATER WHICH IS THE CHART DATUM OF SOUNDINGS.

Table 9.1 Reference Station—Semidiurnal Tide Area

This page from the NOAA 1979 Tide Table for the East Coast of North and South America lists the predicted times of high and low tides at Newport, Rhode Island, U.S.A. Simple inspection of the column labeled "Ht." (height) shows whether the time given under "h.m." (hours, minutes) refers to high or low water. Thus the first entry for May 26 is 0133 −0.5. This indicates low tide will be at 1:33 A.M. Eastern Standard Time at which time the tide is expected to reach a level of one-half foot *below* (−0.5) the depths shown on the standard charts for the area. Likewise, the first high tide of the day will occur at 7:42 A.M. and is predicted to reach a height 3.7 feet *above* the depths shown on the standard charts.

No.	PLACE	POSITION		DIFFERENCES				RANGES		Mean Tide Level
				Time		Height				
		Lat.	Long.	High water	Low water	High water	Low water	Mean	Spring	
		° ′	° ′	h. m.	h. m.	feet	feet	feet	feet	feet
	RHODE ISLAND and MASSACHUSETTS Narragansett Bay — Continued *Time meridian, 75°W.*	N.	W.			on NEWPORT, p.40					
1159	Fall River, Massachusetts----------	41 44	71 08	+0 31	+0 34	+0.9	0.0	4.4	5.5	2.2
1161	Taunton, Taunton River, Mass--------	41 53	71 06	+1 09	+2 23	-0.7	0.0	2.8	3.5	1.4
1163	Bristol----------------------------	41 40	71 16	+0 10	0 00	+0.6	0.0	4.1	5.1	2.0
1165	Warren-----------------------------	41 44	71 17	+0 21	+0 04	+1.1	0.0	4.6	5.7	2.3
1167	Nayatt Point-----------------------	41 43	71 20	+0 12	+0 03	+1.1	0.0	4.6	5.7	2.3
1169	Providence-------------------------	41 48	71 24	+0 14	+0 05	+1.1	0.0	4.6	5.7	2.3
1171	Pawtucket, Seekonk River------------	41 52	71 23	+0 21	+0 14	+1.1	0.0	4.6	5.8	2.3
1173	East Greenwich---------------------	41 40	71 27	+0 16	+0 08	+0.5	0.0	4.0	5.0	2.0
1175	Wickford---------------------------	41 34	71 27	+0 12	+0 07	+0.3	0.0	3.8	4.7	1.9
1177	Narragansett Pier------------------	41 25	71 27	-0 08	+0 16	-0.3	0.0	3.2	4.0	1.6
	RHODE ISLAND, Outer Coast									
1179	Point Judith Harbor of Refuge-------	41 22	71 29	-0 07	+0 22	-0.4	0.0	3.1	3.9	1.5
1181	Block Island (Great Salt Pond)------	41 11	71 35	+0 05	+0 12	-0.9	0.0	2.6	3.2	1.3
1183	Block Island (Old Harbor)----------	41 10	71 33	-0 14	+0 17	-0.6	0.0	2.9	3.6	1.4
1185	Watch Hill Point-------------------	41 18	71 52	+0 44	+1 21	-0.9	0.0	2.6	3.2	1.3
						on NEW LONDON, p.44					
1186	Westerly, Pawcatuck River-----------	41 23	71 50	-0 27	+0 02	+0.1	0.0	2.7	3.2	1.3
	CONNECTICUT, Long Island Sound									
1187	Stonington, Fishers Island Sound----	41 20	71 54	-0 33	-0 41	+0.1	0.0	2.7	3.2	1.3
1189	Noank, Mystic River entrance--------	41 19	71 59	-0 23	-0 08	-0.3	0.0	2.3	2.7	1.2
1191	West Harbor, Fishers Island, N. Y---	41 16	72 00	-0 01	-0 06	-0.1	0.0	2.5	3.0	1.2
1192	Silver Eel Pond, Fishers I., N. Y---	41 15	72 02	-0 17	-0 04	-0.3	0.0	2.3	2.7	1.1
	Thames River										
1193	NEW LONDON, State Pier-----------	41 22	72 06		Daily predictions			2.6	3.1	1.3
1195	Smith Cove entrance-------------	41 24	72 06	-0 01	+0 10	-0.1	0.0	2.5	3.0	1.2
1197	Norwich------------------------	41 31	72 05	+0 09	+0 20	+0.4	0.0	3.0	3.6	1.5
1199	Millstone Point--------------------	41 18	72 10	+0 08	+0 01	+0.1	0.0	2.7	3.2	1.3
	Connecticut River										
1200	Saybrook Jetty-----------------	41 16	72 21	+1 10	+0 45	+0.9	0.0	3.5	4.2	1.7
1201	Saybrook Point-----------------	41 17	72 21	+1 10	+0 53	+0.6	0.0	3.2	3.8	1.6
1202	Lyme, highway bridge-----------	41 19	72 21	+1 24	+1 10	+0.5	0.0	3.1	3.7	1.5
1203	Essex--------------------------	41 21	72 23	+1 38	+1 38	+0.4	0.0	3.0	3.6	1.5
1204	Hadlyme†-----------------------	41 25	72 26	+2 18	+2 23	+0.1	0.0	2.7	3.2	1.3
1205	East Haddam--------------------	41 27	72 28	+2 41	+2 53	+0.3	0.0	2.9	3.5	1.4
1206	Haddam†------------------------	41 29	72 30	+2 47	+3 08	-0.1	0.0	2.5	3.0	1.2
1207	Higganum Creek-----------------	41 30	72 33	+2 54	+3 25	0.0	0.0	2.6	3.1	1.3
1209	Portland†----------------------	41 34	72 38	+3 50	+4 28	-0.4	0.0	2.2	2.6	1.1
1211	Rocky Hill†--------------------	41 39	72 38	+4 43	+5 44	-0.6	0.0	2.0	2.4	1.0
1213	Hartford†----------------------	41 46	72 40	+5 29	+6 52	-0.7	0.0	1.9	2.3	1.0
						on BRIDGEPORT, p.48					
1214	Westbrook, Duck Island Roads--------	41 16	72 28	-0 23	-0 34	-2.6	0.0	4.1	4.7	2.0
1215	Duck Island------------------------	41 15	72 29	-0 25	-0 37	-2.2	0.0	4.5	5.2	2.2
1217	Madison---------------------------	41 16	72 36	-0 20	-0 32	-1.8	0.0	4.9	5.6	2.4
1219	Falkner Island---------------------	41 13	72 39	-0 13	-0 27	-1.3	0.0	5.4	6.2	2.7
1220	Sachem Head-----------------------	41 15	72 42	-0 10	-0 17	-1.3	0.0	5.4	6.2	2.7
1221	Money Island-----------------------	41 15	72 45	-0 11	-0 25	-1.1	0.0	5.6	6.4	2.8
1223	Branford Harbor--------------------	41 16	72 49	-0 07	-0 20	-0.8	0.0	5.9	6.8	2.9
1225	New Haven Harbor entrance-----------	41 14	72 55	-0 08	-0 16	-0.5	0.0	6.2	7.1	3.1
1227	New Haven (city dock)--------------	41 18	72 55	+0 02	-0 03	-0.7	0.0	6.0	6.9	3.0
1229	Milford Harbor--------------------	41 13	73 03	-0 07	-0 12	-0.7	0.0	6.6	7.6	3.3
1231	Stratford, Housatonic River--------	41 11	73 07	+0 27	+0 59	-1.2	0.0	5.5	6.3	2.7
1233	Shelton, Housatonic River----------	41 19	73 05	+1 36	+2 42	-1.7	0.0	5.0	5.8	2.5

†Tidal information applies only during low river stages.

Table 9.2   List of Intermediate Stations

Places for which tide predictions can be worked using the base data on the table for Newport are listed in the upper left of this sample page. Thus, for the time of high water at Fall River, Massachusetts, 31 minutes is to be added to the times given for high water in Newport and .9 feet to the Newport heights.

TIMES AND HEIGHTS OF HIGH AND LOW WATERS

JANUARY

DAY	TIME h.m.	HT. ft.	DAY	TIME h.m.	HT. ft.
1 M	1049	-0.5	16 TU	0006	0.9
				1045	-0.2
2 TU	0036	1.1	17 W	0031	0.8
	1117	-0.3		1050	-0.1
3 W	0115	0.9	18 TH	0057	0.6
	1125	-0.1		1042	0.0
4 TH	0133	0.6	19 F	0101	0.5
	1105	0.0		1023	0.1
	2026	0.5		1930	0.4
5 F	0957	0.1	20 SA	0920	0.1
	1856	0.6		1757	0.5
6 SA	0706	0.0	21 SU	0556	0.1
	1857	0.8		1801	0.7
7 SU	0611	-0.2	22 M	0451	-0.1
	1923	0.9		1830	0.8
8 M	0629	-0.3	23 TU	0520	-0.3
	1955	1.0		1906	1.0
9 TU	0701	-0.4	24 W	0558	-0.5
	2031	1.1		1945	1.2
10 W	0736	-0.5	25 TH	0646	-0.6
	2110	1.1		2033	1.3
11 TH	0813	-0.5	26 F	0733	-0.7
	2148	1.1		2126	1.3
12 F	0850	-0.5	27 SA	0824	-0.7
	2224	1.1		2215	1.3
13 SA	0926	-0.4	28 SU	0911	-0.6
	2259	1.1		2307	1.2
14 SU	0955	-0.4	29 M	0950	-0.5
	2331	1.0		2357	1.0
15 M	1022	-0.3	30 TU	1015	-0.3
			31 W	0042	0.8
				1015	-0.1

FEBRUARY

DAY	TIME h.m.	HT. ft.	DAY	TIME h.m.	HT. ft.
1 TH	0128	0.5	16 F	0125	0.4
	0934	0.1		0845	0.2
	1651	0.4		1512	0.4
				2206	0.2
2 F	0757	0.1	17 SA	0251	0.3
	1637	0.6		0702	0.2
				1524	0.5
3 SA	0416	0.0	18 SU	0110	0.1
	1706	0.7		1549	0.7
4 SU	0429	-0.2	19 M	0238	-0.1
	1745	0.9		1631	0.9
5 M	0505	-0.3	20 TU	0338	-0.2
	1831	1.0		1721	1.0
6 TU	0547	-0.4	21 W	0430	-0.4
	1916	1.0		1816	1.1
7 W	0631	-0.4	22 TH	0526	-0.5
	2006	1.0		1919	1.2
8 TH	0713	-0.4	23 F	0619	-0.5
	2054	1.0		2018	1.2
9 F	0751	-0.4	24 SA	0711	-0.5
	2139	1.0		2121	1.2
10 SA	0829	-0.3	25 SU	0757	-0.3
	2215	1.0		2221	1.1
11 SU	0854	-0.3	26 M	0839	-0.2
	2254	0.9		2325	0.9
12 M	0927	-0.2	27 TU	0857	0.0
	2330	0.8			
13 TU	0941	-0.1	28 W	0024	0.7
				0830	0.2
				1331	0.3
				1843	0.2
14 W	0007	0.7			
	0939	0.0			
15 TH	0046	0.6			
	0920	0.1			

MARCH

DAY	TIME h.m.	HT. ft.	DAY	TIME h.m.	HT. ft.
1 TH	0155	0.5	16 F	0300	0.5
	0725	0.4		0518	0.4
	1336	0.5		1229	0.7
	2144	0.2		2118	0.2
2 F	1401	0.7	17 SA	1301	0.8
				2254	0.1
3 SA	0018	0.0	18 SU	1338	0.9
	1443	0.9			
4 SU	0157	-0.1	19 M	0024	-0.1
	1536	1.0		1429	1.1
5 M	0306	-0.2	20 TU	0136	-0.2
	1633	1.0		1522	1.1
6 TU	0402	-0.2	21 W	0242	-0.2
	1733	1.0		1626	1.2
7 W	0457	-0.2	22 TH	0343	-0.3
	1831	1.0		1734	1.2
8 TH	0545	-0.2	23 F	0436	-0.3
	1929	1.0		1847	1.2
9 F	0629	-0.1	24 SA	0533	-0.2
	2028	1.0		1959	1.1
10 SA	0711	-0.1	25 SU	0615	0.0
	2117	0.9		2119	1.0
11 SU	0741	0.0	26 M	0640	0.2
	2206	0.9		2248	0.8
12 M	0803	0.1	27 TU	0645	0.4
	2248	0.8		1139	0.5
				1716	0.3
13 TU	0800	0.2	28 W	0041	0.6
	2354	0.7		0543	0.5
				1112	0.7
				1924	0.2
14 W	0737	0.3	29 TH	1134	0.9
	1213	0.4		2103	0.1
	1729	0.3			
15 TH	0054	0.6	30 F	1209	1.0
	0706	0.4		2229	0.0
	1214	0.5			
	1929	0.3	31 SA	1251	1.1
				2348	-0.1

TIME MERIDIAN 90° W. 0000 IS MIDNIGHT. 1200 IS NOON.
HEIGHTS ARE REFERRED TO MEAN LOW WATER WHICH IS THE CHART DATUM OF SOUNDINGS.

Table 9.3 **Reference Station—Diurnal Tide Area**

Nathaniel Bowditch. What you need in order to use this table is some source of information on the basic phases of the moon, and I have included that for the years 1981 through 2003. So with this information you have a tide table for the world and will be able to predict for yourself to practical accuracy when the tides will change and, thus, know what to expect in the way of current directions.

A practical way to train yourself to think about the tides is to use this method for the waters you normally cruise. That way, you'll develop a feel for the basic mechanics involved and a habit of taking account of this important factor in planning your boating activities.

This tide table begins in the North American Arctic and then moves south along the coast through the West Indies, East Coast of South America, up the West Coast of South and North America, north to the Arctic again, then down the East Coast of Asia and so on around the world. For each place listed, latitude and longitude are given, as well as the mean and spring range of the tides. Most places in the world have two high tides daily, and here the tides are said to be semidiurnal. Those that have only one (tides said to be diurnal) are marked with an asterisk (*).

Now, look at the first page of the tide table at the entry for Thank God Harbor in Greenland (last entry for Greenland). The third column is headed High Water Interval and the numbers in that column are hours (h.) and minutes (m.). The number in this column for Thank God Harbor is 1214. What this means is that on the days of the full and new moon, high tide occurs twelve hours and fourteen minutes after the moon passes the longitude of Thank God Harbor.

Suppose it is July 24, 1979, the day of a new moon. By the table, the time of high tide at Thank God Harbor would be 12:14 A.M. (0014) on July 25th, since on the day of the new moon the moon is alongside the sun, the moon passes the longitude of Thank God Harbor with the sun at noon. Checking this against the NOAA tide table for 1979, I got

1:09 A.M. (0109), which I feel is acceptable agreement, considering that the Bowditch table will give useful approximations forever, whereas the modern tables have to be scrapped annually.

The full moon for July 1979 occurred on the ninth, which means it passed the longitude of Thank God Harbor about midnight local time. Twelve hours and fourteen minutes from midnight would make the next high tide occur at 12:14 P.M., or a little after noon. The government table gives the time of high tide at Thank God Harbor as 11:34 A.M.

In comparing these tables with the NOAA tables the greatest differences I have found have been in the order of an hour and a half. In actually using the tables in various places on the East Coast of the United States, I have most often found that the differences between them and the NOAA tables are indistinguishable due to the fact that the tide "stands" for a time at each end of its cycle; and there are daily, unpredictable influences such as barometric pressure and wind, which affect the tide.

For practical purposes in areas where the tides are semidiurnal you can consider the high water interval to be the time of day, A.M. and P.M., at which the two high tides will occur when the moon is full or new.

In areas where the tides are diurnal you need to do a little more work in order to be able to tell whether the one high for the day will occur in the A.M. or P.M. We'll get to that shortly.

Now, to repeat, the moon takes about twenty-four hours and forty-eight minutes to circle the earth; and, for numerous reasons, when there is a high tide on your side of the earth, there is also another high tide directly opposite you on the other side of the earth. This tide will reach you in twelve hours and twenty-four minutes, and, in the meantime, low tide occurs. The sequence of tides, then, for places having the normal two high tides per day (semidiurnal) is this:

high tide
low tide
high tide
low tide

Since this complete cycle takes twenty-four hours and forty-eight minutes, the timing cycle looks like this:

high tide
six hours twelve minutes
low tide
six hours twelve minutes
high tide
six hours twelve minutes
low tide
six hours twelve minutes
high tide

Thus, if you know the time of high tide, you can figure the time of the following low by adding six hours and twelve minutes, or the time of the next high by adding twelve hours and twenty-four minutes. If, as in the first example, the predicted high tide is for the day after the one you want, you subtract twelve hours twenty-four minutes to find the previous high tide.

To figure tides for days other than full or new moons you would *add* forty-eight minutes to find the time for days after a new or full moon and *subtract* forty-eight minutes for days before a new or full moon.

It needs to be said that the high-water intervals are *averages* and so is the figure of forty-eight minutes per day that the moon lags behind. The difference between consecutive passages of the moon past a given longitude ranges from about twenty minutes to a little over an hour, so extrapolating too many days from the day of the new or full moon must be done with awareness of this fact. If you are

107

on a cruise, though, you can go from day to day with this figure if you note (by looking) either the time of high water or the time of slack current, since they generally coincide reasonably closely.

There is a rather elegant wrinkle that occurs with this way of predicting tides and that is this: if you note the bearing (compass direction) of the moon when it is high tide in your area, every time the moon is at that bearing the tide will be high. It does not matter what phase the moon is in. So once you have coordinated the moon's position in the sky with high tide for your usual sailing area, you won't have to refer to a table when the moon's up.

On a day or night when the moon is visible in one of its phases other than new or full you can determine the time of the next high tide by noting the time on your watch when the moon bears true south or north. When it is on either of these bearings, it is on your meridian—i.e., on the same line of longitude as you. Then look up the tide interval in the table for the place closest to you and add this to your watch time. This will give you the time of the next high tide. To find the time of the preceding low, subtract six hours and twelve minutes; for the preceding high, subtract twelve hours and twenty-four minutes.

For places where the tide sequence is one high and one low per day (diurnal), this is the pattern:

high tide
twelve hours twenty-four minutes
low tide
twelve hours twenty-four minutes
high tide

In the Bowditch table (table 9.4) these places are marked with an asterisk (*) and the high-water interval is followed with an *a* or *b* to indicate whether you start counting from midnight or noon. Here's the way it works:

Dates between March 22–September 21
Suffix a—apply high-water interval to noon
Example: 24 June 1979, Port Royal, Jamaica (new moon)
high-water interval = 10:00
+ 12:00 (noon)

high tide = 10:00 P.M.
Suffix b—apply high-water interval to midnight
high-water interval = 12:25
+ 00:00 (Midnight)

high tide = 12:25 P.M.

Dates between September 22–March 21
Suffix a—apply high-water interval to midnight
Example: 19 December 1979, St. Thomas, Virgin Islands
high-water interval = 7:30
+ 0:00 (midnight)

high tide = 7:30 A.M.
Suffix b—apply high-water interval to noon
high-water interval = 10:30
+ 12:00 (noon)

high tide= 10:30 P.M.

TIDAL DATA.

EAST COAST OF NORTH AMERICA.

Place.	Lat. N.	Long. W.	High water interval.	Mean range.	Spring range.
	° ′	° ′	h. m.	Feet.	Feet.
ARCTIC ARCHIPELAGO.					
Herschel Island	69 34	138 50	0 25	0.8	1.2
Prince of Wales Strait	72 50	117 45	12 00	2.3	3.0
Mercy Bay, Banks Island	74 07	118 15	0 26	1.6	2.1
Winter Harbor, Melville Island	74 47	110 48	1 06	2.6	3.5
Bridport Inlet, Melville Island	74 55	108 47	1 38	3.1	4.0
Byam Martin Island	75 10	103 34	11 29	2.8	3.7
Cambridge Bay, Dease Strait	69 06	105 25	11 06	1.8	2.3
Fury and Hecla Strait, Igloolik	69 21	81 49	6 29	6.2	8.0
Port Kennedy, Bellot Strait	72 01	94 12	11 20	3.6	4.5
Port Bowen, Prince Regent Inlet	73 14	88 55	11 37	3.4	4.5
Port Leopold, Prince Regent Inlet	73 50	90 20	11 06	4.4	5.6
Beechy Island, Barrow Strait	74 43	92 00	11 56	4.3	5.6
Assistance Harbor, Barrow Strait	74 37	94 15	0 06	3.1	4.1
Griffiths Island, Barrow Strait	74 35	95 30	0 05	2.9	3.8
Refuge Cove, Wellington Channel	75 31	92 10	11 58	4.4	5.8
Penny Strait	76 52	97 00	0 05	1.4	1.8
Cape Columbia, Grant Land	83 05	69 35	7 58	0.8	1.1
Cape Sheridan, Grant Land	82 27	61 21	10 30	1.8	2.5
Cape Bryant, North Greenland	82 21	55 30	0 03	1.1	1.4
Cape Morris Jesup, North Greenland	83 40	33 35	10 49	0.4	0.6
GREENLAND.					
East Coast.					
Cape Borgen	75 26	18 00	12 06	3.0	3.9
Cape Philip Broke	74 55	17 37	11 25	3.5	4.6
Pendulum Island	74 37	18 29	11 31	3.0	4.0
Jackson Island	73 54	20 00	11 01	3.2	4.2
Cape Hold With Hope (Broer Ruys)	73 28	20 30	10 46	3.0	3.9
Angmagsalik	65 37	37 30	7 00	4.1	5.3
Nubarlik	63 24	42 02	6 43	3.8	4.9
Cape Farewell	59 45	43 56	6 00	4.0	5.2
West Coast.					
Fredericksdal	60 00	44 40	6 10	7.1	9.5
Nennortalik	60 02	45 10	6 14	6.2	8.2
Julianshaab	60 43	46 01	6 20	5.7	7.4
Kajartalik, Arsuk Fiord	61 10	48 33	6 25	8.0	10.4
Frederickshaab	62 00	49 43	6 35	6.7	8.7
Godthaab	64 10	51 35	6 42	8.3	10.8
Holsteinborg	66 56	53 42	6 12	7.7	10.0
Godhaven, Disco Island	69 12	53 20	8 42	5.8	7.5
Upernivik	72 47	56 03	10 42	6.2	8.1
North Star Bay, Wolstenholm Sound	76 30	68 50	11 05	5.6	7.3
Pandora Harbor	78 15	72 45	11 14	7.0	9.1
Port Foulke (Etah)	78 18	73 00	11 14	7.7	10.0
Rensslaer	78 37	70 53	11 43	8.0	10.8
Thank God Harbor, Polaris Bay	81 37	61 40	12 14	3.9	5.4
BAFFIN BAY.					
West Side.					
Fort Conger, Discovery Harbor	81 44	64 44	11 33	4.3	6.0
Cape Lawrence	81 21	69 15	11 30	5.5	7.2
Payer Harbor (Cape Sabine)	78 45	74 10	11 20	7.0	9.1
Cape Adair, Scott Inlet	71 18	70 55	10 50	6.0	7.8
Cape Hewett, River Clyde	70 22	68 26	10 40	5.5	7.2
DAVIS STRAIT.					
West Side.					
Cumberland Sound, Kingna Fiord	66 36	67 19	5 38	15.4	20.0
Frobisher Bay, N. W. Arm	63 45	68 40	6 30	34.6	45.0
HUDSON STRAIT AND BAY.					
Button Islands	60 37	64 44	8 30	12.5	18.0
Port Burwell, Ungava Bay	60 22	64 46	8 54	14.6	19.0
Koksoak River, Ungava Bay	58 33	68 05	8 21	29.6	38.5
Ashe Inlet, Big Island	62 30	70 38	8 01	23.1	30.0
Stupart Bay	61 35	71 32	7 40	18.5	24.0
Port Laperriere, Digges Island	62 37	78 10	8 22	6.6	9.0
Port Boucherville, Nottingham Island	63 12	77 25	8 59	10.0	13.0
Bowdoin Harbor	64 24	77 52	10 33	14.2	18.9
Repulse Bay, near head of	66 31	86 30	11 55	9.9	12.9
Winter Island	66 11	83 10	12 02	9.7	12.6
Cape Welsford, Southampton Island	65 28	84 40	11 44	12.8	16.6
Fullerton Harbor	63 59	89 06	2 19	12.3	16.0
Marble Island Harbor	62 42	91 10	3 39	9.2	12.0
Port Churchill	58 46	94 10	7 00	11.0	14.5
York Factory	57 02	92 22	11 00	10.5	13.7
North Bluff Beacon, James Bay	51 30	80 40	11 15	8.0	10.4

Table 9.4 **Tide Tables for Entire World**

TIDAL DATA.

EAST COAST OF NORTH AMERICA—Continued.

Place.	Lat. N.	Long. W.	High water interval.	Mean range.	Spring range.
	° ′	° ′	h. m.	Feet.	Feet.
LABRADOR.					
Eclipse Harbor	59 50	64 10	8 00	3.7	5.0
Nachvak Bay	59 05	63 20	7 00	3.8	5.2
Nain	56 34	61 44	7 00	4.9	6.5
Hopedale Harbor	55 25	60 20	5 30	5.2	6.9
Indian Harbor	54 30	57 30	6 10	5.3	7.0
Independent Harbor	53 51	56 55	6 40	4.4	5.8
Indian Tickle	53 34	56 00	6 27	4.6	6.0
Seal Islands	53 14	55 42	6 30	4.2	5.5
Venison Tickle	52 58	55 46	6 37	4.2	5.5
Occasional Harbor	52 40	55 47	6 38	3.8	5.0
Fishing Ship Harbor	52 36	55 45	6 44	4.2	5.5
Spear Harbor	52 26	55 38	7 12	3.4	4.5
St. Lewis Sound	52 19	55 44	6 30	2.7	3.5
Chateau Bay, Strait of Belle Isle	52 00	55 53	7 30	2.4	3.1
Red Bay, Strait of Belle Isle	51 45	56 26	9 00	2.4	3.1
Forteau Bay, Strait of Belle Isle	51 27	56 23	10 00	3.1	4.0
NEWFOUNDLAND.					
East Coast.					
Pistolet Bay	51 32	55 45	7 29	2.5	3.3
Hare Bay	51 17	55 55	8 28	5.3	7.0
Canada Bay	50 45	56 08	6 36	4.0	5.2
Cat Head, White Bay	50 08	56 41	6 50	3.5	4.6
Fortune Harbor, Notre Dame Bay	49 32	55 15	7 04	3.2	4.0
Fogo Harbor	49 44	54 16	7 05	3.4	4.5
Barrow Harbor, Bonavista Bay	48 40	53 36	6 03	3.3	4.4
Hearts Content, Trinity Bay	47 53	53 23	7 23	3.1	4.1
Grace Harbor, Conception Bay	47 42	53 13	7 15	3.4	4.5
St. Johns	47 34	52 42	7 12	2.5	3.3
South Coast.					
Cape Race	46 39	53 07	6 50	4.9	6.0
Trespassey Harbor	46 43	53 22	6 50	5.0	6.0
St. Mary Harbor, St. Mary Bay	46 55	53 35	7 30	5.7	7.5
Cape St. Mary, Placentia Bay	46 50	54 12	8 20	5.4	7.2
Woody Island, Placentia Bay	47 47	54 13	8 00	5.3	7.0
Burin Harbor, Placentia Bay	47 02	55 11	8 35	4.9	6.5
Great Laun	46 56	55 33	8 05	5.3	7.0
Miquelon or St. Pierre Island	46 47	56 09	8 23	5.0	6.6
Brunet Islands	47 16	55 55	8 53	4.9	6.5
Grand Bank Harbor, Fortune Bay	47 06	55 44	8 38	4.7	6.2
Grand le Pierre H., Fortune Bay	47 09	54 46	9 00	5.2	6.9
Breton Harbor, Fortune Bay	47 30	55 47	8 42	5.4	7.1
Hermitage Cove	47 32	55 55	8 35	5.3	7.0
Rencontre Bay	47 37	56 37	8 45	4.8	6.3
La Hune Bay	47 33	56 50	8 30	4.9	6.4
Burgeo Islands	47 36	57 37	8 22	4.7	6.2
La Poile Bay	47 40	58 23	8 50	4.6	6.0
Port Basque	47 35	59 07	8 52	4.2	5.5
West Coast.					
Codroy Road	47 53	59 24	8 50	3.3	4.3
St. George Harbor	48 28	58 21	9 05	3.0	3.9
Frenchman Cove, Bay of Islands	49 00	58 09	9 20	3.5	4.5
Bonne Bay	49 34	57 57	9 30	3.6	4.6
Cowhead Harbor	49 55	57 47	9 40	3.8	4.9
Hawke Harbor	50 37	57 12	9 55	3.7	4.8
Port au Choix	50 44	57 21	9 50	5.0	6.5
Good Bay	50 48	57 12	9 56	4.9	6.4
Castors Harbor, St. John Bay	50 54	56 57	10 00	3.2	4.1
St. Genevieve Bay	51 09	56 48	10 10	4.0	5.2
QUEBEC.					
Gulf of St. Lawrence.					
Belles Amour Bay	51 27	57 26	8 45	2.8	3.6
Mistanoque Harbor	51 16	58 12	10 15	3.7	4.8
Antrobus Island	50 33	59 17	10 15	3.1	4.0
Wapitagun Harbor	50 12	60 01	10 15	3.1	4.0
Kegashka Bay	50 11	61 16	10 30	3.1	4.0
Little Natashquan Harbor	50 12	61 50	10 45	3.1	4.0
Appeetetat Bay	50 19	63 00	10 55	3.1	4.0
Mingan Harbor	50 17	64 02	1 01	3.7	4.8
Anticosti Island.					
West Point Light	49 52	64 32	1 45	3.7	4.8
Bear Bay	49 31	62 26	0 10	3.1	4.0
East Point	49 08	61 39	11 05	2.8	3.6
Southwest Point Light	49 24	63 36	1 12	4.9	6.0
St. Lawrence River.					
Cape Rosier Light	48 52	64 12	1 25	4.9	5.5
Cape Magdalen Light	49 16	65 19	1 33	5.6	6.4
Martin River Light	49 13	66 09	1 37	6.4	7.3

TIDAL DATA.
EAST COAST OF NORTH AMERICA—Continued.

Place.	Lat. N.	Long. W.	High water interval.	Mean range.	Spring range.
QUEBEC—Continued.					
St. Lawrence River—Continued.					
	° ′	° ′	h. m.	Feet.	Feet.
Carousel Light	50 06	66 23	1 43	7.1	8.1
Cawee Island	49 50	67 07	1 45	7.0	9.0
Cape Chatte Light	49 06	66 45	1 55	9.5	12.0
Pointe de Monts Light	49 20	67 22	1 53	9.5	12.0
Matane Light	48 52	67 33	1 55	9.0	11.5
Little Metis	48 41	68 01	1 55	10.5	13.0
Manicouagan Shoal Light	49 06	68 12	1 57	10.0	12.5
Father Point Light	48 31	68 28	1 56	11.0	14.0
Bic Island	48 24	68 53	1 59	11.1	14.0
Tadousac, Saguenay River	48 09	69 43	2 23	13.5	17.0
Chicoutimi, Saguenay River	47 52	69 41	2 34	12.5	16.0
Brandy Pots Light	47 39	70 08	2 37	13.5	17.0
Murray Bay	47 30	70 02	3 17	13.5	17.0
Orignaux Point Light	47 21	70 26	3 25	14·0	17.5
Coudres Island	47 08	70 22	3 51	14.0	17.5
L'Islet	47 05	70 29	4 54	14.5	18.0
Beaujeu Channel	47 02	70 40	5 12	15.0	18.5
Grosse Isle	46 56	70 43	5 09	15.0	19.0
Berthier	46 52	71 03	5 26	14.5	18.0
St. Laurent Light, Orleans Island	46 49	71 11	5 49	14.0	17.5
Quebec Dry Dock	46 42	71 24	6 04	13.1	16.5
St. Nicholas	46 43	71 28	6 38	12.5	16.0
St. Augustin Bar	46 37	71 45	6 49	12.5	15.5
Ste. Croix	46 40	71 51	7 33	12.0	14.0
Point Platon	46 36	72 04	7 43	11.5	13.5
Grondine Light	46 33	72 10	8 21	7.0	8.5
Cape Roche Light	46 31	72 15	8 44	5.5	7.0
Batiscan Light	46 26	72 21	9 41	2.5	3.5
Champlain Light	46 20	72 33	10 12	2.0	3.0
Three Rivers			10 44	1.1	1.3
Gulf of St. Lawrence.					
O'Hara Point Light, Gaspe Bay	48 50	64 32	2 09	4.1	5.0
Cape Despair Light	48 26	64 18	1 29	3.5	4.5
Maquereau Point, Chaleur Bay	48 12	64 46	1 54	3.6	4.7
Carlisle, Chaleur Bay	48 01	65 20	2 19	3.7	4.8
Carleton Point, Chaleur Bay	48 05	66 07	2 28	6.6	8.0
NEW BRUNSWICK.					
Campbellton, Chaleur Bay	48 01	66 40	3 28	8.3	10.0
Dalhousie, Chaleur Bay	48 04	66 21	2 38	7.4	9.0
Bathurst, Chaleur Bay	47 39	65 37	2 29	4.9	6.3
Caraquette, Chaleur Bay	47 50	64 54	2 14	4.2	5.4
Miscour Harbor, Chaleur Bay	47 55	64 29	1 59	3.1	4.0
North Tracadio Gully Light	47 30	64 52	3 14	1.9	2.4
Lower Neguac, Miramichi Bay	47 16	65 03	4 50	1.8	2.3
Richibucto Head Light	46 40	64 42	5 50	2.2	2.8
Shediac Island Light	46 15	64 32	7 30	2.2	2.8
Jourimain Islet Light	46 10	63 48	9 05	3.2	4.2
Cape Tormentine	46 07	63 46	10 09	3.3	4.0
PRINCE EDWARD ISLAND.					
North Point Light	47 04	63 59	4 19	i.9	2.4
Alberton	46 48	64 03	5 42	1.9	2.4
Richmond Harbor	46 34	63 45	5 50	1.4	1.8
Grand Rustico Light	46 28	63 17	5 47	1.2	1.6
St. Peters Harbor Light	46 26	62 45	6 10	1.0	1.3
East Point Light	46 27	61 58	8 16	1.1	1.4
Souris	46 20	62 17	8 35	2.5	3.2
Georgetown Harbor Light	46 10	62 31	8 59	2.3	3.0
Cape Bear Light	46 01	62 27	8 54	3.2	4.2
Charlottetown	46 12	63 07	10 21	4.9	6.4
Hillsboro River Head	46 23	62 49	11 21	6.9	9.0
Crapaud Light	46 13	63 29	9 39	4.9	6.4
Summerside, Bedeque Bay	46 24	63 47	10 36	4.3	5.6
Minimegash Light	46 53	64 14	5 00	1.9	2.4
St. Paul Island, Northeast Light	47 14	60 08	8 30	2.1	2.7
Magdalen Islands, Grindstone Island	47 23	61 57	8 45	1.8	2.3
NOVA SCOTIA.					
Pugwash Harbor Light	45 52	63 40	10 22	4.2	5.4
Tatamagouche Harbor	45 45	63 10	9 52	4.6	6.0
Pictou Harbor Light	45 41	62 40	9 50	3.0	3.9
Cape George Light	45 53	61 55	9 08	2.2	2.8
Pomquet Harbor	45 39	61 55	9 25	2.4	3.1
CAPE BRETON ISLAND.					
Gut of Canso, North Entrance	45 42	61 32	9 26	2.4	3.1
Port Hood Light	46 00	61 32	8 53	2.7	3.5
Chetican Island Light	46 38	61 00	8 50	2.1	2.7
Cape North	47 02	60 23	8 35	2.4	3.1

TIDAL DATA.

EAST COAST OF NORTH AMERICA—Continued.

Place.	Lat. N.	Long. W.	High water interval	Mean range.	Spring range.
	° ′	° ′	h. m.	Feet.	Feet.
CAPE BRETON ISLAND—Continued.					
Neal Harbor	46 49	60 20	8 11	3.7	4.5
St. Anne Harbor Light	46 17	60 32	8 25	4.9	5.0
Sydney Harbor Light	46 13	60 13	8 06	4.1	5.0
Menadou Bay	45 59	59 48	8 00	4.5	5.5
Louisburg Harbor Light	45 55	59 57	7 45	4.1	5.0
St. Peter Bay Light	45 41	60 50	7 15	4.9	6.0
Arichat Harbor Light	45 30	61 03	7 55	4.1	5.0
NOVA SCOTIA.					
Gut of Canso, South Entrance	45 31	61 15	8 05	4.6	5.6
Guysboro Light	45 23	61 29	8 05	5.2	6.4
Canso Harbor Light	45 21	60 59	7 43	5.3	6.5
Whitehaven	45 12	61 08	7 45	5.4	6.6
Country Harbor, Island Harbor	45 10	61 41	7 25	5.3	6.5
Liscomb Harbor Light	44 59	61 58	7 45	5.3	6.5
Sheet Harbor	44 53	62 31	7 50	5.4	6.5
Ship Harbor	44 46	62 48	7 39	5.3	6.5
Jedore Harbor	44 42	63 01	7 30	5.2	6.4
Halifax	44 39	63 35	7 33	4.3	5.2
Sable Island, north side	43 57	59 55	7 15	3.3	4.0
Sable Island, south side	43 55	60 00	6 15	3.4	4.1
Blind Bay	44 28	63 50	7 30	6.1	7.5
St. Margaret Bay	44 35	63 58	7 32	6.1	7.1
Mahone Bay	44 28	64 17	7 30	6.1	7.5
Lunenburg	44 23	64 15	7 39	5.7	7.0
Port Medway	44 08	64 35	7 31	6.4	7.9
Liverpool Bay	44 02	64 42	7 35	6.5	8.0
Port Mouton	43 56	64 49	7 49	6.1	7.5
Port Ebert	43 48	64 56	7 46	6.4	7.8
Rugged Island Harbor	43 42	65 06	7 38	6.1	7.5
Shelburne	43 45	65 19	7 49	5.7	7.0
Negro Harbor	43 34	65 25	7 49	5.7	7.0
Barrington	43 33	65 34	8 48	9.0	11.0
Cape Sable Light	43 23	65 37	8 42	9.1	11.0
Seal Island Light	43 24	66 01	9 35	11.2	12.8
Pubnico	43 38	65 47	9 11	10.5	12.0
Argyle	43 42	65 50	9 13	11.2	12.8
Yarmouth	43 50	66 08	10 01	14.0	16.0
Grand Passage, St. Mary Bay	44 15	66 20	10 37	18.2	20.8
Petite Passage, St. Mary Bay	44 23	66 12	10 34	19.3	22.0
Weymouth, St. Mary Bay	44 27	66 01	10 43	21.1	24.1
Digby Pier	44 41	65 46	10 52	24.1	27.5
Annapolis	44 45	65 30	11 17	25.1	28.7
Port George	45 00	65 09	11 05	27.8	32.0
Isle Haute Light	45 15	65 01	11 09	28.9	33.0
Black Rock Light	45 10	64 46	11 17	31.5	36.0
Spencer Anchorage	45 20	64 42	11 31	34.0	39.0
Parrsboro, Minas Basin	45 23	64 19	12 09	37.7	43.0
Horton Bluff, Minas Basin	45 07	64 13	12 21	42.0	48.0
Noel Bay, Minas Basin	45 19	63 45	0 07	44.2	50.5
Spicer Cove	45 25	64 54	11 25	32.2	37.0
NEW BRUNSWICK.					
Sackville	45 53	64 22	11 46	39.6	45.2
Grindstone Island Light	45 43	64 27	11 36	35.9	41.0
Folly Point	45 52	64 34	11 39	39.4	45.0
Monckton Railway	46 06	64 47	12 00	41.2	47.0
Quaco	45 21	65 32	11 23	26.3	30.0
St. John	45 16	66 03	11 08	20.9	23.8
Lepreau Bay	45 07	66 31	11 06	21.5	24.5
L'Etang	45 04	66 50	11 07	20.3	23.3
Welchpool, Campobello Island	44 53	66 57	11 07	19.7	22.5
Fish Head, Grand Manan Island	44 47	66 44	11 03	19.2	22.0
Seal Cove, Grand Manan Island	44 38	66 50	10 44	17.5	20.0
Machias Seal Island Light	44 30	67 06	10 57	15.7	18.0
MAINE.					
Eastport	44 54	66 59	11 09	18.2	20.7
Gleason Cove, Western Passage	44 58	67 03	11 14	18.4	20.9
Robbinston, St. Croix River	45 05	67 06	11 15	19.2	21.8
Dochet Island Light, St. Croix River	45 08	67 08	11 16	19.6	22.3
Ledge, St. Croix River, N. B	45 10	67 12	11 23	20.0	22.8
Calais, St. Croix River	45 11	67 17	11 36	20.0	22.8
Deep Cove, Cobscook Bay	44 54	67 01	11 14	18.7	21.3
Garnet Point, Cobscook Bay	44 56	67 07	11 20	19.1	21.8
Coffin Point, Cobscook Bay	44 52	67 07	11 39	18.3	20.8
Bitch Islands, Cobscook Bay	44 52	67 09	12 11	17.6	20.0
Federal Harbor, Cobscook Bay	44 52	67 04	11 24	19.2	21.9
Lubec	44 52	66 59	11 04	17.5	20.0
West Quoddy Head	44 49	66 59	10 58	15.7	17.9
Moose Cove	44 44	67 06	10 57	14.8	16.9
Cutler, Little River	44 39	67 13	10 56	13.9	15.9
Starboard Island, Machias Bay	44 36	67 23	10 54	12.9	14.7
Machiasport, Machias River	44 42	67 24	10 59	13.0	14.8
Bare Cove, Little Kennebec Bay	44 37	67 26	10 52	12.4	14.2

TIDAL DATA.

EAST COAST OF NORTH AMERICA—Continued.

Place.	Lat. N.		Long. W.		High water interval.		Mean range.	Spring range.
	°	′	°	′	h.	m.	Feet.	Feet.
MAINE—Continued.								
Roque I. Harbor, Englishman Bay	44	34	67	31	10	53	12.3	14.0
Moose Peak Light	44	28	67	32	10	52	11.8	13.5
Jonesport, Mooseabec Reach	44	32	67	36	10	58	11.5	13.1
Nash Island Light	44	28	67	45	10	50	11.0	12.5
Gibbs Island, Pleasant River	44	33	67	46	11	00	11.3	12.9
Addison Point, Pleasant River	44	37	67	45	11	21	11.8	13.4
Trafton Island, Narraguagus Bay	44	29	67	50	10	57	11.1	12.6
Millbridge, Narraguagus Bay	44	32	67	53	11	00	11.3	12.9
Pigeon Hill Bay	44	27	67	52	10	59	11.1	12.7
Goods Point, Dyer Bay	44	27	67	55	10	57	10.9	12.4
Jetteaus Point, Gouldsboro Bay	44	28	67	59	10	56	10.8	12.3
Indian Harbor	44	24	67	58	10	55	10.5	12.0
Prospect Harbor	44	24	68	01	10	56	10.7	12.2
Winter Harbor, Frenchman Bay	44	23	68	05	10	57	10.3	11.7
Eastern Pt. Harbor, Frenchman Bay	44	28	68	11	10	59	10.5	12.0
Sullivan, Frenchman Bay	44	31	68	12	11	09	10.5	12.0
Mount Desert Narrows	44	26	68	22	11	10	10.5	12.0
Salisbury Cove, Mount Desert Island	44	26	68	17	11	03	10.6	12.1
Bar Harbor, Mount Desert Island	44	23	68	12	10	58	10.5	12.0
Southwest Harbor, Mount Desert Island	44	16	68	19	10	58	10.3	11.7
Somesville, Mount Desert Island	44	22	68	20	11	02	10.6	12.0
Bass Harbor, Mount Desert Island	44	14	68	21	11	02	10.2	11.6
Pretty Marsh Harbor, Mount Desert Island	44	20	68	25	11	05	10.2	11.7
Union River, Blue Hill Bay	44	30	68	26	11	09	10.4	11.9
Blue Hill Harbor, Blue Hill Bay	44	24	68	34	11	07	10.3	11.7
Allen Cove, Blue Hill Bay	44	18	68	32	11	05	10.3	11.7
Mackerel Cove, Blue Hill Bay	44	10	68	26	11	02	10.2	11.7
Penobscot Bay.								
Naskeak Harbor, Eggemoggin Reach	44	13	68	33	11	01	10.2	11.6
Center Harbor, Eggemoggin Reach	44	16	68	35	11	04	10.1	11.5
Sedgwick, Eggemoggin Reach	44	18	68	37	11	06	10.2	11.7
Head Harbor, Isle au Haut	44	01	68	37	10	49	9.1	10.4
Kimball Island	44	04	68	39	10	57	9.6	10.9
Oceanville, Deer Isle	44	12	68	38	10	59	10.1	11.5
Stonington, Deer Isle	44	09	68	40	10	59	9.7	11.0
Northwest Harbor, Deer Isle	44	13	68	41	11	05	10.1	11.5
Matinicus Island	43	52	68	53	10	55	9.1	10.4
Carvers Harbor, Vinal Haven Island	44	03	68	50	11	01	9.4	10.7
Iron Point, North Haven Island	44	08	68	52	11	03	9.5	10.8
Pulpit or North Harbor, North Haven Island	44	09	68	53	11	09	9.8	11.1
Castine	44	23	68	48	11	12	9.7	11.1
Bangor, Penobscot River	44	49	68	47	11	20	13.1	14.9
Belfast	44	25	69	00	11	10	9.7	11.1
Camden	44	12	69	03	11	09	9.6	10.9
Rockland	44	06	69	06	11	08	9.7	11.0
Owlshead Light	44	06	69	03	11	08	9.4	10.7
Tenants Harbor	43	58	69	12	11	04	9.3	10.6
Monhegan Island Light	43	46	69	19	11	00	9.3	10.6
Port Clyde	43	56	69	16	11	00	9.3	10.6
Thomaston, St. George River	44	04	69	11	11	12	9.3	10.6
New Harbor, Muscongus Bay	43	52	69	29	11	02	8.9	10.1
Muscongus Harbor, Muscongus Bay	43	58	69	27	11	05	9.5	10.9
Pemaquid Harbor, Johns Bay	43	52	69	32	11	04	8.8	10.0
Boothbay Harbor	43	51	69	37	11	05	8.8	10.0
Heals Cove, Hockomoc Bay	43	53	69	44	11	33	9.3	10.5
Kennebec River.								
Hunniwell Point	43	45	69	47	11	11	8.3	9.5
Parkers Head	43	47	69	47	11	20	7.9	9.0
Phippsburg	43	49	69	48	11	30	7.5	8.6
Bath	43	55	69	49	12	15	6.4	7.3
Casco Bay.								
Small Point Harbor	43	44	69	51	11	00	8.8	10.1
Birch Point, New Meadow River	43	50	69	52	11	08	9.2	10.4
Lowell Cove, Orrs Island	43	45	69	59	11	04	8.8	10.1
Harpswell Harbor	43	46	70	00	11	09	9.0	10.4
Potts Harbor	43	44	70	02	11	05	8.8	10.1
Middle Bay Cove, Middle Bay	43	51	69	58	11	11	9.0	10.3
Flying Point	43	49	70	04	11	09	9.0	10.3
South Freeport	43	49	70	06	11	10	9.2	10.6
Chebeag Point, Great Chebeag Island	43	46	70	06	11	07	9.0	10.4
Prince Point	43	46	70	10	11	09	9.0	10.4
Peaks Island	43	39	70	12	11	02	9.0	10.5
Portland	43	39	70	15	11	11	8.9	10.2
Richmond Island	43	33	70	14	11	07	9.0	10.1
Old Orchard Beach	43	31	70	23	11	10	8.8	10.1
Wood Island Harbor	43	27	70	21	11	08	8.7	9.9
Cape Porpoise	43	22	70	26	11	06	8.7	9.9
NEW HAMPSHIRE								
Portsmouth Harbor Light	43	04	70	43	11	21	8.7	9.9
Portsmouth, Piscataqua River	43	05	70	45	11	30	7.8	8.9

TIDAL DATA.

EAST COAST OF NORTH AMERICA—Continued.

Place.	Lat. N.	Long. W.	High water interval.	Mean range.	Spring range.
	° ′	° ′	h. m.	Feet.	Feet.
NEW HAMPSHIRE—Continued.					
Dover Point, Piscataqua River	43 07	70 50	0 15	6.4	7.4
Isles of Shoals Light	42 58	70 37	11 19	8.7	9.9
Hampton Harbor	42 54	70 49	11 26	7.7	8.8
MASSACHUSETTS.					
Merrimack River Entrance	42 49	70 49	11 30	7.9	9.1
Newburyport, Merrimack River	42 49	70 52	11 40	7.8	8.8
Ipswich River Entrance	42 42	70 48	11 24	8.7	9.9
Annisquam	42 40	70 41	11 18	8.8	10.1
Rockport	42 40	70 37	11 13	8.8	10.1
Gloucester	42 37	70 40	11 14	8.9	10.1
Salem	42 32	70 53	11 16	9.0	10.3
Nahant	42 25	70 54	11 15	9.1	10.3
Lynn Harbor	42 27	70 57	11 24	9.2	10.4
Boston (Commonwealth Pier 5)	42 21	71 03	11 18	9.4	10.8
(Navy Yard)	42 22	71 03	11 28	9.6	10.9
Boston Light	42 20	70 53	11 18	9.0	10.3
Sheppards Ledge, Cohasset Harbor	42 15	70 46	11 16	9.0	10.3
Gurnet Lights	42 00	70 36	11 20	9.2	10.5
Plymouth	41 57	70 40	11 21	9.6	10.9
Canal Entrance, Cape Cod Bay	41 46	70 30	11 23	9.4	10.8
Sandy Neck Light	41 43	70 17	11 27	9.4	10.8
Wellfleet, Cape Cod	41 56	70 02	11 20	10.7	12.2
Provincetown, Cape Cod	42 03	70 11	11 22	9.2	10.5
Race Point, Cape Cod	42 04	70 15	11 16	9.0	10.4
Pamet River Coast Guard Station, CapeCod	42 00	70 01	11 30	7.1	8.3
Nauset Harbor, Cape Cod	41 48	69 56	11 50	6.0	7.0
Pleasant Bay, Cape Cod	41 44	69 59	0 30	3.5	4.1
Chatham Light, Cape Cod	41 40	69 57	11 50	6.7	7.9
Monomoy Point	41 33	70 01	12 00	3.7	4.4
Georges Shoal	41 40	67 45	10 18	4.9	5.6
Nantucket Sound, North Side.					
Stage Harbor	41 40	69 58	12 11	3.9	4.7
Dennisport	41 39	70 07	12 01	3.7	4.4
South Yarmouth, Bass River	41 40	70 11	0 00	2.9	3.5
Hyannisport	41 38	70 18	12 16	3.3	3.9
Succonnesset Point	41 33	70 29	12 10	1.9	2.3
Monant Hill	41 33	70 33	11 15	1.2	1.4
Nantucket Island.					
Great Point	41 23	70 03	12 01	3.1	3.7
Wauwinet (outer shore)	41 20	70 00	0 01	3.3	4.0
Siasconset	41 16	69 58	11 35	1.2	1.5
Tom Nevers Head	41 14	69 59	10 23	1.2	1.4
Forked Pond	41 14	70 02	8 40	1.4	1.6
Weweeder	41 14	70 06	8 08	1.7	2.0
Smith Point, south side	41 17	70 15	7 56	2.2	2.7
Eel Point	41 17	70 12	11 43	2.4	2.9
Nantucket Harbor	41 17	70 06	12 24	3.1	3.7
East Pond, Tuckernuck Island	41 18	70 15	12 05	2.6	3.2
Muskeget Island Coast Guard Station	41 20	70 19	11 27	1.6	1.9
Marthas Vineyard.					
Cape Poge Light, Chappaquiddick Island	41 25	70 27	12 02	2.2	2.7
Wasque Point, Chappaquiddick Island	41 21	70 27	9 12	1.6	2.0
Edgartown	41 23	70 31	12 09	2.0	2.4
Katama Point, Katama Bay	41 21	70 30	9 30	1.4	1.7
Pahognet	41 21	70 35	7 52	2.7	3.2
Chilmark Pond	41 20	70 43	7 34	2.9	3.5
No Mans Land Island	41 16	70 49	7 32	3.2	3.8
Gay Head Light	41 21	70 50	7 45	3.0	3.6
Menemsha Bight	41 21	70 47	7 51	3.0	3.6
Cedar Tree Neck	41 26	70 42	7 58	2.3	2.8
Chappaquonsett	41 28	70 38	8 59	2.1	2.5
West Chop Light	41 29	70 36	11 34	1.6	1.9
Vineyard Haven	41 28	70 36	11 43	1.7	2.0
East Chop Light	41 28	70 34	11 45	1.7	2.0
Cottage City	41 27	70 33	12 00	1.9	2.3
Vineyard Sound					
Falmouth	41 32	70 37	10 24	1.3	1.6
Nobska Point Light	41 31	70 39	8 32	1.5	1.8
Woods Hole, Fish Commission Wharf	41 31	70 40	8 26	1.8	2.1
Tarpaulin Cove	41 28	70 45	7 59	2.3	2.8
Quicks Hole, south side	41 26	70 51	7 38	3.1	3.8
Buzzards Bay.					
Cuttyhunk Light	41 25	70 57	7 36	3.4	4.1
Penikese Island	41 27	70 55	7 37	3.6	4.3
Quicks Hole, north side	41 27	70 50	7 38	3.7	4.5
Kettle Cove	41 28	70 47	7 44	4.0	4.8

TIDAL DATA.
EAST COAST OF NORTH AMERICA—Continued.

Place.	Lat. N.		Long. W.		High water interval.		Mean range.	Spring range.
	°	′	°	′	h.	m.	Feet.	Feet.
MASSACHUSETTS—Continued.								
Buzzards Bay—Continued.								
Uncatena Island, Woods Hole, north side	41	31	70	42	7	59	3.9	4.7
West Falmouth	41	37	70	38	7	50	4.1	4.9
Pocasset Harbor	41	41	70	37	7	55	4.2	5.0
Cape Cod Canal Entrance	41	44	70	37	8	00	4.1	4.9
Wareham River	41	44	70	43	8	00	4.1	4.9
Bird Island Light	41	40	70	43	7	55	4.2	5.0
Mattapoisett	41	39	70	49	7	53	4.1	5.0
Clark Point	41	36	70	54	7	51	3.9	4.6
New Bedford	41	38	70	55	7	57	4.0	4.8
Dumping Rock Light	41	32	70	55	7	50	3.7	4.5
Westport River Entrance	41	31	71	04	7	58	3.1	3.7
RHODE ISLAND.								
Narragansett Bay.								
Sakonnet Point Light	41	27	71	12	7	40	3.3	4.0
Fogland Point, Sakonnet River	41	34	71	13	7	50	3.8	4.6
Beavertail Light	41	27	71	24	7	42	3.5	4.3
Newport	41	29	71	20	7	44	3.5	4.3
Prudence Island Light	41	36	71	18	7	55	3.8	4.7
Bristol Ferry Light	41	39	71	16	8	00	4.0	4.8
Fall River, Mass	41	42	71	10	8	10	4.9	5.9
Taunton, Taunton River, Mass	41	53	71	06	8	55	2.8	3.5
Bristol	41	40	71	16	8	02	4.1	5.0
Warren	41	44	71	17	8	06	4.6	5.5
Nayat Point	41	43	71	21	8	05	4.6	5.5
Providence	41	49	71	24	8	12	4.6	5.6
East Greenwich	41	40	71	27	8	00	4.4	5.3
Wickford	41	34	71	27	7	50	4.1	4.9
Narragansett Pier	41	26	71	27	7	42	3.5	4.2
Point Judith Light	41	22	71	29	7	45	3.1	3.8
Block Island, Basin Harbor	41	10	71	33	7	33	3.0	3.6
Watch Hill Light	41	18	71	52	8	49	2.7	3.3
CONNECTICUT.								
Long Island Sound.								
Stonington	41	20	71	54	8	59	2.7	3.2
Noank, Mystic River Entrance	41	19	71	59	9	05	2.6	3.0
New London, Customhouse Wharf	41	21	72	06	9	26	2.5	2.9
Naval Station	41	24	72	06	9	30	2.5	2.9
Norwich, Thames River	41	32	72	05	10	07	3.1	3.7
Millstone Point	41	18	72	10	9	39	2.7	3.2
Saybrook Light, Connecticut River	41	16	72	21	10	29	3.6	4.3
Willets Point	40	48	73	47	11	18	7.2	8.5
Hewletts Point	40	50	73	45	11	15	7.2	8.5
Execution Rocks Light	40	53	73	44	11	12	7.3	8.6
Glen Cove, Hempstead Harbor	40	51	73	39	11	12	7.3	8.6
Oyster Bay	40	52	73	31	11	15	7.3	8.6
Cold Spring Harbor, Oyster Bay	40	52	73	28	11	15	7.4	8.7
Lloyd Harbor Light, Huntington Bay	40	55	73	26	11	10	7.4	8.7
Northport Harbor	40	54	73	21	11	10	7.3	8.6
Nissequogue River, Smithtown Bay	40	54	73	13	11	10	7.3	8.6
Stony Brook, Smithtown Bay	40	55	73	09	11	05	7.0	8.3
Stratford Shoal Light	41	04	73	06	11	25	6.1	7.2
Port Jefferson Entrance	40	58	73	05	11	03	6.6	7.8
Port Jefferson	40	57	73	04	11	06	6.2	7.3
Setauket	40	56	73	06	11	35	6.4	7.5
Conscience Bay	40	57	73	07	12	10	6.5	7.6
Herod Point	40	57	72	50	12	20	5.0	5.9
Jacob Point	40	59	72	39	11	02	5.9	7.0
Duck Pond Point	41	02	72	31	11	00	4.9	5.8
Horton Point Light	41	05	72	27	10	57	4.5	5.3
Truman Beach	41	08	72	19	10	51	4.0	4.7
Orient Point	41	10	72	14	10	30	3.4	4.0
Little Gull Island Light	41	12	72	06	10	00	2.7	3.2
West Harbor, Fishers Island	41	16	72	00	9	26	2.5	3.0
Gardiners Point	41	09	72	09	9	31	2.5	3.0
Orient Harbor	41	08	72	18	9	50	2.7	3.2
Greenport	41	06	72	21	10	20	2.5	3.0
Southold Landing	41	04	72	25	10	24	2.4	2.8
Cutchogue Harbor	41	00	72	27	11	12	2.5	3.0
Jamesport	40	56	72	34	11	48	2.6	3.1
Sag Harbor	41	00	72	17	12	11	2.4	2.8
Cedar Island Light	41	02	72	16	10	30	2.5	2.9
Acabonack Harbor	41	01	72	08	10	07	2.6	3.1
Napeague Harbor	41	00	72	03	9	25	2.7	3.1
Fort Pond Bay	41	03	71	58	9	15	2.5	3.0
Montauk Point Light	41	04	71	51	8	50	2.2	2.6
					8	20	2.0	2.4
NEW YORK.								
Long Island, South Side.								
Amagansett Coast Guard Station	40	58	72	07	8	10	2.2	2.6
Mecox Coast Guard Station	40	54	72	18	8	00	2.3	2.8

TIDAL DATA.

EAST COAST OF NORTH AMERICA—Continued.

Place.	Lat N.	Long. W.	High water interval.	Mean range.	Spring range.
	° ′	° ′	h. m.	Feet.	Feet.
NEW YORK—Continued.					
Long Island, South Side—Continued.					
Southampton Coast Guard Station	40 52	72 23	7 54	2.4	2.9
Shinnecock Coast Guard Station	40 51	72 28	7 48	2.5	3.0
Quogue Coast Guard Station	40 48	72 36	7 42	2.7	3.2
Moriches Coast Guard Station	40 46	72 43	7 36	2.9	3.4
Bellport Coast Guard Station	40 43	72 56	7 30	3.1	3.6
Bellport, Great South Bay	40 45	72 56	10 55	1.1	1.4
Patchogue, Great South Bay	40 45	73 01	10 38	1.0	1.1
Lone Hill Coast Guard Station	40 40	73 04	7 25	3.3	3.9
Fire Island Inlet, Great South Bay	40 38	73 14	7 19	2.0	2.3
Jones Inlet, Hempstead Bay	40 41	73 19	9 50	1.2	1.4
Babylon, Great South Bay	40 36	73 32	7 30	3.8	4.5
East Rockaway Inlet, Hempstead Bay	40 36	73 41	7 36	4.1	4.9
Barren Island, Rockaway Inlet	40 35	73 53	7 42	4.6	5.6
Holland Landing, Jamaica Bay	40 35	73 49	8 18	4.8	5.8
Norton Point, Jamaica Bay	40 38	73 45	8 45	4.8	5.8
Canarsie, Jamaica Bay	40 38	73 53	8 20	4.8	5.8
Coney Island	40 34	73 59	7 35	4.7	5.7
Staten Island.					
Elm Tree Beacon	40 34	74 06	7 38	4.9	5.9
Great Kills	40 32	74 08	7 36	5.1	6.1
Princess Bay Light	40 30	74 13	7 39	5.3	6.4
Great Beds Light	40 29	74 15	7 41	5.3	6.4
Tottenville, Arthur Kill	40 31	74 15	7 45	5.3	6.4
Rossville, Arthur Kill	40 33	74 13	8 10	5.3	6.3
Chelsea, Arthur Kill	40 36	74 12	8 22	5.0	6.0
Port Richmond, Kill van Kull	40 38	74 09	8 11	4.5	5.4
New Brighton, Kill van Kull	40 39	74 06	7 56	4.5	5.4
St. George	40 39	74 04	7 53	4.4	5.3
Fort Wadsworth Light, The Narrows	40 36	74 03	7 40	4.6	5.6
New York Harbor.					
Bath, Gravesend Bay	40 36	74 00	7 35	4.8	5.7
Fort Hamilton, The Narrows	40 37	74 02	7 40	4.7	5.7
Bay Ridge	40 38	74 02	7 49	4.5	5.4
Gowanus Bay	40 40	74 01	7 56	4.4	5.3
New York, Governors Island	40 42	74 01	8 04	4.4	5.4
NEW JERSEY.					
Atlantic Highlands	40 25	74 02	7 37	4.7	5.6
Sandy Hook, The Horseshoe	40 27	74 00	7 35	4.7	5.6
Seabright	40 22	73 58	7 25	4.4	5.3
Long Branch	40 18	73 59	7 21	4.3	5.1
Asbury Park	40 13	74 00	7 18	4.1	4.9
Seagirt	40 08	74 02	7 20	3.8	4.5
Seaside Park	39 55	74 05	7 25	3.8	4.5
Little Egg Inlet, Sea Haven Light	39 30	74 18	7 42	3.3	3.9
Great Bay (entrance)	39 30	74 22	8 05	2.9	3.5
Mullica River Entrance, Great Bay	39 32	74 24	8 34	2.6	3.2
Main Marsh Thorofare	39 29	74 23	8 15	2.8	3.4
Simkins Thorofare	39 28	74 22	8 24	2.9	3.5
Grassy Bay	39 26	74 24	8 45	3.2	3.8
Golden Thorofare	39 24	74 24	8 15	3.6	4.3
Absecon Bay	39 24	74 29	8 37	3.9	4.7
Atlantic City (near the bridges), Inlet, Gardiners Basin	39 22	74 25	7 20	3.8	4.6
Atlantic City (near the bridges)	39 22	74 27	8 35	3.6	4.3
Million Dollar Pier	39 21	74 26	7 11	4.0	4.8
Persimmon Point	39 21	74 30	8 30	3.5	4.2
Risley Channel	39 19	74 32	7 50	3.8	4.6
Great Egg Inlet	39 18	74 33	7 36	4.1	4.9
Ocean City, Fourth Street (inside)	39 17	74 35	7 50	3.7	4.4
Crook Horn Thorofare	39 14	74 39	8 25	3.9	4.7
Corson Inlet	39 12	74 39	7 35	4.2	5.0
Ben Hands Thoroughfare	39 12	74 41	8 05	3.9	4.7
Sea Isle City (inside)	39 09	74 42	8 10	4.0	4.8
Townsend Inlet (entrance)	39 07	74 43	7 32	4.2	5.1
Leaming Channel	39 05	74 46	8 30	3.4	4.1
Hereford Inlet	39 02	74 49	7 55	3.6	4.3
Grassy Sound Channel	39 01	74 47	7 30	4.2	5.1
Richardson Channel	38 59	74 49	8 05	3.6	4.3
Grassy Sound	38 58	74 51	7 40	4.0	4.8
Jarvis Sound	38 57	74 52	7 55	4.4	5.3
Cold Spring Inlet, Sewell's Point	38 56	74 52	7 37	4.4	5.3
Cape May City	38 56	74 55	7 50	4.6	5.5
Five Fathom Bank	38 51	74 38	7 35	4.1	4.9
McCries Shoal	38 51	74 51	7 55	4.3	5.2
Cape May Point Light	38 56	74 58	8 14	4.7	5.6
Wilmington, Del	39 44	75 33	12 05	5.6	6.4
Edgemoor, Cherry Landing Front Light, Del	39 45	75 30	12 07	5.5	6.3
Oldmans Point	39 46	75 28	12 14	5.4	6.3
Marcus Hook, Pa	39 49	75 25	0 08	5.4	6.2
Chester, Pa	39 51	75 21	0 24	5.4	6.0

TIDAL DATA.

EAST COAST OF NORTH AMERICA—Continued.

Place.	Lat. N.	Long. W.	High water interval.	Mean range.	Spring range.
	° ′	° ′	h. m.	Feet.	Feet.
NEW JERSEY—Continued.					
League Island Navy Yard, Pa	39 53	75 11·	1 02	5.3	5.8
Gloucester	39 54	75 08	1 10	5.3	5.8
Philadelphia, Washington Avenue, Pa	39 56	75 08	1 25	5.2	5.7
Chestnut Street, Pa	39 57	75 08	1 29	5.2	5.7
Pier 80	39 58	75 07	1 38	5.2	5.7
Bridesburg, Pa	40 00	75 04	1 56	5.1	5.6
Camden, Cooper Point, N. J	39 57	75 08	1 32	5.2	5.7
DELAWARE.					
Renoboth	38 43	75 05	8 01	4.0	4.8
Indian River Inlet (outside)	38 37	75 04	7 56	3.9	4.6
MARYLAND.					
Fenwick Island Light	38 27	75 03	7 48	3.7	4.4
Ocean City	38 20	75 05	7 41	3.6	4.4
Great Machipongo Inlet (inside, near Hog Island Light)	37 22	75 43	7 47	4.1	4.9
Upshur Neck (south end)	37 28	75 48	8 20	4.4	5.3
Sand Shoal Inlet (inside, near Cobb Island Coast Guard Station)	37 18	75 47	7 45	4.0	4.8
Ship Shoal Inlet (inside)	37 13	75 48	7 56	4.0	4.8
Smith Island (inside, at Cape Charles Light)	37 08	75 55	7 57	4.0	4.8
Baltimore, Fort McHenry	39 16	76 35	6 32	1.1	1.3
Fells Point	39 17	76 35	6 34	1.2	1.3
Washington, D. C., Seventh Street	38 53	77 01	7 49	2.9	3.3
Navy Yard, Anacostia River	38 52	77 00	7 52	2.9	3.3
Arsenal Wharf	38 52	77 01	7 47	2.9	3.3
Old Point Comfort	37 00	76 19	8 44	2.5	3.0
Craney Island Light, Elizabeth River	36 54	76 20	9 00	2.6	3.0
Norfolk, Elizabeth River	36 51	76 18	9 12	2.8	3.5
Portsmouth Navy Yard, Elizabeth River	36 50	76 18	9 16	2.8	3.2
Newport News, James River	36 58	76 26	9 03	2.6	3.0
Cape Henry Light	36 56	76 00	8 00	2.8	3.3
VIRGINIA.					
Virginia Beach	36 50	75 58	7 56	3.0	3.5
False Cape Coast Guard Station	36 36	75 53	7 47	3.6	4.2
NORTH CAROLINA.					
Currituck Beach Light	36 23	75 50	7 40	3.6	4.2
Oregon Inlet	35 48	75 32	7 20	2.0	2.4
New Inlet	35 41	75 29	7 18	2.0	2.4
Cape Hatteras	35 14	75 31	6 56	3.6	4.2
Hatteras Inlet	35 12	75 44	7 10	2.0	2.4
Ocracoke Inlet	35 04	76 01	7 10	1.9	2.3
Cape Lookout	34 37	76 32	6 29	3.7	4.4
Beaufort	34 43	76 40	7 30	2.7	3.2
Bogue Inlet	34 39	77 06	7 10	2.2	2.6
New River Inlet	34 32	77 20	7 12	2.5	3.0
New Topsail Inlet	34 22	77 38	7 15	3.0	3.5
Masonboro Inlet	34 11	77 49	7 20	3.4	4.0
Bald Head	33 52	78 00	7 26	4.3	4.9
Wilmington	34 14	77 57	9 44	2.7	2.9
SOUTH CAROLINA.					
Little River	33 51	78 34	7 15	4.8	5.6
North Inlet	33 20	79 10	7 10	4.5	5.3
Georgetown, Winyah Bay	33 13	79 11	7 37	3.5	4.1
Georgetown, Winyah Bay	33 22	79 17	8 39	3.3	4.0
Cape Romain	33 01	79 21	6 59	4.7	5.5
Jacks Creek Entrance, Bull Bay	32 56	79 35	7 05	5.0	5.8
Capers Inlet	32 51	79 42	7 10	5.2	6.1
North Jetty, Charleston Harbor Entrance	32 44	79 48	7 10	5.2	6.1
Fort Sumpter	32 45	79 52	7 17	5.0	5.8
Charleston, Customhouse Wharf	32 47	79 55	7 25	5.2	6.1
Navy Yard	32 52	79 58	7 50	5.3	6.2
Bee Ferry Bridge, Ashley River	32 51	80 03	8 00	5.8	6.8
Legareville, Stono River	32 40	80 00	7 25	5.0	5.8
North Edisto River Entrance	32 34	80 11	7 08	5.8	6.8
Bluff Point, Wadmelaw River	32 39	80 15	7 40	6.5	7.6
Big Bay Creek, South Edisto River	32 30	80 20	7 12	6.2	7.3
Peters Point, St. Pierre Creek, South Edisto River	32 32	80 21	7 38	6.2	7.3
Salt Landing, South Edisto River	32 34	80 23	7 35	6.1	7.1
Coosaw R., Mining Co.'s Wharf	32 31	80 40	8 50	7.5	8.8
Hunting Island Light, St. Helena Sound	32 23	80 25	7 14	6.0	7.0
Martin Industry Shoal	32 07	80 35	6 50	6.4	7.5
Hilton Head, Port Royal Sound	32 14	80 40	7 12	6.6	7.7
Naval Station, Beaufort River	32 21	80 40	7 51	7.1	8.3
Port Royal, Battery Creek	32 22	80 41	7 57	7.2	8.4
Beaufort, Beaufort River	32 26	80 40	8 10	7.3	8.5
Colleton River Entran e	32 19	80 48	8 00	7.5	8.8
Whale Island, Broad River	32 29	80 48	8 40	8.0	9.4
Braddock Point, Calibogue Sound	32 07	80 49	7 15	6.8	1.0

TIDAL DATA.

EAST COAST OF NORTH AMERICA—Continued.

Place.	Lat. N.	Long. W.	High water interval.	Mean range.	Spring range.
	° ′	° ′	h. m.	Feet.	Feet.
GEORGIA.					
Savannah, Savannah River	32 05	81 05	8 26	6.5	7.6
Oglethorpe, Savannah River	32 05	81 02	8 13	6.6	7.7
Fort Pulaski, Savannah River	32 02	80 53	7 20	6.9	8.1
Tybee Light, Savannah River Entrance	32 02	80 51	7 11	6.8	8.0
Wassaw Sound	31 55	80 58	7 24	6.8	8.0
Ossabaw Sound	31 50	81 05	7 19	6.6	7.7
St. Catherine Sound	31 40	81 09	7 39	7.0	8.2
National Quarantine Station, Sapelo Sound	31 32	81 12	7 30	7.3	8.6
Sapelo Light, Doboy Sound	31 23	81 17	7 30	6.8	8.0
Altamaha Sound	31 18	81 18	7 40	6.4	7.5
Brunswick Outer Bar	31 06	81 19	7 18	6.3	7.5
St. Simon Light	31 08	81 24	7 30	6.6	7.7
Brunswick	31 09	81 30	8 00	7.0	8.2
Jekyl Island, St. Andrews Sound	31 06	81 26	7 43	6.8	8.0
FLORIDA.					
East Coast.					
Fernandina Entrance (outer end of jetty)	30 43	81 25	7 27	5.9	7.0
Fernandina, Desoto Street	30 41	81 28	8 00	6.0	7.0
Nassau Sound	30 31	81 27	7 41	5.4	6.3
Fort George Inlet	30 26	81 26	7 43	5.4	6.3
St. Johns River, South Jetty	30 24	81 23	7 13	5.0	5.8
Jacksonville	30 20	81 39	9 03	1.0	1.2
St. Augustine Light	29 53	81 17	7 50	4.5	5.3
St. Augustine	29 54	81 18	7 58	4.2	5.0
Matanzas Inlet	29 42	81 13	7 35	2.5	3.0
Mosquito Inlet Light	29 05	80 56	7 43	2.3	2.7
Cape Canaveral Light	28 28	80 32	8 00	5.0	5.9
Indian River Inlet	27 30	80 18	7 30	1.7	2.0
Jupiter Inlet Light	26 57	80 05	8 00	1.5	1.8
Lake Worth Inlet	26 48	80 02	8 03	1.6	1.9
Hillsboro Inlet	26 15	80 05	8 20	1.7	2.0
Miami, Key Biscayne Bay	25 46	80 11	9 30	1.4	1.7
Cape Florida, Key Biscayne	25 40	80 09	8 24	1.7	2.2
Fowey Rocks Light	25 35	80 06	8 20	2.0	2.6
Point Elizabeth, Key Largo	25 14	80 19	8 25	2.3	2.9
Carysfort Reef Light	25 13	80 13	8 21	2.1	2.7
Alligator Reef Light	24 51	80 37	8 22	2.0	2.6
Indian Key	24 53	80 41	8 23	1.8	2.3
Tom Harbor Keys	24 46	80 56	8 25	1.6	2.0
Knights Key	24 42	81 07	8 30	1.4	1.8
Sombrero Key Light	24 38	81 07	8 30	1.5	1.9
Bahia Honda, south side	24 40	81 16	8 50	1.5	1.9
American Shoal Light	24 31	81 31	8 50	1.6	2.0
Sand Key Light	24 27	81 53	8 50	1.2	1.5
Key West, Currys Wharf	24 34	81 48	9 52	1.2	1.6
Rebecca Shoal Light	24 35	82 35	9 45	1.2	1.5
Tortugas Harbor Light	24 38	82 53	10 00	1.2	1.5
Gulf of Mexico.					
Cape Sable, East Cape	25 07	81 05	1 05	2.9	3.7
Lostmans River	25 32	81 12	0 46	3.7	4.7
Pavilion Key	25 42	81 21	0 36	3.5	4.5
Round Key	25 50	81 31	0 25	3.4	4.4
Cape Romano	25 51	81 41	0 15	2.6	3.3
Big Marco Pass	25 58	81 45	0 05	2.3	2.9
Sanibel I. Light, San Carlos Entrance	26 27	82 01	12 17	1.8	2.3
Puntarasa, San Carlos Bay	26 29	82 00	12 19	1.7	2.1
Fort Myers, Caloosahatchee River	26 39	81 52	1 45	0.8	1.0
Boca Grande, Charlotte Harbor	26 43	82 16	0 42	1.4	1.8
Punta Gorda, Charlotte Harbor	26 55	82 05	2 00	1.4	1.8
Sarasota Point	27 17	82 ·34	12 15	1.5	2.0
Egmont Key Light, Tampa Bay	27 36	82 46	11 32	1.4	1.8
Palma Sola, Manatee River, Tampa Bay	27 31	82 37	11 55	1.6	2.1
St. Petersburg, Tampa Bay	27 46	82 38	0 03	2.0	2.6
Tampa, Hillsboro Bay, Tampa Bay	27 57	82 27	1 20	2.2	2.9
Dunedin, St. Josephs Sound	28 01	82 48	12 15	1.8	2.4
Anclote Keys Light	28 10	82 51	12 20	2.0	2.6
Bayport	28 32	82 39	0 34	2.4	3.2
Cedar Keys	29 08	83 02	0 55	2.4	3.1
Suwanee River Entrance	29 17	83 09	1 00	2.4	3.1
Pepperfish Keys	29 30	83 22	1 05	2.4	3.1
Steinhatchee River, Deadman Bay	29 40	83 24	1 10	2.4	3.1
Point Edward	29 44	83 32	1 10	2.4	3.1
Warrior River	29 55	83 41	1 15	2.4	3.1
Rock Island	29 58	83 50	1 20	2.4	3.1
Aucilla River Entrance	30 05	84 00	1 25	2.4	3.2
St. Marks Light, Apalachee Bay	30 04	84 11	1 29	2.5	3.2
St. Marks, St. Marks River	30 09	84 12	2 00	2.0	2.6
Ocklockonee Point	29 58	84 20	1 20	2.0	3.0

TIDAL DATA.

EAST COAST OF NORTH AMERICA—Continued.

Place.	Lat. N.		Long. W.		High water interval.		Mean range.	Spring range.
	°	′	°	′	h.	m.	Feet.	Feet.
FLORIDA—Continued.								
Gulf of Mexico—Continued.								
*Apalachicola, Apalachicola Bay	29	43	84	59	11	05b	1.5	1.9
*St. Vincents Island, West Pass	29	38	85	06	10	25b	1.5	1.9
*Cape San Blas	29	40	85	22	10	05b	1.5	1.9
*St. Josephs, St. Josephs Bay	29	48	85	18	10	30b	1.5	1.9
*St. Andrews, St. Andrews Bay	30	10	85	41	10	30b	1.4	1.8
*East Pass, Choctawhatchee Bay	30	23	86	29	10	10b	1.4	1.8
*Fort Pickens, Pensacola Bay	30	20	87	17	10	05b	1.3	1.6
*Warrington Navy Yard, Pensacola Bay	30	21	87	16	10	10b	1.3	1.6
*Pensacola, Pensacola Bay	30	24	87	13	10	30b	1.3	1.6
ALABAMA.								
*Mobile Point Light, Mobile Bay	30	14	88	01	10	00b	1.2	1.5
*Mobile, Mobile River	30	41	88	02	12	25b	1.5	1.9
MISSISSIPPI.								
*Horn Island Light	30	13	88	32	10	10b	1.7	2.0
*Pascagoula Light	30	21	88	34	10	40b	1.8	2.0
*Biloxi Light	30	24	88	54	10	50b	1.8	2.3
*Cat Island Light	30	14	89	09	10	50b	1.7	2.1
LOUISIANA.								
*Lake Borgne, The Rigolets	30	09	89	38	11	00b	0.9	1.1
*Chandeleur Light	30	03	88	52	10	00b	1.3	1.6
*Pass a Loutre Light, Mississippi River	29	12	89	02	9	00b	1.2	1.5
*Port Eads, South Pass, Mississippi River	29	01	89	10	8	45b	1.3	1.6
*Southwest Pass Light, Mississippi River	28	58	89	24	8	45b	1.4	1.7
*Barataria Bay Light	29	17	89	57	8	50b	1.3	1.6
*Grand Pass, Timbalier Light	29	03	90	21	8	50b	1.3	1.6
*Ship Shoal Light	28	55	91	04	8	00b	1.1	1.4
*Point au Fer Reef Light, Atchafalaya Bay	29	22	91	23	8	15b	1.2	1.5
*Atchafalaya River Entrance	29	28	91	16	8	30b	1.1	1.4
*Cote Blanche, Cote Blanche Bay	29	44	91	43	8	30b	1.1	1.4
*Southwest Pass, Vermillion Bay	29	35	92	02	7	00b	1.0	1.3
Mermentau River Entrance	29	45	93	06	2	00	1.2	1.4
Calcasieu Light	29	47	93	21	2	17	1.5	1.7
Sabine Pass Light	29	43	93	51	3	17	1.4	1.6
TEXAS.								
*Bolivar Point Light	29	22	94	46	5	15b	1.1	1.4
*Galveston, Twentieth Street	29	19	94	48	5	50b	1.0	1.3
*Morgans Point, Galveston Bay	29	41	94	58	8	50b	0.5	0.8
*Brazos River Entrance	28	56	95	18	5	40b	1.9	2.4
*Pass Cavallo, Matagorda Bay	28	22	96	24	6	00b	1.0	1.3
*Aransas Pass Light	27	52	97	03	5	50b	1.0	1.3
*Corpus Christi Pass	27	36	97	13	5	30b	1.0	1.3
*Brazos Santiago Light	26	04	97	10	5	00b	0.8	1.0
*Rio Grande Entrance	25	57	97	09	4	30b	1.0	1.3
MEXICO.								
*Tampico	22	10	97	49	5	50b	1.0	1.3
*Vera Cruz	19	12	96	08	6	15b	1.8	2.3
*Arcas Cays	20	15	91	58	3	05b	1.3	1.7
*Triangles	20	54	92	08	3	00b	1.3	1.7
*Laguna de Terminos	18	36	91	53	3	15b	1.3	1.7
Campeche	19	50	90	32	2	59	1.7	2.1
Sisal	21	10	90	03	10	20	1.4	1.8
Cape Catoche	21	32	87	04	9	30	1.2	1.5
Mugeres Harbor	21	14	86	52	9	20	1.3	1.6
Cozumel	20	28	86	48	8	20	1.2	1.5
BELIZE								
Belize	17	33	88	14	8	00	1.2	1.5
GUATEMALA.								
Dulce River Entrance	15	50	88	45	9	00	1.6	2.0
HONDURAS.								
Roatan Island	16	23	86	28	7	35	2.7	3.5
Bonacca Island	16	29	85	54	8	50	1.2	1.5
NICARAGUA.								
Serranilla Bank	15	50	79	48	4	25	1.6	2.0
Serrana Bank	14	20	80	17	4	25	1.6	2.0
Old Providence Island	13	21	81	18	4	25	0.8	1.0
Cape Gracias a Dios Harbor	14	52	83	14	10	20	1.6	2.0

*Tide is chiefly diurnal.
b=mean higher high-water interval, referring to lower transit of moon at north declination or upper transit at south declination.

TIDAL DATA.

EAST COAST OF NORTH AMERICA—Continued.

Place.	Lat. N.	Long. W.	High water interval.	Mean range.	Spring range.
	° ′	° ′	h. m.	Feet.	Feet.
NICARAGUA—Continued.					
Pearl Cays	12 23	83 26	1 50	1.6	2.0
Corn Islands	12 10	83 03	1 35	1.6	2.0
Bluefields, Lagoon Entrance	12 01	83 42	1 04	0.7	0.8
San Juan del Norte (Greytown)	10 55	83 41	1 00	1.2	1.5
COSTA RICA.					
Point Blanco	10 00	83 02	1 00	1.3	1.6
CANAL ZONE.					
Boca del Toro, Almirante Bay	9 21	82 15	0 51	0.8	1.0
Colon (Aspinwall)	9 22	79 55	0 06	0.9	1.1
Caledonia Harbor	8 56	77 47	11 30	1.2	1.5

WEST INDIA ISLANDS.

Place.	Lat. N.	Long. W.	High water interval.	Mean range.	Spring range.
BERMUDA ISLANDS.					
Ireland Island, dockyard	32 20	64 50	7 04	3.3	4.0
BAHAMAS.					
Memory Rock	26 59	79 09	7 40	2.5	3.2
Great Bahama Island	26 29	78 40	7 45	3.0	3.8
Whale Key	26 42	77 08	7 50	3.5	4.5
Great Abaco	26 17	77 08	7 52	2.4	3.1
Gun Key	25 34	79 18	8 20	2.3	3.0
Andros Island	24 29	77 44	7 40	2.3	3.0
Nassau, New Providence Island	25 05	77 21	7 23	2.6	3.1
Eleuthera Island	25 08	76 08	7 00	3.1	4.0
Cat Island	24 20	75 24	7 00	3.1	4.0
San Salvador, or Watling Island	24 06	74 26	7 00	3.1	4.0
Clarence Harbor, Long Island	23 06	74 58	8 20	3.2	4.1
Crooked Island	22 49	74 21	6 50	2.0	2.5
Mariguana Island	22 26	73 00	7 20	2.3	3.0
Inagua Island	20 56	73 41	7 50	2.7	3.5
Turks Islands	21 26	71 09	7 30	2.3	3.0
Cuba.					
Isabela de Sagua	22 56	80 00	8 52	1.6	2.0
Cayo Paredon Grande	22 29	78 09	7 20	2.2	2.8
Nuevitas Bay Entrance	21 38	77 07	8 30	1.3	1.5
Nuevitas, Nuevitas Bay	21 35	77 15	10 15	1.4	1.6
Port Padre	21 12	76 36	8 41	2.1	2.4
Port Gibara	21 06	76 08	7 48	1.9	2.2
Port Nipe Entrance	20 48	75 35	7 55	2.0	2.3
Livisa Bay Entrance	20 45	75 48	7 48	1.9	2.2
Port Tanamo	20 43	75 19	7 51	1.9	2.2
Cape Maisi	20 15	74 08	7 40	2.2	2.8
Guantanamo Bay Entrance	19 55	75 09	8 47	1.0	1.3
Santiago Bay Entrance	20 00	75 50	9 09	1.1	1.4
Ensenada de Mora	19 51	77 30	8 59	0.8	1.0
Manzanillo	20 19	77 10	11 00	3.1	4.0
Port Xagua Entrance (Cienfuegos)	22 08	80 28	9 04	0.8	1.0
Cape San Antonio	21 52	84 58	8 30	1.2	1.5
Bahia Honda	22 58	83 13	8 24	1.0	1.4
Habana	23 08	82 22	8 36	0.9	1.3
Matanzas	23 02	81 45	8 40	1.7	2.2
Cardenas	23 04	81 12	9 25	1.4	1.8
Jamaica.					
*Morant Point	17 55	76 11	9 00a	0.7	0.9
*Port Royal	17 56	76 47	10 00a	0.7	0.9
*South Negril Point	18 18	78 24	13 00a	0.7	0.9
*St. Anns Bay	18 30	77 16	10 00a	0.8	1.0
*Grand Cayman Island	19 20	81 21	8 00a	0.9	1.1
Haiti and Santo Domingo (Hispaniola).					
Port au Prince	18 33	72 21	8 23	1.2	1.5
Puerto Plata	19 48	70 42	8 08	1.6	2.0
Sanchez, Samana Bay	19 13	69 36	8 40	2.3	3.0
*Saona Island	18 08	68 40	9 25a	0.4	0.5
*Santo Domingo	18 27	69 53	9 40a	0.6	1.0
*Jacmel	18 13	72 32	9 40a	0.7	1.1
Puerto Rico.					
*Parguera	17 58	67 03	10 25a	0.7	0.9
*Port Guanica	17 58	66 56	10 25a	0.7	0.9
*Port of Ponce	17 59	66 40	10 25a	0.6	0.8

* Tide is chiefly diurnal.
a = mean higher water interval, referring to upper transit of moon at north declination or to lower transit at south declination.

121

TIDAL DATA.

WEST INDIA ISLANDS—Continued.

Place.	Lat. N.	Long. W.	High water interval.	Mean range.	Spring range.
	° ′	° ′	h. m.	Feet.	Feet.
Porto Rico—Continued.					
*Point Tuna Light	17 59	65 53	10 00a	0.7	0.9
*Culebrita Island Light	18 19	65 14	9 00a	0.7	0.9
*Port Ferro, Vieques or Crab Island	18 06	65 26	8 40a	0.7	0.9
Port Mulas	18 09	65 27	8 11	0.8	1.0
Great Harbor, Culebra Island	18 18	65 17	8 04	0.7	0.8
Fajardo Harbor	18 20	65 38	7 55	1.1	1.4
San Juan	18 29	66 07	8 23	1.1	1.3
Mayaguez	18 13	67 08	8 00	1.1	2.0
Port Real	18 05	67 11	7 57	0.8	1.2
Lesser Antilles.					
*St. Thomas Island, Virgin Islands	18 25	64 58	7 30a	0.8	1.0
*St. Bartholomew Island	17 54	62 51	7 40a	1.0	1.2
*Antigua Island	16 59	61 48	8 40a	1.3	1.6
*Guadaloupe	16 12	61 27	9 40a	0.9	1.1
Dominica	15 34	61 30	1 20	1.2	1.6
Martinique	14 35	61 03	3 50	1.0	1.5
St. Vincent, Kingstown	13 10	61 13	2 50	2.0	2.7
Barbados	13 07	59 36	2 50	2.3	3.1
Grenada	12 04	61 45	2 30	1.2	1.5
Tobago	11 10	60 42	3 50	1.6	2.1

NORTH AND EAST COASTS OF SOUTH AMERICA.

Place.	Lat. N.	Long. W.	High water interval.	Mean range.	Spring range.
COLOMBIA.					
Savanilla	11 00	74 58	11 00	2.0	2.5
Cartagena	10 26	75 34	10 50	1.3	1.6
VENEZUELA.					
Maracaibo	10 43	71 39	5 05	2.0	2.5
La Guaira	10 40	66 58	6 00	2.3	2.8
Parlamar, Margarita Island	10 58	63 51	4 20	1.3	1.6
Orinoco River Entrance, Cangrejo Island	8 39	60 35	4 50	5.4	6.5
TRINIDAD.					
Port of Spain	10 39	61 31	4 20	3.2	4.0
Galeota Point	10 08	60 59	4 00	2.6	3.2
GUIANA.					
Georgetown, Demerara River	6 52	58 11	4 18	6.4	8.6
Paramaribo, Surinam River	5 50	55 09	5 50	7.1	9.5
Cayenne, Cayenne River	4 56	52 20	4 27	4.5	6.0
BRAZIL.					
Vape Cachipour	3 49	51 01	5 42	7.2	9.5
Conani River	2 50	50 53	6 28	14.5	19.0
Maraca Island Anchorage	2 09	50 30	6 00	22.9	30.0
Balique Island Light, Amazon River Entrance	0 54	49 55	8 30	10.9	14.3
Point Pedrere, Amazon River	0 11	50 43	10 50	12.3	16.2
	Lat. S.				
Dentro Channel, Para River Entrance	0 23	47 55	10 40	7.9	10.4
Para, Para River	1 27	48 31	11 50	8.1	9.6
San Joao Islands Light	1 17	44 55	6 14	10.7	14.1
Maranhao, or San Luiz	2 32	44 14	6 50	12.6	16.5
Santa Anna Reefs Light	2 16	43 36	5 35	10.0	13.1
Tutoia Anchorage	2 46	42 21	5 05	9.7	12.8
San Joao de Paranahiba	2 59	41 47	5 18	9.8	12.9
Camocim	2 53	40 52	6 07	7.6	9.7
Point Jericoacoara	2 48	40 32	5 15	6.0	7.9
Mandahi River Entrance	3 10	39 23	5 20	6.6	8.6
Ceara	3 42	38 31	4 58	6.4	8.0
Aracati, Jaguarybe River	4 28	37 45	5 50	6.1	8.0
Povoacao, Mossoro River	4 57	37 10	4 45	6.5	8.5
Cape St. Roque	5 29	35 16	4 05	6.7	8.8
Parahiba River Light	6 57	34 50	5 00	6.0	7.9
Pernambuco (Recife Arsenal)	8 04	34 54	4 33	5.3	7.0
Maceio	9 35	35 41	4 20	6.5	8.5
San Francisco River Entrance	10 28	36 23	4 17	5.9	7.8
Bahia	12 58	38 31	4 10	5.8	7.6
Morro de Sao Paulo	13 21	38 54	3 50	4.6	6.0
Fort Camamu	13 54	39 02	3 50	4.8	6.3
San Jorge dos Ilheos	14 47	39 03	3 35	4.9	6.4
Santa Cruz	16 17	39 02	3 25	4.6	6.0
Comoxatiba	17 06	39 10	3 20	4.3	5.6

* Tide is chiefly diurnal.
a = mean higher water interval, referring to upper transit of moon at north declination or to lower transit at south declination.

TIDAL DATA.

NORTH AND EAST COASTS OF SOUTH AMERICA—Continued.

Place.	Lat. S.		Long. W.		High water interval.		Mean range.	Spring range.
	°	′	°	′	h.	m.	Feet.	Feet.
BRAZIL—Continued.								
Caravellas	17	43	39	09	3	10	4.9	6.4
Abrolhos Island Light	17	57	38	40	3	15	5.1	6.6
Aldeia Velha, Barra de Santa Cruz	19	55	40	08	2	55	3.2	4.2
Victoria, Espirito Santo Bay	20	19	40	20	2	50	3.0	4.0
Benevente	20	49	40	41	2	40	3.8	5.0
Itabapuana	21	20	40	59	2	30	4.0	5.3
Macahe	22	23	41	47	2	20	3.4	4.5
Porto Frio	22	58	42	00	2	30	3.4	4.5
Rio de Janeiro (Arsenal)	22	54	43	10	2	24	2.5	3.5
Parati, Ilha Grande Bay	23	18	44	42	1	35	4.0	5.3
San Sebastiao	23	48	45	23	1	50	3.0	4.0
Santos	23	56	46	20	2	50	3.8	5.0
Paranahua	25	31	48	30	2	55	4.9	6.4
Cape Joao Diaz, San Francisco River	26	11	48	32	2	20	3.6	4.7
Santa Catharina Island	27	27	48	31	2	35	4.5	5.9
Rio Grande do Sul	32	07	52	04	9	20	1.5	2.0
URUGUAY.								
Castillo Bay	34	22	53	48	8	20	1.5	2.0
Montevideo, Plata River	34	53	56	12	2	00	1.4	1.7
Colonia, Plata River	34	28	57	52	6	30	3.4	4.0
ARGENTINA.								
Buenos Aires, Plata River	34	36	58	22	6	50	1.8	2.1
Barragan Bay	34	49	57	54	6	00	3.0	3.6
San Boronbon Bay	35	54	57	22	4	30	4.4	5.2
Cape San Antonio	36	20	56	46	9	50	4.5	5.3
Point Mogotes	38	09	57	30	9	48	7.6	9.8
Port Belgrano, Bahia Blanca	38	58	61	51	4	25	12.3	15.8
Point Medano, Rio Negro Entrance	41	03	62	46	10	50	11.5	14.7
Port San Antonio, San Matias Gulf	40	46	64	47	10	35	18.3	23.5
Port San Josef	42	23	64	20	10	05	22.4	28.7
Port Madryn, Nuevo Gulf	42	45	64	59	7	05	10.3	13.2
Port Santa Elena	44	31	65	22	3	50	13.1	16.8
Port Desire	47	45	65	55	0	00	14.3	18.3
Port San Julian	49	15	67	42	10	35	23.0	29.5
Port Santa Cruz	50	08	68	23	9	20	30.9	39.6
Coy Inlet	50	58	69	10	9	00	31.2	40.0
Port Gallegos	51	33	69	01	8	40	35.6	45.6
Tierra del Fuego.								
San Sebastian Bay	53	15	68	27	6	50	15.6	20.0
Cape Penas	53	52	67	33	6	32	9.2	11.8
Cape San Diego	54	42	65	10	4	20	7.7	9.9
Staten Island, east end	54	45	63	46	4	19	6.9	7.8
DETACHED ISLANDS.								
As Rocas Reef Light	3	51	33	49	5	05	7.5	10.0
Fernando Noronha	3	50	32	25	5	00	4.5	6.0
Trinidad Islands	20	30	29	22	3	40	3.0	4.0
Martin Vaz Islets	20	29	28	53	3	35	2.6	3.5
South Georgia (Royal Bay)	54	31	36	01	7	19	1.7	2.3
FALKLAND ISLANDS.								
Port Louis, Berkeley Sound	51	29	58	00	5	31	3.3	4.3
Bay of Harbors	52	15	59	16	5	50	3.7	4.8
Port Stephens	52	12	60	40	7	35	5.5	7.1
Port Egmont	51	18	60	05	7	20	8.3	10.7
CHILE.								
Magellan Strait.								
Sarmiento Bank	52	30	68	03	8	00	30.0	38.5
Cape Virgins	52	19	68	22	8	18	30.2	38.7
Dungeness	52	24	68	26	8	19	30.7	39.4
Cape Espiritu Santo	52	39	68	34	8	20	30.4	39.0
Catherine Point	52	32	68	45	8	24	23.4	30.0
Possession Bay, Stonewall Anchorage	52	16	69	10	8	35	30.4	39.0
Direction Hill	52	21	69	29	8	43	29.6	38.0
First Narrows	52	30	69	36	8	47	30.4	39.0
Philip Bay, east side	52	40	69	37	9	05	14.0	18.0
St. Jago Bay	52	32	69	55	9	14	15.6	20.0
Gregory Bay	52	37	70	08	9	23	16.4	21.0
Second Narrows	52	45	70	17	9	50	17.9	23.0
Gracia Point	52	44	70	32	10	07	6.2	7.9
Port Zenteno	52	47	70	48	10	28	5.5	7.0
Royal Road, Elizabeth Island	52	49	70	36	10	24	6.2	8.0
Santa Magdalena Island	52	56	70	35	10	25	7.7	9.9
Sandy Point	53	10	70	54	11	03	3.9	5.0
Port Famine	53	38	70	59	11	58	4.7	6.0
Cape San Isidro	53	47	70	55	12	21	6.2	8.0
Cape Froward	53	54	71	18	0	28	5.5	7.0

123

TIDAL DATA.

NORTH AND EAST COASTS OF SOUTH AMERICA—Continued.

Place.	Lat. S.	Long. W.	High water interval.	Mean range.	Spring range.
	° ′	° ′	h. m.	Feet.	Feet.
CHILE—Continued.					
Magellan Strait—Continued.					
Woods Bay	53 48	71 38	0 54	6.2	8.0
Port Gallant, Fortescue Bay	53 42	72 00	1 20	6.2	8.0
Borja Bay	53 32	72 29	1 54	4.3	5.5
Swallow Bay	53 30	72 48	1 53	4.5	5.0
Playa Parda Cove	53 19	73 00	1 31	4.0	4.5
Port Angosto	53 14	73 22	1 09	3.6	4.0
Sylvia Cove	52 59	73 33	1 00	3.8	4.3
Port Tamar	52 56	73 45	0 55	5.3	6.0
Tuesday Bay	52 51	74 27	0 44	5.2	5.8
Cape Pillar	52 43	74 42	0 32	3.6	4.0
Goree Road	55 12	67 05	3 50	6.0	6.7
St. Martin Cove, Hermite Island	55 51	67 33	4 07	4.3	4.8
Cape Horn (Orange Bay)	55 31	68 05	3 33	4.2	4.8
Diego Ramirez Islands	56 28	68 43	3 50	4.5	5.0
New Year Sound	55 30	69 06	3 20	4.5	5.0

WEST COAST OF SOUTH AMERICA.

Place.	Lat. S.	Long. W.	High water interval.	Mean range.	Spring range.
Noir Island	54 26	73 03	2 20	4.3	4.8
Week Island	53 12	74 21	1 50	4.2	4.7
Evangelistas Island	52 21	75 08	0 55	3.9	4.4
Guia Narrows	50 45	74 27	2 10	6.1	6.9
Port Henry, Gulf of Trinidad	50 03	75 18	0 30	4.0	4.5
English Narrows	49 04	74 21	1 00	5.3	6.0
Port Barbara, Penas Gulf	48 01	75 24	0 15	4.7	5.3
Port Otway, Penas Gulf	46 54	75 22	0 10	4.7	5.3
San Andres Bay	46 36	75 31	0 05	4.3	4.8
Cape Taytao, Anna Pink Bay	45 52	75 06	0 00	3.9	4.4
Vallenar Road	45 19	74 35	12 15	4.0	5.0
Port Yates	45 26	74 26	0 10	5.5	7.0
Port Italiano	45 23	74 08	0 20	6.5	8.0
Port Lagunas	45 17	73 46	0 55	5.5	7.0
Port Tangbac	45 03	73 45	1 25	7.0	9.0
CHILE.					
Huamblin Island	44 49	75 02	12 15	5.0	6.0
Huafo Island	43 36	74 43	12 10	5.0	6.0
Cucao Bay, Chiloe I.	42 40	74 06	12 05	4.0	5.2
Port Low, Corcovada Gulf	43 50	73 57	12 20	5.5	7.0
Port Melinca	43 54	73 45	0 00	6.5	8.0
Tictoc Bay	43 37	72 56	0 05	7.0	9.0
Port San Pedro	43 20	73 41	0 10	9.5	12.0
Port Quellon	43 07	73 36	0 15	10.0	12.5
Castro	42 28	73 44	0 25	13.5	17.0
Port Quemchi, Gulf of Ancud	42 09	73 28	0 40	14.5	18.0
Linao Bay	41 56	73 32	0 45	12.0	15.0
Tres Cruces Point	41 50	73 29	0 50	12.0	15.0
Huito Inlet	41 45	73 10	1 00	12.0	15.0
Port Montt, Reloncavi Sound	41 29	72 56	1 00	15.0	19.0
Chacao Narrows, Remolinos Rock	41 48	73 31	0 35	12.0	15.0
Ancud Bay	41 52	73 50	0 04	4.6	5.9
Maullin, Maullin River	41 36	73 38	0 20	6.1	7.9
Bueno River Entrance	40 14	73 42	0 00	5.6	7.2
Chaihuin Bay	39 58	73 37	11 00	3.3	4.3
Corral, Port Valdivia	39 53	73 27	10 25	4.3	5.6
Valdivia	39 50	73 18	11 25	3.0	3.9
Queule	39 23	73 14	10 18	3.8	4.9
Imperial or Cautin River Entrance	38 48	73 23	10 00	3.9	5.0
Mocha Island	38 20	73 57	10 20	2.6	3.3
Lebu, Lebu River	37 37	73 42	10 15	3.8	4.9
Yeñez Cove	37 22	73 41	10 10	4.1	5.3
Santa Maria Island Light	37 03	73 32	10 10	4.7	6.0
Lota, Arauco Bay	37 06	73 11	10 05	3.8	4.9
Talcaguano, Concepcion Bay	36 43	73 08	10 04	4.1	5.3
Tome	36 37	72 59	10 05	3.9	5.0
Dichato, Coliumo Bay	36 32	72 58	10 06	3.8	4.9
Buchupureo	36 04	72 47	10 07	2.4	3.1
Curanipe	35 48	72 38	10 21	2.6	3.4
Maule River Entrance	35 19	72 25	9 45	2.8	3.6
Constitucion, Maule River	35 20	72 24	10 06	3.0	3.9
Llico	34 45	72 07	9 57	3.2	4.1
Pichilemo	34 23	72 00	9 53	3.1	4.0
Matanza Anchorage	33 58	71 54	9 49	3.1	4.0
Toro Point	33 45	71 48	9 45	2.9	3.7
Juan Fernandez Island	33 38	78 53	9 30	2.9	3.8
Port San Antonio	33 34	71 39	9 44	3.1	4.0
Quintai Road	33 11	71 42	9 39	3.0	3.9
Valparaiso	33 02	71 39	9 37	3.0	3.9
Quintero Bay	32 46	71 31	9 35	3.2	4.1
Port Papudo	32 30	71 28	9 32	3.2	4.1

TIDAL DATA.

WEST COAST OF SOUTH AMERICA—Continued.

Place.	Lat. S.		Long. W.		High water interval.		Mean range.	Spring range.
	°	′	°	′	h.	m.	Feet.	Feet.
CHILE—Continued.								
Pichidanqui	32	06	71	33	9	30	3.0	3.9
Vilos	31	54	71	32	9	26	3.3	4.2
Oscuro Cove	31	28	71	37	9	20	3.5	4.5
Tongoi	30	15	71	31	9	15	3.2	4.1
Guayacan, Port Herradura	29	58	71	23	9	10	3.6	4.7
Coquimbo	29	57	71	22	8	58	3.8	4.9
Totoralillo	29	29	71	21	8	50	3.8	4.9
Pena Blanco Road	28	43	71	23	8	29	3.3	4.3
Port Huasco	28	27	71	15	8	23	3.8	4.9
Port Carrizal Bajo	28	04	71	12	8	50	3.8	4.9
Port Copiapo	27	20	70	59	8	21	3.9	5.0
Caldera	27	04	70	52	8	50	3.8	4.9
Port Flamenco	26	34	70	44	9	00	3.9	5.0
Chanaral de las Animas	26	20	70	41	9	05	3.8	4.9
Lavata Bay	25	39	70	44	9	10	3.9	5.0
Port Taltal	25	25	70	34	9	20	3.8	4.9
Grande Point	25	07	70	30	9	35	3.9	5.0
Paposo	25	03	70	30	9	30	3.8	4.9
Blanco Encalada Road	24	22	70	34	9	50	2.7	3.5
Antofagasta, Moreno Bay	23	38	70	25	9	05	3.6	4.7
San Luciano, Mejillones del Sur Bay	23	06	70	28	9	35	3.0	3.9
Cobija	22	34	70	18	9	44	3.1	4.0
Tocopilla	22	05	70	13	8	55	3.7	4.8
Point Lobos	21	05	70	13	9	00	3.8	4.9
Iquique	20	12	70	10	8	35	3.9	5.0
Buena Cove	19	52	70	09	8	35	4.2	5.4
Pisagus River	19	33	70	14	8	32	3.9	5.0
Arica	18	28	70	20	7	49	4.3	5.6
PERU.								
Ilo Road	17	35	71	23	7	55	4.1	5.3
Islay Road	16	58	72	10	7	39	4.8	6.2
Port San Juan	15	20	75	09	6	47	3.0	3.9
Pisco Bay	13	40	76	14	6	16	2.9	3.8
Callao Bay	12	02	77	09	5	47	2.7	3.5
Huacho Bay	11	08	77	35	5	29	2.3	3.0
Huarmey Bay	10	05	78	08	5	08	1.6	2.1
Ferrol Bay	9	07	78	33	4	50	1.6	2.0
Port Malabrigo	7	40	79	24	4	19	1.6	2.1
Eten Point	6	55	79	52	4	04	1.9	2.5
Paita	5	05	81	06	3	20	2.7	3.5
ECUADOR.								
Santa Clara Island	3	12	80	23	4	00	7.8	10.0
Guayaquil	2	17	79	49	7	00	8.5	11.0
Santa Elena Bay	2	11	80	56	3	00	6.1	7.9
Port Manta	0	56	80	30	3	10	5.8	7.5
Cape Pasado	0	22	80	30	3	15	7.7	9.9
GALAPAGOS ISLANDS.								
Charles Island	1	13	90	30	2	10	4.7	6.0
Iguana Cove, Albermarle Island	0	58	91	29	2	00	4.8	6.2
Chatham Island	0	47	89	27	2	20	5.0	6.5
Indefatigable Island	0	30	90	15	2	00	4.8	6.0
James Island, north side	0	13	90	44	2	45	4.0	5.2
ECUADOR.								
	Lat. N.							
Padernales	0	02	80	05	3	20	8.4	10.8
Atacames Bay	0	53	79	54	3	25	9.9	12.8
Santiago River	1	16	79	03	3	20	9.9	12.7
COLOMBIA.								
Tumaco Road	1	51	78	40	3	35	10.3	13.2
Buenaventura	3	52	77	03	4	10	10.3	13.2
Negrillas Rocks	3	52	77	24	4	00	10.0	12.8
Cabita Bay	5	28	77	28	3	40	10.2	13.1
Cupica Bay	6	35	77	23	3	30	10.4	13.3

WEST COAST OF NORTH AMERICA.

Place.	Lat. N.		Long. W.		High water interval.		Mean range.	Spring range.
PANAMA CANAL ZONE.								
Pinas Bay	7	34	78	11	3	00	10.8	13.8
Rey Island	8	17	78	54	3	00	12.3	16.0
Chepo River	8	59	79	07	3	05	12.5	16.2
Balboa	8	58	79	34	3	05	12.5	16.2
Taboga	8	48	79	33	3	00	12.5	16.2
Chame Bay	8	41	79	45	3	02	12.5	16.2
Cape Mala	7	30	80	00	3	00	10.3	13.0
Bahia Honda	7	43	81	30	3	10	8.7	11.0
Parida Island	8	07	82	20	3	15	8.3	10.5

TIDAL DATA.
WEST COAST OF NORTH AMERICA—Continued.

Place.	Lat. N.	Long. W.	High water interval.	Mean range.	Spring range.
	° ′	° ′	h. m.	Feet.	Feet.
COSTA RICA					
El Rincon Harbor, Gulf of Dulce	8 44	83 28	2 45	7.9	10.0
Uvita Bay	9 08	83 46	2 20	7.5	9.5
Port Herradura	9 39	84 39	2 35	7.1	9.0
Port Culebra	10 38	85 40	2 45	7.1	9.0
Port Elena	10 58	85 42	2 50	7.5	9.5
NICARAGUA					
Port San Juan del Sur	11 15	85 53	3 00	7.9	10.0
Corinto Harbor	12 28	87 12	2 55	8.3	10.5
HONDURAS					
Amapala	13 20	87 34	3 00	8.7	11.0
SALVADOR					
Port la Union	13 20	87 51	3 15	8.3	10.5
Libertad	13 29	89 19	3 05	7.9	10.0
Acajutla Bay	13 34	89 50	2 55	7.5	9.5
GUATEMALA					
San Jose	13 56	90 49	2 50	7.1	9.0
Champerico	14 17	91 55	2 50	6.7	8.5
Soconuso Bar	15 05	92 54	2 50	6.3	8.0
MEXICO					
La Puerta	15 57	93 48	2 50	5.9	7.5
Salina Cruz	16 10	95 12	2 50	5.5	7.0
Port Sacrificios	15 41	96 14	2 50	4.7	6.0
Maldonado	16 33	98 45	2 45	3.2	4.0
Acapulco	16 52	99 56	2 40	1.6	2.0
Port Sihuatanejo	17 36	101 32	8 50	1.7	2.0
Manzanillo	19 03	104 20	9 07	1.8	1.9
Chamela or Perula Bay	19 32	105 07	9 07	2.0	2.5
San Blas	21 30	105 19	9 08	2.3	3.2
Mazatlan	23 11	106 26	9 08	2.6	3.8
Altata, Culiacan River	24 38	107 57	10 07	4.0	5.8
San Lorenzo Channel	24 22	110 20	9 35	3.6	5.3
La Paz Harbor	24 20	110 21	9 40	3.7	5.4
San Lucas Bay	27 14	112 13	11 15	3.2	4.7
Guaymas Harbor	27 55	110 51	11 30	3.4	5.0
Santa Teresa Bay	28 25	112 52	11 50	7.7	11.2
Puerto Refugio	29 33	113 35	0 25	8.1	11.8
Tepoca Bay	30 15	112 50	1 20	11.8	17.2
Colorado River Entrance	31 45	114 48	2 15	21.6	31.5
San Jose del Cabo	23 03	109 42	8 36	3.1	4.5
Pequeña Bay, Santa Margarite Island	24 24	111 49	8 17	4.0	5.3
Magdalena Bay	24 34	112 09	8 25	3.8	5.5
San Juanico Bay	26 15	112 28	8 29	3.9	5.7
Abreojos Pt., Ballenas Bay	26 43	113 34	9 00	4.7	6.7
San Bartolome Bay	27 40	114 51	9 00	5.8	8.2
Cerros Island	28 12	115 14	9 05	5.9	7.8
Playa Maria Bay	28 55	114 48	9 15	5.7	7.6
Rosario Bay	29 54	115 43	9 19	4.8	6.4
San Quentin Bay	30 25	115 54	9 23	3.7	4.9
Colnett Bay	30 57	116 15	9 27	4.4	5.8
Ensenada, Todos Santos Bay	31 51	116 36	9 28	3.8	5.0
CALIFORNIA					
San Diego Bar	32 40	117 14	9 29	3.7	5.0
San Diego	32 42	117 14	9 32	3.9	5.6
San Juan Capistrano	33 27	117 41	9 42	3.7	5.4
Newport Landing	33 38	117 54	9 45	3.5	5.1
Anaheim Landing	33 43	118 05	9 43	3.9	5.6
San Pedro	33 43	118 16	9 36	4.0	5.8
Santa Monica	34 01	118 30	9 37	3.8	5.4
Hueneme Light	34 09	119 13	9 32	3.7	5.4
Ventura	34 16	119 17	9 53	3.7	5.4
Santa Barbara	34 24	119 41	9 30	3.6	5.4
Gaviota	34 28	120 14	9 34	3.6	5.4
Santa Catalina Harbor, Catalina Island	33 26	118 29	9 28	3.8	5.4
Corral Harbor, San Nicholas Island	33 17	119 31	9 20	3.7	5.2
Prisoner Harbor, Santa Cruz Island	34 01	119 41	9 29	3.7	5.2
Cuyler Harbor, San Miguel Island	34 03	120 21	9 23	3.7	5.2
Lompoc Landing	34 44	120 37	9 55	3.7	5.0
Point Sal	34 54	120 40	10 02	3.6	5.0
San Luis Obispo	35 11	120 44	10 17	3.7	5.1
Morro, Morro Bay	35 21	120 50	10 45	3.2	4.7
Cayucos, Estero Bay	35 27	120 55	10 33	3.8	5.3
San Simeon	35 39	121 11	10 38	4.0	5.5
Monterey Harbor Light	36 37	121 52	10 43	4.0	5.6
Santa Cruz Harbor Light	36 57	122 02	10 54	4.3	6.2
Half Moon Bay	37 30	122 27	10 48	4.1	5.8

TIDAL DATA.
WEST COAST OF NORTH AMERICA—Continued.

Place.	Lat. N.	Long. W.	High water interval.	Mean range.	Spring range.
	° ′	° ′	h. m.	Feet.	Feet.
CALIFORNIA—Continued.					
Southeast Farallon Light	37 42	123 00	10 40	3.7	5.6
San Francisco Bar	37 46	122 38	11 15	3.8	5.6
San Francisco (Fort Point)	37 49	122 29	11 39	3.9	5.6
Presidio	37 48	122 27	11 40	3.9	5.7
Alcatraz Light	37 49	122 25	11 50	4.0	5.8
San Francisco, North Beach	37 48	122 24	12 05	4.0	5.8
Mission Street	37 48	122 24	12 07	4.2	6.0
Goat Island (Yerba Buena Light)	37 48	122 22	12 08	4.2	6.0
Oakland Harbor	37 47	122 16	12 15	4.4	6.1
Sausalito	37 51	122 29	11 44	3.7	5.4
Angel Island	37 51	122 26	11 48	3.8	5.6
Mare Island Light	38 04	122 15	1 00	4.8	6.6
Point Reyes Light	37 54	122 41	11 10	3.9	5.7
Bolinas Bay	38 00	123 01	11 00	3.9	5.7
Bodega Head	38 18	123 03	11 05	3.9	5.8
Fort Ross	38 31	123 15	11 05	3.9	5.8
Point Arena Light	38 57	123 44	11 00	3.9	5.8
Navarro River Entrance	39 12	123 45	11 00	3.9	5.8
Little River Harbor	39 16	123 47	11 00	4.0	6.1
Mendocino Bay	39 18	123 47	11 00	3.8	5.8
Fort Bragg Landing	39 26	123 49	11 00	3.9	5.9
Westport	39 38	123 47	11 00	4.0	6.1
Shelter Cove	40 02	124 03	11 00	4.2	6.1
Cape Mendocino	40 26	124 25	11 00	3.9	5.9
Eel River Bar	40 38	124 19	11 10	4.4	6.3
Humboldt Bay Bar	40 46	124 15	11 33	4.3	6.2
Humboldt Bay (S. Jetty Landing)	40 45	124 14	11 47	4.5	6.4
Trinidad Harbor Light	41 03	124 09	11 27	4.6	6.2
Crescent City Light	41 45	124 12	11 33	5.0	6.8
OREGON.					
Chetko Cove	42 03	124 16	11 41	4.5	6.0
Rogue River	42 25	124 25	11 42	4.5	6.0
Port Orford	42 44	124 30	11 32	4.8	6.4
Bandon, Coquille River	43 07	124 25	11 53	5.0	6.7
Coos Bay Bar	43 21	124 21	11 55	4.8	6.4
Empire	43 24	124 17	0 02	4.9	6.7
Umpqua River Entrance Bar	43 41	124 12	0 05	5.0	6.8
Gardiner	43 44	124 06	0 36	5.1	6.8
Suislaw River Entrance	44 01	124 07	12 09	5.2	6.9
Alsea Bay Entrance	44 25	124 05	12 01	5.8	7.6
Yaquina River Entrance Bar	44 37	124 05	11 50	5.9	7.7
Newport	44 38	124 04	11 54	6.1	8.0
Nestucca Bay Entrance	45 09	123 59	12 12	5.8	7.6
Hobsonville, Tillamook Bay	45 34	123 57	12 31	6.3	8.2
Nehalem River Entrance	45 40	123 56	12 08	6.1	8.0
Columbia River Entrance Jetty	46 14	124 05	11 59	6.3	8.3
Cape Disappointment, Wash	46 17	124 03	12 08	6.3	8.3
Point Adams	46 12	123 59	0 00	6.5	8.5
Astoria	46 11	123 50	0 34	6.4	8.3
Portland	45 31	122 40	6 43	1.0	1.2
WASHINGTON.					
Willapa Bay Entrance	46 39	124 03	0 00	6.2	8.1
Toke Point	46 42	123 58	0 15	6.9	9.1
South Bend, Willapa Bay	46 40	123 48	0 45	7.8	9.8
Grays Harbor Entrance	46 54	124 10	12 15	6.9	9.1
Destruction Island	47 40	124 30	12 00	6.6	8.9
Quillayute River	47 53	124 39	12 18	6.3	8.7
Cape Alava (Flattery Rocks)	48 10	124 44	12 07	6.0	8.5
Juan de Fuca Strait.					
Cape Flattery Light, Tatoosh Island	48 23	124 44	0 08	5.7	8.3
Neah Bay	48 22	124 38	0 10	5.8	8.4
Port Angeles	48 08	123 26	2 10	4.4	7.5
New Dungeness Light	48 11	123 07	2 42	4.2	7.4
Washington Harbor	48 04	123 02	3 06	4.6	7.7
Port Discovery	48 02	122 52	3 19	4.6	7.8
Smith Island Light	48 19	122 51	3 40	4.7	7.9
Partridge Point	48 14	122 46	3 46	5.0	8.3
Port Townsend	48 07	122 45	3 47	5.2	8.8
Marrowstone Point	48 06	122 41	3 56	5.6	9.2
Oak Bay	48 01	122 43	3 58	6.0	9.6
Seattle	47 37	122 20	4 29	7.6	11.3
Bremerton, Port Orchard	47 34	122 37	4 35	7.8	11.5
Tacoma	47 16	122 26	4 35	8.0	11.8
Bellingham	48 43	122 31	4 30	5.3	8.5
BRITISH COLUMBIA.					
Esquimalt Harbor, Vancouver Island	48 26	123 27	1 15b	....	6.5
Victoria Harbor, Vancouver Island	48 27	123 23	1 05b	....	6.5
Discovery Island Light	48 25	123 13	3 00b	....	6.0

b=mean higher high water interval, referring to lower transit of the moon at north declination or upper transit at south declination.

127

TIDAL DATA.
WEST COAST OF NORTH AMERICA—Continued.

Place.	Lat. N.	Long. W.	High water interval.	Mean range.	Spring range.
	° ′	° ′	h. m.	Feet.	Feet.
BRITISH COLUMBIA—Continued.					
Active Pass, Mayne Island	48 52	123 18	5 05	5.9	9.5
Cowichin Harbor, Vancouver Island	48 46	123 37	5 04	5.9	9.5
Maple Bay, Vancouver Island	48 50	123 36	5 10	5.9	9.5
Oyster Harbor, Vancouver Island	49 00	123 48	5 30	6.4	10.0
North Sand Heads Light, Fraser R.	49 05	123 16	5 11	6.0	9.5
Atkinson Point Light, Burrard Inlet	49 20	123 16	5 20	6.7	10.2
Vancouver, Burrard Inlet	49 17	123 07	5 28	6.8	10.3
Race Rocks Light, Fuca Strait	48 18	123 32	1 45	4.8	8.0
Sooke Inlet, Fuca Strait	48 21	123 43	1 27	5.0	8.3
Jordan River, Fuca Strait	48 25	124 03	1 10	5.4	8.8
Port San Juan, Fuca Strait	48 33	124 26	0 45	6.0	8.0
Carmanah Point Light	48 37	124 46	0 20	6.0	8.0
Cape Beale Light, Barclay Sound	48 48	125 14	12 20	8.0	10.2
Stamp Harbor	49 16	124 51	0 45	10.0	12.4
Clayoquot Sound	49 14	126 00	12 15	8.1	10.3
Hesquiat Harbor	49 25	126 28	12 05	8.3	10.5
Nootka Sound	49 36	126 38	12 05	7.9	10.0
Esperanza Inlet	49 50	126 58	11 55	7.8	9.9
Kyuquot Sound	50 00	127 12	11 50	7.5	9.5
Ou-Ou-Kinsh Inlet	50 08	127 34	11 47	7.5	9.5
Klaskino Inlet	50 18	127 52	11 35	6.9	8.9
Quatsino Sound Entrance	50 28	127 56	11 35	6.9	8.9
Takush Harbor	51 17	127 39	0 25	9.2	11.5
Port Kuper	52 57	132 16	0 00	9.0	11.2
Skidegate Inlet	53 13	131 59	0 07	10.0	12.4
Parry Passage, Graham Island	54 11	133 00	0 00	9.5	11.5
Naden Harbor Harrows, Graham Island	54 03	132 34	0 04	14.0	17.0
Entry Point, Masset Harbor	54 02	133 12	0 05	7.7	9.2
ALASKA.					
Cape Muzon, Dall Island	54 40	132 40	0 02	9.5	11.7
Nichols Bay	54 43	132 08	0 10	11.1	13.4
Cape Chacon	54 42	132 01	0 04	11.1	13.6
Brundige Inlet, Dundas Island	54 37	130 51	0 06	13.5	16.2
Barren Island Light	54 45	131 21	0 06	11.6	13.9
Cape Fox	54 46	130 51	0 07	12.4	14.6
Cape Ommaney	56 10	134 40	0 05	7.6	9.6
Whale Bay	56 38	135 07	0 06	7.7	9.7
Sitka	57 03	135 20	0 07	7.7	9.8
Gilmer Bay, Kruzof Island	57 13	135 50	0 05	8.0	10.1
Falcon Arm, Slocum Arm	57 33	135 56	0 07	8.1	10.2
Elbow Passage, Klag Bay	57 37	136 05	0 20	8.4	10.4
Dry Pass, Hill Island	57 46	136 17	0 10	7.9	10.2
Cape Bingham	58 05	136 34	0 10	8.1	10.3
Cape Spencer	58 12	136 40	0 08	8.1	10.3
Dixon Harbor	58 23	136 52	0 09	8.2	10.4
Lituya Bay	58 37	137 38	0 08	8.0	10.2
Dry Bay	59 10	138 37	0 07	7.7	9.8
Port Mulgrave, Yakutat Bay	59 34	139 46	0 06	7.4	9.4
Icy Bay	59 53	141 28	0 05	7.6	9.9
Wingham Island, Controller Bay	60 05	144 48	12 20	7.7	10.1
Orca	60 35	145 44	0 05	9.9	12.3
Port Etches, Hinchinbrook I.	60 20	146 35	12 15	9.0	11.2
Valdez	61 07	146 17	12 20	9.7	12.2
Seward	60 06	149 26	12 05	8.4	10.0
Port Chatham	59 13	151 44	0 24	12.1	14.4
Port Graham	59 21	151 50	0 45	14.4	15.5
Seldovia, Kachemak Bay	59 26	151 43	0 46	15.4	17.8
Cape Ninilchick	60 01	151 44	1 28	16.5	19.1
Chinulna Point, Kenai River Entrance	60 31	151 18	2 41	17.7	20.7
East Foreland	60 44	151 20	3 25	18.0	21.0
Fire Island	61 09	150 15	5 15	24.4	27.6
Sunrise, Turnagain Arm	60 53	149 26	6 15	30.3	33.3
Anchorage, Knik Arm	61 14	149 55	5 45	27.2	30.3
Tyonek	61 01	151 19	4 18	17.5	20.6
Tuxedni Harbor	60 09	152 38	1 22	14.0	16.6
Iliamna Bay	59 36	153 37	0 51	12.3	14.5
Danger Bay, Marmot Bay	58 07	152 33	0 15	7.2	9.4
Fox Bay, Whale Island	57 58	152 46	0 23	8.1	10.3
Kizhuyak Bay	57 49	152 54	0 21	7.6	9.8
Uzinki Point, Spruce Island	57 55	152 32	0 20	7.2	9.4
Kodiak, Kodiak Harbor	57 47	152 24	0 17	6.9	9.0
Lazy Bay, Alitak Bay	56 53	154 15	0 08	9.5	11.8
Uyak, Uyak Bay, Shelikof Strait	57 38	154 00	0 21	11.5	14.1
Uganik Passage	57 48	153 17	0 33	11.9	14.6
Onion Bay, Kupreanof Strait	58 03	153 13	0 41	11.8	14.4
Dry Spruce Island, Kupreanof Strait	57 57	153 02	0 43	11.4	13.9
Malina Bay, Shelikof Strait	58 10	152 57	0 28	12.0	14.5
Katmai Bay, Shelikof Strait	58 05	154 49	0 20	9.5	12.5
Kanatak, Portage Bay	57 34	156 02	0 20	9.8	11.9
Lees Cabin, Wide Bay	57 26	156 18	0 13	9.8	11.9
Anchorage Bay	56 18	158 23	0 03	6.6	8.7
Sand Pt., Popof I., Shumagin Is.	55 20	160 31	0 11	5.1	7.0
Sanborn Harbor, Nagai I.	55 09	159 59	0 10	5.2	7.2
Dolgoi Harbor, Dolgoi I.	55 07	161 48	0 13	4.7	6.7

TIDAL DATA.

WEST COAST OF NORTH AMERICA—Continued.

Place.	Lat. N.	Long. W.	High water interval.	Mean range.	Spring range.
	° ′	° ′	h. m.	Feet.	Feet.
ALASKA—Continued.					
Kings Cove	55 04	162 19	0 06	4.7	6.8
Ikatan Bay, Unimak I	54 45	163 19	0 06	4.6	6.5
Peterson Bay	54 23	162 38	12 13	4.4	6.2
Acherk Harbor	54 29	162 48	12 15	4.5	6.3
Aleutian Islands.					
Tigalda Bay, Tigalda Island	54 07	164 59	2 08	1.6	3.0
Unalga Bay, Unalga Island	54 00	166 10	3 28	1.8	3.3
Dutch Harbor, Unalaska Island	53 54	166 32	3 51	2.1	3.7
Iliuliuk, Unalaska Island	53 53	166 32	3 50	2.3	4.2
Kashega Bay, Unalaska Island	53 28	167 05	3 12	2.5	4.1
Eagle Bay, Unalaska Island	53 28	166 54	0 47	3.8	5.4
Idak Cove, Umnak Island	53 27	167 42	1 00	3.7	5.3
Adak Island	51 49	176 52	1 35	2.8	4.4
Kiska Harbor, Kiska Island	51 59	182 27	2 07	1.9	3.6
Attu Island	52 56	186 48	3 00	2.0	3.6
Bering Sea.					
St. Paul Island, Pribilof Islands	57 08	170 18	4 17	2.1	3.5
Nunivak Island	60 04	167 15	7 20	3.0	4.6
St. Matthew Island	60 20	172 25	4 40	2.4	3.9
St. Lawrence Island	63 20	170 00	5 35	1.3	1.9
Port Moller, Bristol Bay	55 56	160 33	8 15	7.5	10.6
Clark Point, Nushagak, Bristol Bay	58 51	158 32	1 00	15.2	19.5
Goodnews Bay Entrance	59 03	161 47	7 07	6.2	8.9
Carter Spit	59 19	161 57	7 26	8.0	10.7
Quinhagak (mid-channel)	59 45	162 15	8 45	9.7	12.3
Warehouse Creek	59 56	162 05	9 12	10.0	12.6
Kuskokwak Creek Entrance	60 02	162 10	10 00	9.6	12.2
Kokokamut Slough Entrance	60 07	162 27	10 22	8.3	10.9
Apokak	60 08	162 10	10 20	9.4	12.0
Eek Island (northwest end)	60 10	162 20	10 38	8.4	11.0
Bethel	60 47	161 46	2 52	2.0	3.4
Cape Dyer	61 49	166 05	12 00	5.2	6.8
Black (Kipniak)	62 20	165 19	0 50	3.8	5.0
Kwikiok Pass, Yukon River, Norton Sound	62 37	164 51	3 05	1.4	2.3
Kwikpak Pass, Yukon River, Norton Sound	63 00	164 45	2 42	1.8	2.8
Apoon Pass, Yukon River, Norton Sound	63 05	163 32	6 20b	_____	4.0
Pitmiktalik, Norton Sound	63 16	162 34	6 40b	_____	4.2
St. Michael, Norton Sound	63 29	162 02	7 44b	_____	3.9
North Bay, Stuart Island, Norton Sound	63 37	162 30	7 20b	_____	2.8
Colofnin Bay, Norton Sound	64 32	163 00	9 00b	_____	1.8
Nome, Norton Sound	64 30	165 26	12 20b	_____	1.6
Port Clarence	65 13	166 24	6 10	1.2	1.4
Arctic Ocean.					
Chamisso Island, Kotzebue Sound	66 15	161 45	5 00	4.0	5.1
Point Barrow	71 18	156 40	11 37	0.4	0.5

EAST COAST OF ASIA.

Place.	Lat. N.	Long. E.	High water interval.	Mean range.	Spring range.
SIBERIA.					
St. Lawrence Bay	65 38	189 00	5 45b	_____	3.5
Cape Chukotski	64 14	186 50	8 01b	_____	4.0
Anadir Bay	64 48	177 30	9 00b	_____	6.0
Cape Oliutorsk	59 50	170 20	8 45b	_____	4.5
Sibir Harbor, Baron Korfa Gulf	60 28	165 25	9 06b	_____	5.0
Kamchatka.					
Nikolski, Komandorski Islands	55 12	165 59	4 00	3.2	4.8
Petropavlovsk, Avatcha Bay	53 00	158 43	4 08	2.5	3.6
Cape Lopatka, Kuril Strait	50 45	156 50	4 11	3.2	4.5
Okhotsk Sea.					
Bolshaya River Entrance	52 46	156 10	4 22a	_____	7.4
Kompakova River Entrance	54 55	155 52	7 00a	_____	10.2
Tigil River Entrance, Kamchatka	58 00	158 20	8 30a	_____	16.0
Gizhiga River Entrance	61 58	160 40	2 20b	_____	18.0
Ola, Tausk Bay	59 34	151 16	8 20	8.5	11.0
Nagaeva, Tausk Bay	59 37	150 40	8 15	8.5	11.0
Port Aian	56 25	138 10	12 15	8.0	10.0
North Bay, Sakhalin Island	54 20	142 17	1 50	4.0	5.0
Langr I., Gulf of Amur	53 19	141 26	6 15b	_____	4.1
Amur River Entrance	53 00	141 10	11 00	2.0	2.5

a = mean higher high water interval, referring to upper transit of the moon at north declination, or to lower transit at south declination.

b = mean higher high water interval, referring to lower transit of the moon at north declination, or to upper transit at south declination. Tide is more or less diurnal.

129

TIDAL DATA.

EAST COAST OF ASIA—Continued.

Place.	Lat. N.		Long. E.		High water interval.		Mean range.	Spring range.
	°	′	°	′	h.	m.	Feet.	Feet.
SIBERIA—Continued.								
Gulf of Tartary.								
Cape Muraveva	52	09	141	33	11	00	4.8	6.1
Castries Bay	51	27	140	50	9	50	4.8	6.1
Alexandrovski, Sakhalin Island	50	54	142	07	9	20	6.3	8.0
Port Imperatorskaya	49	02	140	16	9	00	1.0	1.1
Tobootchi Ko, Aniva Bay	46	31	143	18	4	26	2.2	4.0
Olga Bay	43	43	135	15	2	29	2.0	2.3
Vladivostok	43	07	131	54	2	31	0.6	0.7
JAPAN.								
Northeast Islands.								
Shakotan	43	52	146	49	3	34	1.9	2.6
Taraku Sima	43	38	146	20	3	31	1.9	2.7
Shuisho Sima	43	27	145	52	3	48	2.3	3.1
Hokuhu Island.								
Soya Saki	45	31	141	54	10	30	3.7	4.8
Notsuke Harbor	43	33	145	18	4	50	2.9	3.7
Nemoro	43	20	145	35	3	33	1.5	2.1
Akkeshi	43	02	144	51	3	41	2.2	3.0
Kushiro	43	00	144	22	3	39	1.9	2.6
Mororan, Endermo Harbor	42	20	141	07	3	32	2.6	3.5
Hakodate, Tsugar Strait	41	48	140	42	3	40	2.2	3.0
Otaru, Sea of Japan	43	12	140	54	3	50	0.4	0.5
Honshu Island.								
Moura	40	57	140	52	3	37	1.3	1.8
Ominato	41	15	141	09	3	35	1.5	2.0
Yamada Harbor	39	27	141	59	4	30	2.5	3.4
Tateyama	34	59	139	51	5	04	2.7	3.7
Yokohama (Nishihatoba)	35	27	139	39	5	24	3.5	4.8
Yenoura	35	03	138	54	5	52	3.0	4.2
Shimidzu	35	01	138	31	5	52	2.9	3.9
Sakushima	34	44	137	02	6	06	3.9	5.4
Yokkaichi	34	57	136	38	6	05	4.7	6.4
Toba	34	29	136	50	5	59	3.7	5.0
Matoya	34	22	136	52	5	52	3.2	4.3
Hamashima	34	18	136	45	6	23	3.5	4.7
Osaka Roads, Inland Sea	34	39	135	27	7	30	3.5	4.7
Shimotsui, Inland Sea	34	26	133	48	11	18	6.4	8.4
Tomo, Inland Sea	34	23	133	22	11	16	7.6	10.2
Onomichi, Inland Sea	34	24	133	12	11	04	7.4	9.7
Shimonoseki	33	59	130	53	8	30	4.7	6.7
Setozaki	34	24	131	12	10	55	1.5	2.0
Haigi	34	25	131	24	11	16	1.3	1.7
Yesaki	34	39	131	39	11	41	0.8	1.1
Tonoura	34	54	132	04	12	12	0.6	0.8
Sagiura	35	26	132	41	1	08	0.5	0.6
Yonago	35	22	133	18	4	51	0.4	0.6
Shibayama	35	39	134	39	2	07	0.5	0.6
Tsuiyama	35	39	134	50	2	28	0.5	0.6
Tsuruga Bay	35	43	136	00	2	30	0.5	0.6
Ao	36	53	136	59	2	46	0.5	0.6
Naoyedzu	37	11	138	14	2	48	0.4	0.6
Amaze	37	32	138	41	2	36	0.4	0.6
Funakawa	39	54	139	51	3	07	0.5	0.7
Shikoku Island.								
Urado	33	30	183	35	6	24	3.4	4.5
Susaki, Nomi Harbor	33	23	133	17	5	55	3.6	5.0
Uwajima	33	13	132	33	7	17	3.9	5.3
Aoshima, Inland Sea	33	44	132	29	8	38	6.6	8.9
Kiushu Island.								
Kakaji, Inland Sea	33	40	131	31	8	55	6.7	9.2
Tasman Bay	31	22	131	09	5	45	5.0	6.8
Yamagawa	31	13	130	38	7	20	7.0	9.5
Kagoshima	31	35	130	34	6	40	7.8	10.5
Kabashima	32	34	129	47	0	05	6.2	8.4
Nagasaki	32	45	129	52	7	49	6.2	8.4
Matsushima	32	56	129	36	7	56	6.2	8.6
Tawaranoura	33	07	129	40	8	07	6.1	8.5
Fukushima	33	21	129	49	8	47	5.2	7.0
Kariya	33	28	129	50	9	23	4.6	6.4
Hirugaura, Tsushima Island	34	19	129	16	8	56	4.8	6.7
Riu Kiu (Loo Choo Islands).								
Hancock Bay, Amami Ou Sima	28	17	129	10	7	30	4.6	6.2
Nafa Kiang, Okinawa Sima	26	12	127	40	6	30	4.3	5.8
Miyako Sima Islands.								
Miyako Sima	24	48	125	18	7	27	3.6	4.9

130

TIDAL DATA.

EAST COAST OF ASIA—Continued.

Place.	Lat. N.		Long. E.		High water interval.		Mean range.	Spring range.
	°	′	°	′	h.	m.	Feet.	Feet.
JAPAN—Continued.								
Taiwan.								
Kelung Harbor	25	08	121	46	10	15	2.2	3.9
Sauo Bay	24	46	121	50	6	00	4.3	5.8
Takau Harbor	22	30	120	16	9	45	3.0	4.0
Anping	23	00	120	09	9	50	3.6	4.9
Tamsui Harbor	25	10	121	25	10	00	5.9	8.0
Chosen.								
Yung-hing Bay	39	13	127	18	5	10	1.8	2.5
Tsau-liang-hai or Chosen	35	07	129	03	7	35	5.2	7.0
Port Hamilton	34	01	127	17	9	05	7.7	10.5
Chemulpo (Inner Harbor)	37	29	126	36	4	19	21.1	28.8
Seoul	37	30	127	00	9	20	4.7	6.5
CHINA.								
Port Arthur	38	50	121	16	10	05	6.5	7.5
Newchwang	40	35	122	00	4	30	8.7	10.1
Tientsin Entrance, Taku North Fort	38	59	117	42	2	52	6.8	7.9
Tientsin	39	09	117	11	7	19	1.7	2.0
Hwang Ho River Entrance	37	54	118	34	4	00	9.1	10.5
Chefoo	37	34	121	31	10	25	7.0	8.1
Wei-hai-wei	37	29	122	13	9	20	7.8	9.0
Shantung Promontory	37	24	122	42	4	00	5.9	6.8
Sang-kau Bay	37	08	122	27	0	45	5.4	6.9
Kiaochow Harbor	36	00	120	20	4	50	8.9	11.4
Shanghai, Woosung Bar	31	21	121	30	0	13	7.3	9.2
Nanking, Yangtze River	32	10	118	55	10	50	3.1	4.0
Hang Chu Bay	30	14	120	14	11	35	10.7	13.7
Ning-Po, Yung River	29	57	121	47	1	00	6.9	8.8
Tiachow Islands	28	24	121	52	8	50	11.6	14.1
Namquam or Nam Kwan Harbor	27	12	120	23	9	50	14.1	17.2
Min River Entrance	26	02	119	40	9	45	15.6	19.0
Fuchau, Min River	26	03	119	24	0	30	15.8	19.3
Hungwha Sound	25	24	119	14	11	15	18.9	23.0
Meichen Sound	25	08	119	00	0	20	13.8	16.9
Hui-itau Bay	24	36	118	26	0	05	13.2	16.1
Amoy (Inner Harbor)	24	28	118	03	0	04	12.8	15.6
Tongsang Harbor	23	54	117	31	11	20	9.8	12.0
Swatow	23	20	116	40	1	53	3.0	3.5
Honghai Bay	22	50	115	11	9	50	4.9	6.4
Hongkong	22	18	114	10	9	23	3.3	4.4
Whampoa	23	05	113	26	0	48	4.8	6.0
Canton	23	08	113	16	2	00	3.9	5.1
Macao	22	14	113	34	9	50	4.8	6.3
Hui-ling-san Harbor	21	40	111	46	8	20	5.6	7.4
Tien pak Harbor	21	28	111	13	11	50	6.2	8.2
Nauchau Passage	21	00	110	38	10	10	6.1	8.0
Hoi Hau, Hainan Island	20	04	110	05	7	00	6.1	8.0
Yulinkan Bay, Hainan Island	18	15	109	33	8	55	1.8	2.3
*Hiong Po, Hainan Island	19	44	109	11	5	00a	---------	10.0
*Cape Kami, Hainan Strait	20	13	109	55	3	45a	---------	8.5
*Pakhoi	21	30	109	04	5	40a	---------	10.5
FRENCH INDO-CHINA.								
*Kamfo	21	02	107	22	5	30a	---------	9.5
Do-Son, Kua Kam	20	43	106	48	5	15a	---------	6.5
*Haifong, Kua Kam	17	57	106	40	5	30a	---------	6.5
*Cape Vung Chua	17	57	106	30	5	00a	---------	5.0
Hue River Entrance	16	35	107	40	12	10	2.0	3.0
*Tourane Bay	16	08	108	18	9	30b	---------	2.5
*Kin Hon Harbor	13	45	109	13	9	45b	---------	3.5
Hon Kohe Bay	12	40	109	11	11	20	3.7	5.0
Saigon	10	46	106	42	4	20	7.3	9.8
SIAM.								
Chentabun River Entrance	12	28	102	07	10	00	3.4	4.5
Paknam, Menam River	13	30	100	38	5	10	6.1	8.2
Bangkok, Menam River	13	40	100	32	8	60	5.4	7.3
MALAY PENINSULA.								
East Coast.								
Lakon Roads	8	33	100	05	10	05	3.3	4.5
Singora	7	13	100	40	8	20	2.1	2.8
Tringano River	5	25	103	06	8	20	4.3	5.8
Singapore	1	17	103	51	10	00	5.7	7.4

* Tide is more or less diurnal; higher high water interval and diurnal range are substituted for high water interval and spring range of tide.
  a = mean higher high water interval, referring to upper transit of the moon at north declination or lower transit at south declination.
  b = mean higher high water interval, referring to lower transit of the moon at north declination or upper transit at south declination.

131

TIDAL DATA.
EAST COAST OF ASIA—Continued.

Place.	Lat. N.		Long. E.		High water interval.		Mean range.	Spring range.
	°	′	°	′	h.	m.	Feet.	Feet.
MALAY PENINSULA—Continued.								
West Coast.								
Malakka Road	2	12	102	12	7	20	7.8	10.5
One Fathom Bank	2	52	100	59	5	50	10.7	14.4
Perak River Entrance	4	05	100	44	3	05	6.4	8.6
Georgetown, Penang Island	5	24	100	21	11	50	6.5	8.8
Salang or Junkseylon Island	8	00	98	21	10	00	6.6	8.9
SUMATRA.								
Malakka Strait.								
Acheh Head	5	33	95	18	10	00	3.9	5.2
Diamond Point	5	16	97	30	11	50	6.4	8.7
Deli River Entrance	3	45	98	43	2	48	6.3	8.5
Siak River Entrance	1	20	102	14	8	50	8.4	11.3
Garras Light, Rhio Strait	0	45	104	21	9	40	5.3	7.1
East Coast.								
	Lat. S.							
Linga Linga Island	0	14	104	34	6	00	8.5	11.5
*Tanjong Kalean, Banka Strait	1	58	105	07	7	45a	10.3	
*Nangka Island, Banka Strait	2	24	105	47	8	22a	9.3	
*Banka Point, Banka Strait	2	53	106	08	7	20a	8.4	
*Tobo Ali Bay, Banka Strait	3	00	106	27	10	34a	10.1	
*Clifton Shoal	4	54	106	03	12	03a	4.5	
Sunda Strait.								
Java Fourth Point	6	04	105	53	7	11	1.7	2.4
Krakatoa Island	6	09	105	25	6	50	2.6	3.8
Kalang Bayang Harbor, Sumatra	5	44	105	02	6	10	1.4	2.0
Java First Point	6	44	105	11	5	30	1.7	2.5
EAST INDIES.								
Sumatra, Southwest Coast.								
Flat Cape	5	56	104	33	5	40	1.8	2.6
Benkulen	3	41	102	13	5	50	2.8	4.0
Padang	0	56	100	23	5	35	3.8	5.5
	Lat. N.							
Ayer Bangies	0	12	99	23	5	29	1.9	2.8
Tapanuli Bay	1	35	98	50	5	50	3.9	5.7
Java.								
	Lat. S.							
Batavia (Tandjong Priok)	6	06	106	53	10	05a	2.8	
*Samarang	6	57	110	25	9	23a	4.0	
*Panka Point	6	55	112	34	7	58b	5.0	
*Arisbaya, Surabaya Strait	6	56	112	50	7	28b	5.1	
*Sembilangan, Surabaya Strait	7	04	112	40	10	31b	5.0	
Surabaya, Surabaya Strait	7	12	112	44	12	07	3.6	4.9
Gading, Madura Strait	7	11	112	54	11	52	4.5	6.2
Karang Kleta, Madura Strait	7	20	112	48	11	46	4.5	6.2
Pasuruan, Madura Strait	7	38	112	55	11	44	4.5	6.2
*Sapoedie Island, Madura Strait	7	05	114	16	10	06b	5.0	
*Meinderts Reef, Madura Strait	7	40	114	26	9	53b	4.4	
Banjoewangi, Baly Strait	8	13	114	23	10	00	5.5	7.8
Pangul	8	16	111	26	9	15	4.2	5.9
Tylatiap	7	45	109	04	8	33	3.7	5.2
Wynkoops Bay	6	55	106	30	4	50	3.8	5.3
Bali.								
Tebunkus Road	8	11	115	00	4	55	4.3	6.0
Badong Bay	8	42	115	07	10	50	6.2	8.7
Lombok.								
Ampenam Bay	8	35	116	04	7	50	4.1	5.8
Piju Bay	8	49	116	31	11	30	7.7	10.9
Sumbawa.								
Bima Bay	8	25	118	42	0	00	4.1	5.7
Sapie Bay	8	30	119	01	0	50	6.8	9.6
Sumba Island.								
Palmedo Road	9	22	119	45	12	00	10.0	14.2
Nangamessie Harbor	9	34	120	15	11	20	11.7	16.5
Flores Island.								
Alligator Bay	8	45	119	50	12	20	4.1	5.7
Adenara, Adenara Island	8	14	123	07	11	00	5.4	7.6

* Tide is more or less diurnal; higher high water interval and diurnal range are substituted for high water interval and spring range of tide.

a=mean higher high water interval, referring to upper transit of the moon at north declination or lower transit at south declination.

b=mean higher high water interval, referring to lower transit of the moon at north declination or upper transit at south declination.

TIDAL DATA.

EAST COAST OF ASIA—Continued.

Place.	Lat. S.	Long. E.	High water interval.	Mean range.	Spring range.
	° ′	° ′	h. m.	Feet.	Feet.
EAST INDIES—Continued.					
Timor.					
Koepang	10 10	123 35	10 50	6.0	8.5
Dilhi	8 34	125 48	0 45	4.1	5.7
Cyrus Harbor, Rotti Island	10 51	123 05	11 50	3.9	5.5
Gaspar Strait.					
*Langwas Island, Billiton Island	2 32	107 37	7 45a	6.6	
*Shoalwater Island	3 19	107 13	8 10a	5.6	
Caimata Strait.					
*Montaran Islands	2 35	108 44	3 07b	4.9	
*Kumpul Island	2 43	110 04	3 57b	7.5	
Borneo.					
*Bajor, Koetei River Entrance	0 43	117 33	9 24b	7.0	
*Kotta Baroe Reef	3 12	116 40	7 10b	4.6	
Jelai River Entrance	2 53	110 45	11 30	5.4	7.3
Padang Tikar River	0 38	109 15	7 00	5.3	7.2
	Lat. N.				
Burong Islands	0 47	108 42	4 35	5.0	6.7
Po Point, Sarawak River Entrance	1 43	110 31	4 00	6.7	9.0
Sarawak, Sarawak River	1 32	110 21	5 20	10.4	14.1
Victoria Harbor, Labuan Island	5 20	115 12	9 35	4.1	5.5
*Kudat Harbor	6 53	116 51	8 50b	4.4	
*Sandakan Harbor	5 50	118 07	9 25b	7.0	
Celebes.					
Manado Bay	1 30	124 46	6 00	3.7	4.3
Likupang River, Banka Strait	1 41	125 02	6 35	5.6	6.4
	Lat. S.				
Makassar	5 09	119 22	4 40	3.4	3.9
Brill or Spectacle Reef	6 05	118 54	0 33	1.6	1.9
Molukka Islands.					
Cajeli Bay, Bouro Island	3 19	127 04	1 20	3.7	4.2
Amboina Bay, Amboina Island	3 41	128 07	2 20	6.5	7.5
Wahai Bay, Ceram Island	2 46	129 31	5 50	2.9	3.3
Banda Harbor, Banda Islands	4 33	129 53	1 45	7.8	9.0
Dobbo Harbor, Arru Islands	5 45	134 16	2 20	5.0	5.7
Sannana Bay, Xulla Besi Island	2 03	125 57	2 00	7.7	8.8
Gebi, Fow Island	0 05	129 30	5 00	4.1	4.7
	Lat. N.				
Ternate	0 50	127 20	5 00	3.4	3.9
Manganitu Bay, Sangir Island	3 30	125 28	4 50	5.1	5.8
PHILIPPINE ISLANDS.					
Sulu Islands.					
Sibutu Island	4 45	119 30	6 20	3.5	5.0
Port Bongao, Tawitawi Island	5 02	119 46	6 25	3.0	4.5
Tataan Harbor, Tawitawi Island	5 11	119 56	6 30	3.0	4.5
Port Dos Amigos, Tawitawi Island	5 16	120 04	6 40	3.0	4.5
Port Siasi, Siasi Island	5 32	120 49	5 54	6.0	7.5
Maibun, Jolo Island	5 56	121 02	6 05	3.2	4.1
Jolo, Jolo Island	6 04	120 59	8 30b		3.2
Dalrymple Harbor, Jolo Island	6 00	121 19	8 30b		3.2
Mangal River Entrance, Basilan Island	6 25	121 58	8 00b		3.0
Isabela, Basilan Island	6 42	121 58	8 30b		2.2
Mindanao Island.					
Zamboanga	6 54	122 04	6 32	2.1	3.2
Sibuco Bay	7 19	122 04	10 52	2.5	4.0
Panabutan Bay	7 35	122 08	10 53	2.5	4.1
Port Santa Maria	7 46	122 07	10 54	2.5	4.2
Dapitan	8 40	123 25	10 57	2.6	4.4
Palaridel (Langaran)	8 37	123 43	11 05	2.6	4.1
Oroquieta, Iligan Bay	8 29	123 48	11 16	2.7	4.0
Jimenez, Iligan Bay	8 20	123 51	11 25	2.7	4.1
Misamis, Iligan Bay	8 00	123 51	11 32	2.9	4.4
Iligan, Iligan Bay	8 14	124 14	11 27	2.6	4.2
Macabalan Point, Macajalar Bay	8 30	124 40	11 27	2.7	4.2
Canauayor Anchorage	9 00	124 51	11 25	2.6	4.1
Mambajao, Camiguin Island	9 15	124 43	11 28	2.5	4.1
Nasipit Harbor, Butuan Bay	8 59	125 20	11 25	2.8	4.1
Agusan River Entrance, Butuan Bay	9 00	125 31	11 30	2.8	4.1

* Tide is more or less diurnal; higher high water interval and diurnal range are substituted for high water interval and spring range of tide.

a = mean higher high water interval, referring to upper transit of the moon at north declination or lower transit at south declination.

b = mean higher high water interval, referring to lower transit of the moon at the north declination or upper transit at south declination.

101890°—36——26

TIDAL DATA.

EAST COAST OF ASIA—Continued.

Place.	Lat. N.		Long. E		High water interval.		Mean range.	Spring range.
	°	′	°	′	h.	m.	Feet.	Feet.
PHILIPPINE ISLANDS—Continued.								
Mindanao Island—Continued.								
Surigao	9	48	125	29	10	47b		3.4
Dinagat, Dinagat Island	9	58	125	35	10	20b		3.4
Melgar, Dinagat Island	10	04	125	31	10	00b		3.4
San Roque, Dinagat Island	10	16	125	29	9	40b		3.5
Malinao Inlet, Dinagat Island	10	15	125	38	6	40	3.2	4.0
Gaas Bay, Dinagat Island	10	11	125	39	6	42	3.2	4.0
Cuyamongan, Talabera Island	9	54	125	41	6	49	3.8	4.6
Tayanan, Kangbanyo Island	9	44	125	54	6	37	3.7	4.4
Port Pillar, Siargao Island	9	52	126	06	6	30	3.2	4.0
San Miguel, East Bucas Island	9	44	126	02	6	35	3.2	4.1
Sohutan Bay, Bucas Grande Island	9	36	125	55	6	35	3.8	4.6
Tugas Point	9	29	125	57	6	25	3.8	4.6
Buenavista, General Island	9	25	126	00	6	23	3.8	4.6
Tandag	9	05	126	12	6	22	3.9	4.7
Hinantuan	8	22	126	20	6	21	4.0	4.9
Caraga Bay	7	17	126	35	6	13	4.1	5.0
Mati, Pugada Bay	6	57	126	13	6	12	4.0	4.8
Lavigan Anchorage, Davao Gulf	6	17	126	11	6	09	4.1	4.9
Sigaboy, Davao Gulf	6	39	126	04	6	10	4.1	4.9
Davao, Davao Gulf	7	03	125	35	6	10	4.1	4.8
Bolton, Malalag Bay, Davao Gulf	6	36	125	25	6	09	4.1	4.9
Canalasan Cove, Sarangani Bay	5	45	125	11	6	06	5.0	5.8
Port Lebak	6	32	124	03	6	10	5.0	5.8
Cotabato, Mindanao River	7	13	124	15	7	05	3.0	3.5
Polloc Harbor, Illana Bay	7	21	124	13	6	16	4.8	5.6
Port Baras, Illana Bay	7	38	124	01	6	16	4.8	5.6
Tucuran, Illana Bay	7	51	123	35	6	16	4.8	5.6
Padadian, Illana Bay	7	49	123	27	6	16	4.9	5.7
Port Sambulanan, Illana Bay	7	32	123	24	6	14	4.8	5.6
Limbug Cove, Illana Bay	7	28	123	24	6	12	4.7	5.5
Maligay Bay, Illana Bay	7	32	123	15	6	12	4.8	5.6
Cherif Island, Dumanquilas Bay	7	38	123	06	6	13	4.9	5.8
Port Sibulan	7	26	122	53	6	12	4.9	5.8
Taba Point, Sibuguey Bay	7	35	122	47	6	16	5.1	6.0
Ticanuan Point, Sibuguey Bay	7	45	122	44	6	16	5.2	6.1
Port Banga, Sibuguey Bay	7	3	122	25	6	16	5.0	5.9
Landang, Sacol Island	6	57	122	15	6	12	3.8	4.6
Palawan Islands.								
Secam Island, Balabac Strait	8	11	117	01	10	00b		4.0
Eran Bay	9	05	117	42	9	55b		4.0
Ulugan Bay	10	06	118	47	9	50b		4.0
Port Barton	10	28	119	08	9	45b		4.0
Malampaya Sound	10	52	119	23	9	50b		4.0
Bacuit	11	10	119	23	9	45b		3.9
Northwest Bay, Linapacan Island	11	28	119	46	9	53b		4.1
San Nicolas, Linapacan Island	11	28	119	49	9	55b		4.2
San Miguel, Linapacan Island	11	30	119	52	10	10b		4.4
Batas Island	11	10	119	36	10	10b		4.6
Tatay	10	50	119	31	10	14b		4.6
Paly Island	10	42	119	42	10	15b		4.6
Araceli, Dumaran Island	10	35	119	59	10	17b		4.4
Tinitian, Green Island Bay	10	04	119	12	10	35b		4.4
Puerto Princesa	9	44	118	43	10	00b		4.4
Balabac	8	00	117	04	10	00b		4.3
Cuyo, Cuyo Island	10	51	121	00	10	12b		4.5
Halsey Harbor, Culion Island	11	47	119	58	10	08b		4.0
Culion, Culion Island	11	53	120	01	10	10b		4.5
Coron, Port Uson, Busuanga Island	12	01	120	12	10	10b		4.5
Apo Island, Mindoro Strait	12	40	120	24	10	00b		3.6
Panay and Guimaras Islands.								
Aniniy	10	26	121	55	11	00	3.0	4.9
San Jose de Buenavista	10	44	121	56	10	55	2.7	4.6
Tibiao	11	17	122	02	10	50	3.5	5.4
Borocay Island	11	57	121	56	11	00	3.6	5.3
Aclan River Entrance	11	44	122	22	11	25	3.6	5.3
Port Batan	11	36	122	30	11	31	3.7	5.4
Libas (Capiz Landing)	11	36	122	43	11	35	3.6	5.4
Estancia	11	28	123	09	11	45	4.9	6.9
Concepcion	11	13	123	06	11	45	5.0	7.0
Banate	11	00	122	49	11	51	5.1	7.1
Nabalas, Guimaras Island	10	44	122	41	11	42	4.4	6.4
Inampulugan I., Guimaras Island	10	27	122	43	11	23	3.3	5.1
Lugmayon Point, Guimaras Island	10	25	122	32	11	08	2.7	4.5
Iloilo	10	42	122	34	11	34	3.5	5.4
Miagao	10	38	122	14	11	05	2.7	4.6

b=mean higher high water interval, referring to lower transit of the moon at north declination or upper transit at south declination. Tide is more or less diurnal.

TIDAL DATA.
EAST COAST OF ASIA—Continued.

Place.	Lat. N.		Long. E.		High water interval.	Mean range.	Spring range.
	°	′	°	′	h. m.	Feet.	Feet.
PHILIPPINE ISLANDS—Continued.							
Negros Island.							
Cadiz	10	57	123	19	12 02	4.8	6.6
Humugaan River Entrance	10	57	123	22	11 55	4.5	6.3
Danao River Entrance	10	49	123	33	11 49	4.0	5.8
San Carlos	10	29	123	25	11 48	4.1	5.8
Calagcalag	9	49	123	08	11 42	3.7	5.4
Bais	9	36	123	08	11 40	3.6	5.3
Dumaguete	9	18	123	18	11 10	3.2	4.8
Larena, Siquijor Island	9	15	123	35	11 09	2.7	4.2
Port Bombonon	9	03	123	07	11 00	3.0	4.5
Campomanes Bay	9	42	122	25	10 55	3.1	4.5
Himamaylan	10	06	122	52	11 00	3.3	5.0
Bacolod	10	40	122	57	11 40	4.2	6.1
Cebu Island.							
Moalbual	9	56	123	24	11 45	3.7	5.5
Barili Bay	10	07	123	29	11 45	3.7	5.5
Balamban Bay	10	30	123	43	11 47	3.9	5.7
Tuburan	10	44	123	49	11 49	3.9	5.8
Medellin	11	08	123	58	11 53	4.2	6.0
Bantayan, Bantayan Island	11	10	123	43	11 52	4.2	6.0
Bogo Bay	11	04	124	00	11 54	3.7	5.4
Carmen	10	35	124	01	11 48	3.6	5.3
Cebu, Fort San Pedro	10	18	123	54	11 32	3.3	5.1
Calcar Bay	10	05	123	39	11 28	3.3	5.0
Boljoon	9	38	123	29	11 17	3.0	4.5
Bohol Island.							
Maribojoc	9	44	123	50	11 20	3.0	4.6
Tubigon	9	57	123	58	11 27	3.3	5.1
Ubay	10	04	124	28	11 39	3.4	5.1
Cogton	9	50	124	31	11 26	2.5	4.0
Garcia Hernandez	9	36	124	17	11 20	2.6	4.1
Leyte Island.							
Liloan, Sogod Bay	10	09	125	07	11 00	2.5	4.1
Maasin	10	08	124	50	11 25	3.0	4.6
Baybay	10	41	124	48	11 47	3.9	5.6
Ormoc	11	00	124	36	11 52	3.9	5.6
Palompon	11	03	124	23	11 56	3.8	5.6
Genuruan Island, Biliran Island	11	42	124	21	11 45	3.8	5.5
Poro Island, Biliran Strait	11	28	124	29	11 50	3.8	5.5
Carigara	11	18	124	41	11 55	3.5	5.2
Canauay Island, Janabates Channel	11	26	124	51	11 55	3.2	4.8
Uban Point, San Juanico Strait	11	22	124	59	10 25	2.2	3.4
Tacloban	11	15	125	00	7 04	1.6	2.3
Abuyog	10	43	125	04	6 59	1.5	2.2
Hinunangan	10	24	125	12	8 43	1.5	2.3
Samar Island.							
Guiuan	11	02	125	44	6 31	2.1	2.6
Binatac Point, San Juanico Strait	11	16	125	00	7 04	1.6	2.3
Santa Elena River Entrance, San Juanico Strait	11	21	124	59	10 00	2.0	3.2
Santa Rita Island, San Juanico Strait	11	27	124	57	12 00	2.9	4.3
Talalora	11	32	124	50	11 55	3.4	4.9
Parasan Harbor, Daram Island	11	42	124	45	11 50	3.7	5.2
Catbalogan	11	47	124	52	11 50	3.7	5.2
Santo Nino, Limbancauayan Island	11	56	124	27	11 44	3.5	4.8
Calbayog	12	04	124	35	11 45	2.7	4.1
Mauo	12	26	124	19	10 45b	------	2.4
Macarite Island	12	39	124	22	6 24	2.0	2.4
Catarman	12	31	124	39	6 21	3.6	4.2
Laoang	12	35	125	01	6 22	3.9	4.6
Helm Harbor	12	18	125	22	6 15	4.1	4.8
Hilaban Island	12	02	125	34	6 14	3.8	4.7
Andis Island, Port Borongan	12	39	125	29	6 18	4.0	4.9
Matarinao Bay	11	16	125	34	6 20	4.1	5.0
Masbate Island.							
Port Cataingan	12	00	124	00	11 37	3.4	4.6
Nin Bay	12	14	123	17	11 35	3.6	5.3
Port Barrera	12	30	123	22	11 36	3.6	5.3
Masbate	12	22	123	37	11 37	3.6	5.3
Dimasalang, Naro Bay	12	12	123	51	11 37	3.5	5.0
Port San Miguel, Ticao Island	12	40	123	35	11 38	3.6	5.3
San Jacinto, Ticao Island	12	34	123	44	11 35	3.7	4.6
Port Boca Engano, Burias Island	12	47	123	20	11 35	3.7	5.3
San Pascual, Burias Island	13	08	122	59	11 30	3.9	5.6
Romblon, Romblon Island	12	35	122	16	11 20	3.7	5.5
Guimbilayan, Tablas Island	12	09	122	01	11 21	3.9	5.6
Looc, Tablas Island	12	16	122	00	11 17	3.5	5.2
Port Concepcion, Maestre de Campo Island	12	55	121	44	11 15	3.3	5.1

b=mean higher high water interval, referring to lower transit of the moon at north declination or upper transit at South declination. Tide is more or less diurnal.

TIDAL DATA.

EAST COAST OF ASIA—Continued.

Place.	Lat. N.	Long. E.	High water interval.	Mean range.	Spring range.
	° ′	° ′	h. m.	Feet.	Feet.
PHILIPPINE ISLANDS—Continued.					
Marinduque Island.					
Port Balanacan	13 32	121 52	11 25	3.0	4.9
Santa Cruz	13 30	122 04	11 30	3.1	5.0
Torrijos	13 19	122 05	11 25	3.3	5.2
Mindoro Island.					
Port Galera	13 31	120 58	11 01	2.2	4.0
Calapan	13 36	121 11	11 11	2.8	4.7
Mansalay	12 31	121 26	11 15	3.3	5.1
Mangarin	12 21	121 05	10 10b		3.7
Sablayan	12 50	120 45	10 00b		3.6
Paluan	13 23	120 29	9 55b		3.6
Port Tilig, Lubang I	13 49	120 12	9 50b		3.5
LUZON ISLAND.					
West Coast.					
Anilao, Balayan Bay	13 46	120 55	10 20b		3.7
Corregidor Island, Manila Bay	14 23	120 36	9 51b		3.3
Manila, Pasig River Entrance	14 36	120 57	10 10b		3.5
Olongapo, Subic Bay	14 49	120 17	9 45b		3.1
Port Silanguin	14 46	120 07	9 40b		3.0
Port Masinloc	15 31	119 55	9 30b		2.8
Santa Cruz, Zambales	15 46	119 54	9 20b		2.7
Boliano, Lingayen Gulf	16 24	119 54	9 06b		2.5
Sual, Lingayen Gulf	16 04	120 06	9 17b		2.5
Santo Thomas, Lingayen Gulf	16 17	120 23	9 12b		2.5
San Fernando	16 37	120 18	8 55b		2.4
Solvec Cove	17 27	120 28	8 27b		2.3
Salomague	17 47	120 25	7 44b		2.0
Laoag River Entrance	18 13	120 31	7 32b		1.9
North Coast.					
Aparri, Cagayan River	18 22	121 38	6 18	2.7	3.5
Camalaniugan, Cagayan River	18 17	121 41	6 29	2.8	3.6
Port San Pio V, Camiguin Island	18 55	121 50	6 00	3.5	4.3
East Coast.					
Fort Dimalansan	17 20	122 22	5 55	3.6	4.3
Casiguran Sound	16 05	122 05	5 55	3.7	4.4
Hook Bay, Polillo Island	14 57	121 50	5 55	3.8	4.5
Polillo, Polillo Island	14 43	121 56	5 56	4.1	4.8
Port Lampon, Lamon Bay	14 40	121 37	6 08	4.2	4.9
Sangirin, Alabat Island, Lamon Bay	14 12	121 55	6 08	4.5	5.2
Atimonan, Lamon Bay	14 00	121 55	6 10	4.5	5.2
Apat Bay, Lamon Bay	14 02	122 19	6 12	4.5	5.2
Capalonga, Lamon Bay	14 20	122 29	6 07	4.1	4.9
Mambulao	14 18	122 41	6 10	4.2	4.9
Guintinua Island, Calagua Islands	14 25	122 56	5 58	4.1	4.9
Mercedes	14 07	123 00	6 16	4.0	4.8
Cabgan Island, San Miguel Bay	13 46	123 16	6 16	5.0	5.9
Sisiran Bay	13 56	123 39	6 16	4.0	4.8
Hitoma, Catanduanes Island	13 47	124 08	6 13	4.0	4.8
Port Anajao, Catanduanes Island	13 57	124 20	6 09	3.9	4.7
Tabaco, Tabaco Bay	13 22	123 44	6 18	3.9	4.7
Legaspi, Albay Gulf	13 09	123 45	6 18	3.9	4.7
Gubat	12 55	124 08	6 21	3.7	4.5
San Bernardino Island	12 45	124 17	6 24	2.6	3.4
Matnog	12 35	124 05	7 30	1.6	2.4
South Coast.					
Butag Bay	12 37	123 56	11 35	2.7	3.9
Bagatao Island	12 50	123 48	11 40	3.4	5.0
Sorsogon	12 58	124 00	12 10	3.0	4.1
Pasacao, Ragay Gulf	13 30	123 02	11 30	3.5	5.2
Guinayangan, Ragay Gulf	13 53	122 27	11 45	3.8	5.7
Port Pusgo	13 31	122 36	11 31	4.0	5.5
Aguasa Bay	13 17	122 31	11 32	3.4	5.3
Catanauan	13 36	122 19	11 30	3.3	5.2
Pitogo	13 47	122 05	11 30	2.9	4.8
Lucena	13 54	121 36	11 30	3.0	4.8

ISLANDS OF THE PACIFIC.

Bonin or Arzobispo Islands.					
Newport, Hillsboro Island	26 36	142 09	11 30	2.2	2.8
Port Lloyd, Peel Island	27 05	142 12	6 10	1.9	2.4

b=mean higher high water interval, referring to lower transit of the moon at north declination or upper transit at south declination. Tide is more or less diurnal.

TIDAL DATA.
ISLANDS OF THE PACIFIC—Continued.

Place.	Lat. N.	Long. E.	High water interval.	Mean range.	Spring range.
	° ′	° ′	h. m.	Feet.	Feet.
Marianas.					
Port Apra, Guam Island	13 26	144 39	7 40	1.6	*2.3
Saipan Island	15 19	145 44	7 20	1.6	2.1
Caroline Islands.					
Tomil Bay, Yap or Uap Island	9 30	138 05	7 15	2.7	3.4
Kiti Harbor, Ponapsi Island	6 47	158 08	4 00	3.4	4.3
Kusaie or Ualan Island	5 20	163 05	6 00	2.8	3.5
Marshall Islands.					
Kivajalein Island	8 40	167 45	4 00	3.5	4.4
Ebon Atoll or Boston Islands	4 35	168 40	4 45	3.8	4.7
Ailuk Island	10 25	170 00	4 50	5.0	6.2
Port Rhin, Mulgrave Islands	6 14	171 45	5 00	4.0	5.0
Gilbert Islands.					
Apamama or Hopper Islands	0 30	173 55	4 30	3.8	4.7
Apaiang or Charlotte Island	1 50	172 50	4 45	3.8	4.7
Detached Islands.		Long. W.			
Midway Islands	28 13	177 21	3 05	0.9	1.1
Howland Island	0 53	176 35	7 10	5.0	6.2
Palmyra Island	5 50	162 10	5 25	1.2	1.5
Fanning Island	3 50	159 20	6 00	1.9	2.4
Christmas Island	1 55	157 20	4 25	1.9	2.4
Hawaiian Islands.					
Eleele, Hanapepe Bay, Kauai I	21 54	159 35	2 50	1.0	*1.6
Honolulu, Oahu Islands	21 18	157 52	3 48	1.2	*1.8
Kaunakakai, Molokai Island	21 05	157 02	2 38	1.6	*2.4
Kahului, Maui Island	20 54	156 29	2 08	1.7	*2.4
Kihei, Maalaea B	20 47	156 28	3 43	1.6	*2.3
Lahaina	20 50	156 40	3 32	1.7	*2.5
Mahukona, Hawaii Island	20 11	155 54	3 20	1.4	*2.1
Kealakekua	19 28	155 56	3 10	1.3	*2.0
Hilo	19 44	155 05	2 12	1.5	*2.2
Detached Islands.	Lat. S.				
Sala y Gomez Island	26 19	105 26	4 00	2.7	3.3
Easter Island	27 10	109 21	0 40	2.3	2.8
Rapa or Oparo Island	27 37	144 19	0 10	1.9	2.4
Caroline Atoll	10 00	150 15	4 00	0.9	1.1
Tonga-rewa or Penrhyn Islands	9 00	157 55	6 00	1.2	1.5
Suvarof Island	13 13	163 12	3 10	1.9	2.4
Uea, Uvea, or Wallis Island	13 24	176 08	6 40	3.6	4.4
Tuamotu or Low Archipelago.					
Gambier or Mangareva Island	23 05	135 00	1 50	1.9	2.4
Bow, Harpe, or Hao Island	18 20	140 45	2 40	1.9	2.4
Nairsa or Rangiroa Island	14 58	147 52	4 30	1.7	2.1
Marquesas Islands.					
Santa Christina or Taou-ata Island	9 55	139 08	2 30	2.5	3.1
Tai-o-hae B. Nouka Hiva Island	8 52	140 00	3 50	2.8	3.5
Society Islands.					
Tahiti or Otaheite Island	17 30	149 30	12 00	0.8	1.0
Borabora or Bolabola Island	16 30	151 45	12 10	1.1	1.4
Tubuai or Austral Islands.					
Tubuai Island	23 25	149 33	3 00	1.9	2.4
Cook or Hervey Islands.					
Rarotonga Island	21 15	159 40	6 00	2.2	2.7
Phœnix Islands.					
Enderbury Island	3 09	171 11	5 00	3.7	4.6
Tokelau or Union Islands.					
Fakaofu or Bowditch Island	9 25	171 15	6 00	1.9	2.4
Samoa or Navigator Islands.					
Apia, Upolu Island	13 50	171 44	6 25	2.6	3.2
Pago Pago, Tutuila Island	14 17	170 42	7 00	2.2	2.7
Manua Island	14 15	169 30	6 00	3.7	4.6

* Diurnal range.

TIDAL DATA.

ISLANDS OF THE PACIFIC—Continued.

Place.	Lat. S.	Long. W.	High water interval.	Mean range.	Spring range.
	° ′	° ′	h. m.	Feet.	Feet.
Tonga or Friendly Islands.					
Vavau Island	18 34	173 58	6 20	3.1	3.8
Namuka Island	20 15	174 46	7 50	2.6	3.2
Tongatabu Harbor	21 00	175 10	6 20	3.1	3.8
Fiji Islands.		Long. E.			
Vatoa or Turtle Island	19 49	181 46	6 10	2.5	3.1
Mango Island	17 25	180 50	6 10	2.5	3.1
Totoya Island	18 56	180 10	6 35	2.8	3.5
Savu Savu Bay, Vanua Levu Island	16 43	179 15	6 00	3.5	4.3
Sava Harbor, Viti Levu Island	18 08	178 26	6 30	2.9	3.6
Ngaloa Bay, Kandavu Island	19 02	178 15	6 40	3.2	4.0
Detached Islands.					
Rotumah Island	12 30	177 02	6 15	3.4	4.2
North Minerva Reef	23 36	181 06	7 50	4.5	5.5
Kermadec Islands.					
Raoul or Sunday Island	29 13	182 15	6 00	3.0	3.3
NEW ZEALAND.					
Stewart Island.					
Port Adventure	47 04	168 12	12 24	6.9	8.1
Port Pegasus	47 13	167 43	11 47	7.1	7.9
Mason Bay	46 56	167 45	1 12	6.9	7.7
Paterson Inlet	46 57	168 09	1 04	7.0	7.8
South Island.					
Akaroa Harbor	43 45	172 46	3 23	6.6	7.4
Timaru	44 23	171 18	3 37	5.8	6.5
Oamaru	45 06	171 01	3 10	5.4	6.0
Otago Harbor Entrance	45 46	170 44	3 09	5.0	5.8
Port Chalmers, Otago Harbor	45 49	170 39	3 34	5.0	5.6
Dunedin, Otago Harbor	45 53	170 32	4 03	4.9	5.5
Molyneux Bay	46 23	169 38	2 50	7.0	7.8
Waikawa Harbor	46 39	169 09	2 20	6.8	7.6
Ruapuke Island, Foveaux Strait	46 38	168 33	0 20	6.9	7.7
Awarui or Bluff Harbor	46 36	168 22	1 54	7.0	7.8
North Island.					
Great Barrier Island, Nagle Cove	36 11	175 33	6 55	7.7	8.9
Auckland Harbor	36 51	174 46	7 11	7.7	9.0
River Thames Entrance	37 10	175 35	7 24	9.5	11.0
Coromandel Harbor	36 45	175 31	7 05	9.2	10.7
Mercury Bay	36 46	175 54	7 14	6.2	7.2
Tauranga Harbor	37 36	176 12	7 05	5.3	6.1
Opotiki River	38 00	177 18	7 00	4.3	5.0
Cape Runaway	37 32	178 00	8 10	5.7	6.6
Detached Islands.					
Port Hutt, Chatham Islands	43 47	183 22	5 22	2.3	2.5
Antipodes Islands	49 41	178 42	3 20	4.8	5.3
Perseverance Harbor, Campbell Island	52 34	169 09	1 30	3.0	3.5
Port Ross, Auckland Island	50 32	166 17	11 50	2.9	3.2
Norfolk Island	29 03	167 59	7 30	4.3	4.7
Lord Howe Island	31 34	159 06	8 20	4.4	5.4
Middleton Reef	29 27	159 09	8 15	4.3	5.3
New Caledonia.					
Port Alcmene, Isle of Pines	22 29	167 30	7 55	2.9	3.6
Noumea Bay	22 12	166 30	8 25	2.5	3.1
Port St. Vincent	21 53	166 05	5 40	2.7	3.3
Port Balad	20 15	164 25	6 15	2.8	3.5
Port Yengen	20 39	164 56	6 05	2.9	3.6
Loyalty Islands.					
Wreck Bay, Lifou Island	20 45	167 05	6 30	3.4	4.2
New Hebrides Islands.					
Port Sandwich, Mallicolo Island	16 26	167 47	4 38	2.8	3.8
Havannah Harbor, Efate Island	17 35	168 16	5 15	2.4	3.0
Aneityum Island	20 15	169 44	5 10	2.5	3.1
Banks Islands.					
Patteson, Vanua Lava Island	13 48	167 31	6 40	3.1	3.8
Santa Cruz Islands.					
Vanikoro Island	11 36	166 55	4 50	3.1	3.8

TIDAL DATA.

ISLANDS OF THE PACIFIC—Continued.

Place.	Lat. S.		Long. E.		High water interval.		Mean range.	Spring range.
	°	′	°	′	h.	m.	Feet.	Feet.
Solomon Islands.								
Makira Bay, San Christoval Island	10	30	161	30	6	45	2.7	3.3
Vulavu, Isabel Island	8	30	159	40	5	00	2.8	3.5
Gazelle Harbor, Bougainville Island	6	35	155	05	12	00	2.2	2.7
New Britain Island.								
Blanche Bay	4	13	152	12	9	00	1.7	2.1
New Ireland Island.								
Holz Haven	2	48	150	57	2	50	1.9	2.4
New Hanover Island.								
North Haven	2	26	149	55	2	30	1.9	2.4
Louisiade Archipelago.								
Joannet Harbor, Joannet Island	11	12	153	18	9	50	4.8	5.9
Richards Bay, Woodlark Island	9	03	152	49	7	05	3.4	4.2
NEW GUINEA.								
Dourga Strait	7	27	138	44	11	45	11.3	14.0
Triton Bay	3	47	134	06	0	55	5.9	7.3
Segaar Bay	2	40	132	23	6	20	4.9	6.0
Cape Spencer, Dampier Strait	0	53	131	15	5	45	8.7	10.7
Port Constantine	5	30	145	48	5	15	2.5	3.1
Rook Island	5	33	148	00	4	45	2.4	3.0
Parsee Point	6	38	147	10	5	00	2.6	3.2
Kiriwina, Trobriand Islands	8	28	151	03	4	45	2.4	3.0
Cape Vogel, Ward Hunt Strait	9	40	150	01	4	50	1.9	2.4
East Cape, Goschen Strait	10	13	150	54	7	45	4.0	5.0
China Strait	10	33	150	41	8	25	4.7	5.8
Su-a-u Harbor	10	43	150	14	9	15	6.6	8.1
Port Moresby	9	25	147	07	8	50	6.5	8.0
Fly River Entrance	8	43	143	26	10	15	10.9	13.5

AUSTRALIA.

Place.	Lat. S.		Long. E.		High water interval.		Mean range.	Spring range.
NORTH COAST.								
Turtle Point, Victoria River	14	50	129	14	7	00	15.1	18.6
Pearce Point	14	23	129	20	6	45	18.6	23.0
Port Keats	14	05	129	37	5	45	17.7	21.9
Port Patterson	12	39	130	25	3	50	13.5	16.7
Port Darwin	12	23	130	37	4	57	13.8	17.0
Adelaide River Entrance	12	10	131	13	5	15	13.6	16.8
Port Essington	11	11	132	07	4	00	10.3	12.7
Liverpool River Entrance	12	00	134	15	6	17	9.7	12.0
Cape Wilberforce	11	54	136	34	8	00	7.9	9.8
Sir Edward Pellew Islands	15	34	137	01	7	15	5.4	6.6
Queensland.								
Kimberly	17	27	140	56	5	30	7.0	8.7
Booby Island, Torres Strait	10	36	141	55	4	20	6.3	7.8
Cape York, Torres Strait	10	43	142	31	1	00	6.4	8.0
Murray Islands, Torres Strait	9	57	144	02	9	15	8.0	9.7
Cape Sidmouth	13	24	143	36	9	00	7.8	9.6
Cooktown	15	27	145	15	9	44	4.1	5.5
Cairns Harbor	16	55	145	47	9	44	4.5	6.4
Townsville	19	15	146	50	9	50	7.1	8.7
Bowen, Port Denison	20	01	148	15	10	05	7.3	9.0
Mackay, Pioneer River	21	09	149	16	11	00	13.6	16.8
Rockhampton, Fitzroy River	23	22	150	32	11	45	7.9	9.7
Bundaberg, Burnett River	24	45	152	18	9	15	7.2	8.9
Brisbane Bar	27	19	153	11	10	00	4.7	5.8
New South Wales.								
Ballina, Richmond River	28	52	153	33	9	02	2.3	2.8
Southhead, Clarence River	29	25	153	23	8	15	3.2	4.0
Port Macquarie	31	25	152	56	9	00	3.3	4.1
Crowdy Head	31	51	152	46	9	05	4.0	4.9
Port Stephens	32	45	152	13	8	15	4.8	5.8
Newcastle	32	57	151	44	8	42	3.4	4.2
Sydney (Fort Denison)	33	52	151	12	8	46	3.4	4.2
Botany Bay	33	59	151	09	8	00	5.7	7.0
Ulladulla Harbor	35	22	150	31	8	20	4.4	5.4
Montagu Island	36	15	150	14	8	20	4.3	5.3
Eden, Twofold Bay	37	05	149	55	8	05	4.2	5.2
Victoria.								
Gabo Island	37	35	149	55	8	40	4.0	4.5
Entrance to Gippsland Lakes	37	48	148	32	8	20	2.6	2.2
Corner Inlet	38	43	146	35	0	04	6.4	7.9

TIDAL DATA.

AUSTRALIA—Continued.

Place.	Lat. S.		Long. E.		High water interval.		Mean range.	Spring range.
	°	′	°	′	h.	m.	Feet.	Feet.
Victoria—Continued.								
Venus Bay	38	41	145	46	11	46	5.6	6.3
Port Western	38	31	145	22	0	02	7.6	8.5
Sorrento Back Beach (Ocean Beach)	38	22	144	46	10	55	6.5	7.3
Nepean Point, Port Phillip	38	18	144	39	11	27	2.2	2.5
Geelong, Port Phillip	38	07	144	26	2	02	2.7	3.0
Melbourne (Williamstown)	37	52	144	54	2	10	1.7	2.0
Warrnambool Harbor, Lady Bay	38	23	142	26	0	27	2.5	2.8
Portland Bay	38	20	141	37	0	20	2.4	2.7
Tasmania, Bass Strait.								
Currie Harbor, King Island	39	57	143	51	0	35	2.5	2.8
Port Dalrymple	41	03	146	49	11	10	8.0	9.0
Goose Island, Banks Strait	40	19	147	48	10	38	7.2	8.1
Hobart	42	53	147	21	8	05	3.7	4.2
Macquarie Harbor	42	12	145	13	7	20	2.4	2.7
South Coast.								
Port Macdonnel	38	04	140	40	11	25	2.8	3.9
Kingston	36	50	139	51	11	25	2.9	4.0
Cape Willoughby, Kangaroo Island	35	51	138	10	2	58	3.4	4.7
Port Adelaide	34	51	138	30	4	04	4.5	6.3
Port Wakefield	34	12	138	09	4	51	6.3	8.8
Port Victoria, Spencer Gulf	34	30	137	28	1	25	2.7	3.8
Port Pirie, Spencer Gulf	33	55	137	37	4	30	2.6	3.6
Port Augusta, Spencer Gulf	33	06	138	00	6	44	5.0	7.1
Coffin Bay	32	28	137	46	7	16	6.8	9.4
Port Eyre	34	26	135	22	11	46	3.2	4.5
	31	57	132	30	10	49	3.2	4.5
West Coast.								
*Princess Royal Harbor, King George Sound	35	08	118	00	10	14b	2.2	---------
*Albany, King George Sound	35	01	117	54	9	55b	2.6	---------
*Fremantle, Swan River Entrance	32	03	115	45	8	32b	2.1	---------
*Champion Bay	28	47	114	35	7	40b	3.0	---------
North-West Cape	21	47	114	09	10	15	5.5	8.0
Ashburton Road	21	40	114	58	11	15	4.8	7.0
Sholl Island	20	57	115	54	11	00	6.5	10.0
Fortesque Road	21	00	116	06	10	10	8.5	13.5
Dampier Anchorage	20	25	116	53	10	15	10.5	16.5
Port Walcott	20	39	117	13	11	30	11.5	18.0
Port Hedland (Laurentius Point)	20	18	118	35	10	50	12.2	19.2
Lagrange Bay	18	38	121	43	10	30	18.0	28.0
Pender Bay	16	42	122	43	11	40	13.5	20.5
Cone Bay, King Sound	16	27	123	30	0	35	16.5	25.7
Collier Bay	16	25	124	20	11	35	23.0	36.0
Port Nelson	15	04	125	00	11	30	19.0	30.0
Troughton Island	13	46	126	08	11	15	13.5	21.0
Revely Island	14	22	127	48	6	20	12.0	16.0
Lacrosse Island, Cambridge Gulf	14	36	128	18	6	20	15.5	21.0

SOUTH COAST OF ASIA.

India.	Lat. N.							
Bay of Bengal.								
Nankauri Harbor, Nicobar Islands	8	03	93	30	9	05	5.8	8.3
Port Blair, Andaman Islands	11	41	92	45	9	40	4.4	6.3
Port Cornwallis, Andaman Islands	13	19	93	00	9	50	6.0	8.6
Mergui	12	26	98	36	10	40	13.0	18.0
Reef Island, Tavoy River Entrance	13	36	98	13	10	50	11.2	15.0
Ye, Ye River	15	15	97	53	11	45	13.0	18.1
Amherst, Moulmein River	16	05	97	34	2	12	13.9	19.2
Moulmein, Moulmein River	16	29	97	37	3	07	8.6	11.7
Elephant Point, Rangoon River	16	30	96	18	3	29	13.2	18.1
Rangoon, Rangoon River	16	46	96	08	4	26	12.8	15.5
Bassein, Bassein River	16	47	94	45	1	35	4.9	5.7
Akyab	20	08	92	54	9	40	5.6	7.6
Chittagong	22	20	91	50	1	02	9.6	13.1
Dublat, Hoogly River	21	38	88	06	9	58	10.1	14.1
Diamond Harbor, Hoogly River	22	11	88	12	11	22	11.4	15.9
Calcutta (Kidderpore), Hoogly River	22	33	88	19	1	14	8.0	10.2
False Point	20	23	86	47	9	21	4.9	6.8
Vizagapatam	17	41	83	17	8	48	3.2	4.4
Cocanada	16	56	82	15	8	42	3.3	4.5
Madras	13	06	80	18	8	35	2.2	3.1
Negapatam	10	46	79	51	8	37	1.5	2.1
Pamban Pass, Ramesvaram Island	9	16	79	09	1	37	1.4	2.0
Tuticorin	8	48	78	09	1	52	2.1	3.0

* Tide is more or less diurnal. Tropic interval and range.   b Referring to lower transit of the moon at north declination or upper transit at south declination.

TIDAL DATA.
SOUTH COAST OF ASIA—Continued.

Place.	Lat. N.	Long. E.	High water interval.	Mean range.	Spring range.
	° ′	° ′	h. m.	Feet.	Feet.
Bay of Bengal—Continued.					
Trincomalee, Ceylon	8 33	81 13	8 10	1.4	2.0
Galle, Ceylon	6 02	80 13	2 02	1.2	1.9
Colombo, Ceylon	6 56	79 51	1 47	1.4	2.0
Arabian Sea, East Coast.					
Quilon	8 54	76 37	0 18	2.0	2.5
Cochin	9 58	76 15	11 33	1.6	2.1
Beypore	11 10	75 48	11 21	2.1	2.7
Mangalore	12 52	74 50	10 50	5.1	6.5
Karwar	14 48	74 06	10 34	3.8	5.0
Goa or Mormugoa	15 25	73 48	10 34	4.0	5.2
Bombay, Apollo Bandar	18 55	72 48	11 27	8.8	11.9
Rhaunagar	21 48	72 09	4 27	23.0	30.8
Port Albert Victor (Kathiwadar)	20 58	71 33	2 01	6.8	9.5
Okha Point and Bet Harbor	22 28	69 05	12 05	8.2	10.8
Navanar Point, Gulf of Cutch	22 44	69 43	0 46	13.0	15.5
Hansthal Point, Gulf of Cutch	22 56	70 21	1 24	14.5	16.8
Karachi	24 48	66 58	10 14	5.6	7.4
Detached Islands.					
Suadiva Atoll, Maldive Islands	0 34	73 27	0 50	2.9	3.8
South Male Atoll, Maldive Islands	4 05	73 30	0 20	2.2	2.9
Malcolm Atoll, Maldive Island	6 17	72 33	10 20	2.1	2.7
Minikoi Light	8 16	73 01	11 27	1.9	2.5
Kiltan Island, Laccadive Islands	11 29	73 00	10 20	4.8	6.3
Cherbaniani Reef, Laccadive Island	12 20	71 52	9 50	4.7	6.2
BALUCHISTAN.					
Summiyani Harbor	25 25	66 35	8 50	6.2	8.1
Gwadar Bay	25 10	62 20	9 20	6.1	8.1
Persian Gulf.					
Jask Bay	25 40	57 50	9 20	5.9	7.8
Kishm	26 56	56 15	10 50	8.7	11.6
Jezirat Kais	26 32	53 54	0 30	5.3	6.6
Bushire	29 00	50 52	7 12	2.1	2.6
Euphrates River Entrance	29 51	48 45	11 20	7.6	9.4
Kuweit	29 24	47 58	0 05	6.7	8.3
Menama, Bahrein Harbor	26 16	50 39	5 15	5.2	6.4
Maskat	23 37	58 35	9 30	4.6	6.0
ARABIA.					
Ras-al-Hadd	22 34	59 50	9 15	6.7	8.9
Masira Island	20 28	58 57	9 45	7.2	9.6
Merbat	17 00	54 41	8 50	5.2	7.0
Makalla	14 32	49 06	8 20	5.0	6.8
Aden	12 47	44 59	7 48	3.6	4.8
Red Sea, East Coast.					
Mocha or Mokha	13 19	43 12	11 45	3.3	4.5
Loheiya	15 45	42 40	1 15	2.2	2.9
Jidda	21 28	39 08	3 30	1.5	2.0
Hassani Island	25 00	37 00	5 45	2.3	3.1
Akabah	29 30	35 00	10 00	2.9	3.9
West Coast.					
Suez	29 56	32 33	10 45	5.0	6.8
Zafarana Light	29 06	32 40	10 40	4.1	5.5
Ras Gharib	28 21	33 06	10 35	1.1	1.5
Brothers Islands	26 19	34 51	6 40	1.5	2.0
Suakin	19 06	37 19	2 10	1.3	1.7
Massaua or Massowah	15 37	39 27	0 45	3.0	4.0
Perim Island, Bab el Mandeb Strait	12 38	43 24	7 50	5.3	7.2

AFRICA.

	EAST COAST.					
Zeila	11 24	43 28	7 30	6.2	8.5
Cape Guardafui or Ras Asir	11 53	51 16	6 00	4.5	6.1
Sokotra Island	12 40	53 55	7 05	5.6	7.5
Warsheik Road	2 36	46 11	4 20	5.8	7.8
Brava	1 08	44 04	4 15	5.6	7.5
	Lat. S.				
Juba	0 14	42 38	4 17	6.7	9.0
Port Durnford	1 13	41 55	4 30	8.7	11.7
Malindi	3 07	40 11	4 00	9.0	12.1
Zanzibar	6 09	39 11	4 05	10.7	14.5
Lindi River Entrance	10 00	39 44	3 55	8.1	10.9

TIDAL DATA.
AFRICA—Continued.

Place.	Lat. S.	Long. E.	High water interval.	Mean range	Spring range.
	° ′	° ′	h. m.	Feet.	Feet.
EAST COAST—Continued.					
Cape Delgado	10 41	40 39	3 59	7.8	11.3
Mozambique Harbor	14 58	40 44	4 00	8.1	11.8
Zambezi River Entrance	18 47	36 30	4 15	9.3	13.5
Innamban River Entrance	23 45	35 32	4 30	7.7	11.0
English River, Delagoa Bay	25 59	32 36	5 10	8.2	11.9
MADAGASCAR.					
Diego Suarez Bay	12 15	49 30	3 25	4.4	6.3
Port Choiseul, Antongil Bay	15 29	49 50	3 45	3.5	5.1
Tamatave	18 08	49 26	4 00	5.0	7.3
Fort Dauphin	25 01	47 01	4 15	3.2	4.7
St. Augustine Bay	23 34	43 46	5 40	6.8	9.8
Bembatooka Bay	15 50	46 21	4 15	7.5	10.9
INDIAN OCEAN ISLANDS.					
Maroni Bay, Comoro Islands	11 41	43 21	4 45	6.6	10.0
Zaudzi, Mavotta Island	12 50	45 16	4 00	7.9	11.9
St. Pierre, Reunion or Bourbon Island	21 16	55 35	11 50	2.3	3.5
Port Louis, Mauritius Island	20 08	57 29	0 48	1.1	1.6
Cargados, Carajos Shoals	16 36	59 45	1 50	2.8	4.0
Rodriguez Island	19 45	63 25	0 20	3.8	5.5
Providence Island	9 13	51 01	5 50	5.4	7.8
Mahe Island, Seychelle Islands	4 36	55 32	4 22	2.9	4.3
Diego Garcia Island, Chagos Islands	7 19	72 29	1 30	4.0	5.8
Keeling Islands	12 07	96 55	5 20	3.5	5.1
Christmas Island	10 25	105 43	7 10	3.1	4.5
Amsterdam Island	37 50	77 33	10 50	2.3	3.3
St. Paul Island	38 39	77 34	10 40	2.1	3.0
Betsy Cove, Kerguelen Island	49 09	70 12	0 14	3.2	4.6
SOUTH AND WEST COAST.					
Durban (Port Natal)	29 53	31 04	3 58	3.8	5.6
East London, Buffalo River	33 02	27 55	3 37	3.6	5.0
Port Elizabeth, Algoa Bay	33 58	25 37	3 21	3.9	5.4
Aliwal Harbor, Mossel Bay	34 11	22 09	3 18	4.0	5.6
Cape Agulhas	34 50	20 01	2 40	3.9	5.2
Roman Rocks, Simons Bay	34 11	18 27	2 35	3.9	5.2
Cape Town, Table Bay	33 54	18 25	1 34	3.4	4.7
Saldanha Bay	33 05	17 58	2 20	3.8	5.1
Port Nolloth	29 15	16 51	2 25	4.0	5.3
Elizabeth Bay	26 51	15 11	2 35	4.1	5.5
Port d'Ilheo	23 20	14 28	2 50	6.8	9.0
Great Fish Bay	16 40	11 52	3 00	4.3	5.7
Benguela	12 34	13 23	3 30	4.1	5.5
Loanda	8 43	13 21	3 40	3.6	4.8
Kongo River Entrance	6 07	12 22	4 10	4.5	6.0
Loango Bay	4 38	11 46	4 13	4.9	6.5
Mayumba	3 21	10 40	4 25	5.3	7.0
Cape Lopez	0 48	8 42	4 30	3.9	5.2
	Lat. N.				
Gaboon River Entrance	0 23	9 26	5 10	6.0	8.0
Kamerun River Entrance	3 52	9 38	5 05	5.5	7.3
Niger River, Nun Entrance	4 17	6 05	4 50	4.1	5.4
Lagos River Entrance	6 25	3 25	4 50	2.5	3.3
Volta River Entrance	5 47	0 41	4 20	3.8	4.2
		Long. W.			
Cape Coast Castle	5 06	1 14	4 20	4.5	6.0
Cape Three Points	4 45	2 06	4 00	3.5	4.7
Grand Lahu	5 10	5 03	4 10	3.3	4.4
Cape Palmas	4 22	7 44	4 30	3.2	4.3
Sinu	5 00	9 08	4 50	3.6	4.8
Monrovia	6 19	10 49	5 36	2.3	3.0
Sherbro River, Buoy Point	7 42	12 42	7 45	7.8	10.4
Freetown or Sierra Leone	8 30	13 17	7 40	8.7	11.6
Ponga River	10 09	14 00	7 30	8.6	11.4
Bolama	11 33	15 28	9 20	12.3	16.0
Bissao, Jeba River	11 39	16 01	10 45	5.4	7.2
Bathurst, Gambia River	13 28	16 42	9 00	4.4	5.9
Senegal River Entrance	16 40	16 30	8 30	4.5	6.0
St. Louis, Senegal River	16 11	16 00	9 50	4.4	5.9
Cape Blanco	20 49	17 06	11 35	4.1	5.5
Cape Bojador	26 10	14 29	11 50	5.5	7.3
Cape Juby	27 57	12 54	11 55	6.4	8.5
Santa Cruz or Agadir	30 29	9 35	0 30	6.6	8.8
Mogador	31 31	9 43	1 05	8.2	10.9
Rabat	34 04	6 46	1 35	7.8	10.4
Tangier, Gibraltar Strait	35 47	5 48	1 30	6.9	8.0

TIDAL DATA.
THE MEDITERRANEAN.

Place.	Lat. N.	Long. W.	High water interval.	Mean range.	Spring range.
	° ′	° ′	h. m.	Feet.	Feet.
MOROCCO.					
Ceuta, Gibraltar Strait	35 54	5 17	1 55	2.5	3.3
Tetuan	35 37	5 11	2 00	1.8	2.3
Gomara	35 10	4 18	2 07	1.6	2.1
Melilla	35 18	2 57	2 10	1.7	2.2
ALGERIA.		Long. E.			
Cape Ivi	36 07	0 13	2 27	1.8	2.3
Algiers	36 47	3 04	2 46	2.0	2.6
Port Collo	37 00	6 35	3 09	2.2	2.8
TUNIS.					
Goletta, Tunis Entrance	36 48	10 18	3 33	2.1	3.0
Sfax Road	34 44	10 46	3 35	2.9	4.2
Nathor, Surkenis Bay	34 15	10 04	3 50	3.7	5.4
Humt Suk, Jerba Island	33 53	10 51	4 10	3.5	5.1
Zarzis	33 30	11 07	3 00	1.5	2.2
TRIPOLI.					
Benghazi	32 07	20 03	9 55	0.8	1.2
EGYPT.					
Alexandria	31 12	29 52	9 57	0.4	0.5
Port Said	31 16	32 19	9 40	0.7	1.0
SYRIA.					
Yafa (Joppa or Jaffa)	32 03	34 44	9 40	0.9	1.3
Beirut	33 54	35 28	9 45	0.8	1.2
Tripoli	34 20	35 45	10 00	1.3	1.9
ASIA MINOR.					
Famagusta, Cyprus Island	35 07	33 57	9 40	1.0	1.4
Smyrna Harbor	38 25	27 08	9 15	1.7	2.5
GREECE.					
Volo, Gulf of Volo	39 22	22 58	9 15	1.6	2.3
Patras, Gulf of Corinth	38 15	21 44	3 40	0.7	1.0
ADRIATIC SEA.					
Ragusa	43 42	18 15	4 12	0.7	1.0
Port Comisa, Lissa Island	43 03	16 05	4 00	1.7	2.4
Port Sebenico	43 43	15 51	6 10	0.7	1.0
Port Lussin Piccolo	44 33	14 26	8 10	0.8	1.1
Port Fiume	45 19	14 27	8 15	1.4	2.1
ITALY.					
Port Pola	44 53	13 48	9 00	2.3	3.4
Trieste	45 38	13 45	9 28	2.7	3.9
Port Malamocco	45 20	12 15	10 15	2.3	3.3
Brindisi	40 39	18 00	3 30	1.2	1.8
Port Augusta, Sicily	37 13	15 14	3 00	0.6	0.9
Valetta Harbor, Malta	35 54	14 31	3 12	0.5	0.7
Naples	40 50	14 16	9 15	0.8	1.0
FRANCE.					
Toulon	43 05	5 55	8 22	0.4	0.6
Marseille	43 18	5 21	7 31	0.5	0.6
SPAIN.		Long. W			
Valencia	39 27	0 19	5 00	1.2	1.5
Malaga	36 43	4 24	2 15	2.2	2.9
Gibraltar	36 07	5 22	1 27	2.8	3.7
Tarifa, Gibraltar Strait	36 00	5 36	1 25	4.2	5.6

EUROPE, WEST COAST.

Place.	Lat. N.	Long. W.	High water interval.	Mean range.	Spring range.
SPAIN.					
Conil	36 17	6 15	1 05	8.9	12.0
Cadiz	36 31	6 19	1 00	9.5	12.8
Salmedina Rocks	36 42	6 26	1 00	7.4	10.0
Bonanza, Guadalquivir River	36 48	6 20	2 00	7.4	10.0
Port of Huelva, Odiel River	37 08	6 50	1 40	7.4	10.0
PORTUGAL.					
Guadiana River Entrance	37 10	7 19	1 45	8.9	12.0
Lagos	37 07	8 38	1 55	9.6	13.0
Setubal	38 31	8 45	2 15	8.6	11.6
Lisbon Entrance (Cascaes)	38 42	9 25	1 25	7.4	10.0
Tagus River Entrance	38 42	9 17	1 40	7.8	10.5
Lisbon (Arsenal), Tagus River	38 42	9 08	2 04	8.9	12.0

143

TIDAL DATA.

EUROPE, WEST COAST—Continued.

Place.	Lat. N.	Long. W.	High water interval.	Mean range.	Spring range.
	° ′	° ′	h. m.	Feet.	Feet.
PORTUGAL—Continued.					
Peniche	39 20	9 23	1 40	8.3	11.2
Fort Figueria, Mondego River	40 09	8 52	1 45	9.3	12.5
Oporto, Douro River	41 09	8 41	2 15	7.4	10.0
SPAIN.					
Vigo	42 15	8 41	3 00	8.6	11.5
Salvora Island, Arosa Bay	42 28	9 01	2 45	8.2	11.0
Cape Finisterre	42 53	9 16	2 45	8.1	10.9
Port Camarinas	43 08	9 09	2 43	8.7	12.5
Coruna	43 23	8 24	2 43	8.3	11.5
Ferrol	43 29	8 16	2 44	8.9	12.5
Cedeira	43 39	8 05	2 43	8.0	11.0
Vivero	43 41	7 32	2 44	8.7	11.5
Rivadeo	43 33	7 00	2 45	8.0	11.0
Aviles River	43 38	5 56	2 45	8.8	12.0
Gijon Bay	43 34	5 39	2 50	10.2	13.5
San Vicente de la Barquera	43 24	4 25	3 00	8.5	11.5
Suances, San Martin de la Arena	43 27	4 01	3 00	8.9	11.7
Santander	43 28	3 47	3 05	9.5	12.8
Santona	43 28	3 28	2 55	9.3	12.3
Castro Urdiales	43 24	3 16	2 50	8.9	11.8
Bilbao River Entrance	43 23	3 04	2 50	9.4	12.7
Bilbao	43 16	2 56	3 10	6.7	8.9
Lequeitio	43 23	2 34	2 55	8.0	10.5
San Sebastian	43 19	2 00	2 55	8.9	11.7
FRANCE.					
St. Jean de Luz (Fort Socoa)	43 24	1 40	3 07	9.3	12.3
Boucaut, Adour River	43 34	1 31	3 35	6.3	8.3
Cape Feret	44 38	1 14	3 50	9.6	12.6
Arcachon Basin	44 40	1 09	4 25	9.6	12.7
Cordouan Light, Gironde River	45 35	1 10	3 35	6.8	6.8
Royan, Gironde River	45 37	0 02	3 38	12.7	16.7
Montagne, Gironde River	45 28	0 48	4 14	12.6	16.6
Marechale, Gironde River	45 19	0 46	4 35	12.6	16.7
Pauillac, Gironde River	45 12	0 45	4 51	13.7	18.1
Blaye, Gironde River	45 07	0 40	5 17	12.6	16.6
Bordeaux, Gironde River	44 50	0 34	6 30	11.6	15.3
Marennes, Seudre River Entrance	45 48	1 09	3 25	10.0	13.2
Ile d'Aix, Charente River	46 01	1 11	3 27	12.6	16.6
Rochefort, Charente River	45 57	0 58	3 45	12.6	16.7
Rochelle	46 09	1 09	3 23	12.4	16.2
St. Martin, Ile de Re	46 12	1 22	3 00	12.6	16.8
Les Sables d'Olonne	46 29	1 48	3 20	9.6	12.7
St. Gilles	46 42	1 57	3 20	10.9	14.4
Isle d'Yeu	46 43	2 23	3 18	11.1	14.7
Fromantine Channel	46 53	2 09	3 00	9.5	12.6
Port l'Herbandiere, Noirmoutier Island	47 02	2 18	3 05	12.6	16.7
Port Pornic	47 07	2 07	3 00	12.5	16.5
St. Nazaire, Loire River	47 16	2 12	3 35	12.6	16.6
Paimbœuf, Loire River	47 17	2 03	4 18	12.9	17.0
Pellerin, Loire River	47 13	1 45	5 00	12.3	16.3
Nantes, Loire River	47 12	1 33	5 50	12.5	16.5
Pouliguen	47 16	2 25	3 15	12.6	16.6
Croisic	47 18	2 31	3 25	12.6	16.7
Penerf, Vilaine River	47 31	2 30	3 30	12.7	16.8
Port Navalo, Quiberon Bay	47 33	2 55	3 45	12.6	16.6
Vannes	47 40	2 45	5 47	12.0	15.8
Auray	47 41	2 58	4 00	12.3	16.2
Crac'h River	47 34	3 00	3 30	12.6	16.7
Port Haliguen, Quiberon Bay	47 29	3 06	3 35	12.8	16.9
Hoedic Island	47 20	2 52	3 20	12.6	16.7
Port de Palais, Belle Isle	47 21	3 09	3 25	12.6	16.6
Port Louis	47 42	3 21	3 05	10.4	13.8
Lorient	47 45	3 21	3 09	10.4	13.8
Concarneau	47 53	3 54	3 00	9.7	12.9
Glenan Islands	47 46	4 02	3 00	9.8	13.0
Benodet, Odet River	47 52	4 07	3 15	11.6	15.2
Loctudy	47 50	4 10	3 20	11.5	15.2
Penmarch	47 48	4 23	3 05	10.0	13.3
Audierne	48 01	4 33	3 04	8.4	11.1
Isle de Sein	48 03	4 52	3 25	13.0	17.2
Douarnenez	48 06	4 19	3 20	13.8	18.3
Camaret	48 17	4 36	3 35	13.7	18.2
Brest	48 23	4 29	3 23	14.7	19.5
Port Conquet	48 22	4 47	3 30	14.6	19.3
Molene	48 19	4 55	3 45	14.5	19.2
Ushant or Ouessant Island	48 28	5 08	3 35	14.3	18.9
Abervrach	48 37	4 35	4 00	15.6	20.6
Isle de Bas	48 45	4 02	4 35	16.6	22.0
Roscoff	48 43	3 59	4 40	16.5	21.9
Morlaix	48 40	3 53	5 00	17.4	23.1
Ploumanach	48 50	3 29	5 10	17.6	23.3
Plougrescant, Treguier River	48 51	3 11	5 15	18.7	24.8
Treguier, Treguier River	48 46	3 14	5 25	17.1	22.7
Heaux Light	48 55	3 05	5 35	22.7	30.4

TIDAL DATA.

EUROPE, WEST COAST—Continued.

Place.	Lat. N.		Long. W.		High water interval.		Mean range.	Spring range.
	°	′	°	′	h.	m.	Feet.	Feet.
FRANCE—Continued.								
Brehat	48	51	3	00	5	33	22.8	30.5
Lezardrieux	48	48	3	01	5	35	24.0	32.2
Paimpol	48	47	3	02	5	38	23.6	31.7
Portrieux	48	39	2	49	5	40	23.3	31.3
Binic Harbor	48	36	2	49	5	42	22.4	30.0
Legue or Port de St. Brieuc	48	32	2	43	5	40	23.8	31.9
Dahouet	48	30	2	36	5	37	23.6	31.7
Erquy	48	38	2	26	5	39	24.6	33.0
St. Malo	48	39	2	02	5	43	26.8	36.0
Cancale	48	40	1	51	5	42	27.5	36.8
Granville	48	50	1	36	5	50	27.4	36.7
Regneville	49	00	1	35	5	57	25.9	34.7
St. Germain	49	14	1	35	6	02	25.1	33.7
Carteret	49	22	1	47	6	07	23.0	30.8
Dielette	49	33	1	52	6	21	20.0	26.8
Chausey Islands	48	52	1	49	5	55	25.9	34.7
Les Minquiers	48	59	2	04	5	46	25.9	34.7
St. Helier, Jersey Island	49	11	2	07	6	09	23.3	31.2
St. Peter Port, Guernsey Island	49	27	2	32	6	12	19.4	26.0
Casquets Islands	49	43	2	23	6	20	11.6	15.5
Alderney, Aldernay Island	49	43	2	12	6	21	12.8	17.2
Omonville	49	43	1	51	7	01	11.4	15.2
Cherbourg	49	30	1	37	7	30	13.2	17.6
Barfleur	49	40	1	16	8	14	12.7	17.0
La Houge	49	34	1	16	8	13	13.8	18.5
Port-en-Bessin	49	21	0	46	8	20	14.9	20.0
Courseulles	49	20	0	27	8	40	15.2	19.8
Oystreham	49	17	0	15	8	53	16.0	20.8
Dives	49	18	0	05	9	01	16.0	20.8
			Long. E.					
Havre, Seine River	49	29	0	06	9	03	17.3	22.5
Honfleur, Seine River	49	25	0	13	9	09	17.5	22.8
Quillebœuf, Seine River	49	28	0	31	9	35	7.2	9.4
Fecamp	49	46	0	22	10	06	17.9	23.3
St. Valery-en-Caux	49	52	0	42	10	29	20.6	26.8
Dieppe	49	56	1	05	10	54	20.9	27.3
Treport	50	04	1	22	11	02	21.7	28.3
St. Valery-sur-Somme	50	11	1	38	11	38	22.0	28.5
Boulogne	50	44	1	35	11	18	19.4	25.2
Cape Griznez	50	52	1	35	11	17	16.6	21.5
Calais	50	58	1	51	11	39	16.2	21.0
Gravelines	51	01	2	06	11	59	14.6	19.0
Dunkirk	51	03	2	21	11	58	12.9	16.8

ATLANTIC COAST OF EUROPE.

THE BRITISH ISLANDS.

Scotland, East Coast.

Place.	Lat. N.		Long. W.		High water interval.		Mean range.	Spring range.
Duncansby Head	58	39	3	03	10	00	7.3	9.8
Wick	58	26	3	05	11	10	7.3	9.9
Dornoch Road	57	51	4	00	11	50	8.0	10.8
Cromarty	57	41	4	02	11	45	10.1	13.7
Inverness, Kessock	57	28	4	14	11	55	10.9	14.0
Banff	57	40	2	31	0	18	7.7	10.3
Peterhead	57	30	1	46	0	24	8.9	11.2
Aberdeen	57	09	2	05	0	50	10.2	12.7
Stonehaven	56	58	2	12	1	00	10.9	13.8
Montrose	56	42	2	26	2	07	10.7	13.6
Arbroath	56	33	2	35	1	25	10.8	13.7
Tay River Bar	56	27	2	38	1	56	12.3	15.5
Dundee, Tay River	56	27	2	58	2	22	11.5	14.5
Fife Ness	56	17	2	35	2	00	11.9	14.9
Burntisland, Firth of Forth	56	03	3	14	2	14	12.9	16.3
Alloa, Firth of Forth	56	07	3	47	3	08	13.7	17.3
Granton	55	59	3	13	2	10	13.1	16.4
Edinburgh (Leith)	55	59	3	10	2	00	12.2	16.0
Dunbar	56	00	2	31	1	53	11.3	14.4
Eyemouth	55	52	2	05	2	05	11.9	14.8

England, East Coast.

Place.	Lat. N.		Long. W.		High water interval.		Mean range.	Spring range.
Berwick	55	46	1	59	2	06	11.6	15.0
Holy Island	55	40	1	47	2	20	11.6	15.0
Alnmouth	55	23	1	37	2	28	11.2	14.5
Blyth	55	07	1	29	3	05	11.6	15.0
North Shields	55	01	1	26	3	11	11.4	14.8
Newcastle, Tyne River	54	58	1	36	3	15	11.4	15.0
Sunderland	54	55	1	21	3	12	11.2	14.5
Seaham	54	50	1	19	3	14	11.2	14.5
West Hartlepool	54	41	1	11	3	19	10.9	14.1
Whitby	54	29	0	37	3	35	11.6	15.0
Scarborough	54	17	0	23	4	01	11.9	15.5
Filey Bay	54	13	0	16	4	10	12.2	15.8

TIDAL DATA.
ATLANTIC COAST OF EUROPE—Continued.

Place.	Lat. N.	Long. W.	High water interval.	Mean range.	Spring range.
	° ′	° ′	h. m.	Feet.	Feet.
THE BRITISH ISLANDS—Continued.					
England, East Coast—Continued.					
Flamborough Head	54 07	0 04	4 20	12.5	15.8
Bridlington	54 05	0 11	4 29	12.5	15.8
Grimsby, Humber River	53 35	0 04	5 26	15.1	19.1
Hull, Humber River	53 45	0 19	5 59	16.3	19.9
Goole, Humber River	53 42	0 52	7 15	10.1	12.8
		Long. E.			
Spurn Point, Humber River	53 35	0 07	5 16	14.6	18.5
Boston Dock	52 58	0 01	6 20	16.4	20.8
Lynn Road	52 52	0 15	5 50	18.3	23.1
Wells Harbor	52 57	0 51	6 50	9.3	11.8
Blakeney Bar	52 59	0 59	6 20	11.7	14.8
Yarmouth Road	52 36	1 45	9 05	4.7	5.8
Lowestoft	52 29	1 46	9 47	5.0	6.2
Orford Ness	52 05	1 35	11 05	6.3	7.8
Harwich	51 57	1 17	11 46	10.6	12.7
Nore (light vessel), Thames River	51 29	0 49	0 20	12.3	15.2
Sheerness, Thames River	51 27	0 45	0 14	13.5	16.9
Chatham, Thames River	51 23	0 32	0 50	14.6	18.0
Gravesend, Thames River	51 27	0 23	0 55	14.7	18.2
Woolwich, Thames River	51 29	0 05	1 15	16.8	20.3
Greenwich, Thames River	51 28	0 00	1 20	17.4	20.4
		Long. W.			
London Docks, Thames River	51 30	0 04	1 26	18.2	20.8
London Bridge, Thames River	51 32	0 05	1 31	18.2	20.8
		Long. E.			
Margate	51 23	1 23	11 35	11.7	15.2
Ramsgate	51 20	1 25	11 30	12.1	15.0
Deal	51 13	1 25	11 05	12.2	15.8
South Coast.					
Dover	51 07	1 19	11 08	15.1	18.2
Folkstone	51 05	1 11	10 57	15.3	19.8
Dungeness	50 54	0 58	10 35	16.6	21.5
Rye Bay	50 56	0 45	11 10	16.8	21.8
Hastings	50 51	0 35	10 43	18.3	23.8
Beachy Head	50 44	0 14	11 10	15.3	19.8
Newhaven	50 47	0 03	11 04	14.5	19.0
		Long. W.			
Brighton	50 49	0 00	11 05	15.0	19.5
Shoreham	50 49	0 14	11 24	13.7	17.8
Littlehampton Bar	50 47	0 32	11 10	12.2	15.8
Selsea Bill	50 43	0 47	11 35	12.5	16.2
*Portsmouth Dockyard	50 48	1 06	11 31	10.2	13.2
*Calshot Castle	50 49	1 18	11 20	10.9	14.1
*Southampton	50 54	1 23	11 40	9.9	12.8
*Cowes, Isle of Wight	50 46	1 17	10 35	9.4	12.2
*Bembridge Point, Isle of Wight	50 41	1 04	11 10	9.8	13.0
*Yarmouth, Isle of Wight	50 42	1 30	11 00	5.2	6.8
*Christchurch	50 43	1 44	10 05	8.6	4.8
*Poole Entrance	50 40	1 57	10 40	3.9	6.3
*Portland Breakwater	50 35	2 25	6 21	4.1	6.4
Bridport	50 42	2 45	5 55	6.9	11.1
Lyme Regis	50 43	2 55	6 10	7.1	11.4
Exmouth	50 37	3 25	6 15	8.1	10.8
Teignmouth	50 33	3 30	5 45	9.6	12.8
Torquay, Torbay	50 25	3 32	5 50	10.0	13.4
Dartmouth	50 21	3 34	6 00	10.6	14.1
Start Point	50 13	3 38	5 25	11.2	14.9
Bolt Head	50 12	3 47	5 30	10.9	14.5
Plymouth Breakwater	50 20	4 09	5 45	11.5	15.3
Devenport Yard	50 23	4 11	5 45	11.6	15.4
East Looe	50 21	4 27	5 10	12.5	16.7
Fowey	50 20	4 38	5 00	11.1	14.8
Mevagissey	50 16	4 57	4 50	11.4	15.2
Truro, town quay	50 16	5 03	4 51	7.5	10.0
Falmouth	50 09	5 03	4 42	11.8	15.8
Helford River Entrance	50 05	5 06	4 30	13.8	17.9
Coverack	50 00	5 09	4 20	14.2	18.3
Lizard Head	49 58	5 12	4 45	14.2	17.0
Penzance	50 07	5 31	4 20	12.1	16.1
St. Agnes Island, Scilly Islands	49 53	6 20	4 15	11.9	15.9
St. Mary Island, Scilly Islands	49 55	6 19	4 12	11.9	16.0
Trescoe Island, Scilly Islands	49 57	6 20	4 07	12.1	16.0
West Coast.					
Cape Cornwall	50 07	5 42	4 15	13.8	17.9
St. Ives	50 12	5 28	4 30	16.0	20.8
Towan or New Quay	50 25	5 05	4 28	16.5	21.4
Padstow Bay	50 34	4 56	4 25	16.9	21.9
Boscastle	50 41	4 42	5 00	17.1	22.0
Budehaven	50 50	4 33	5 30	17.6	22.8
Lundy Island	51 11	4 40	5 00	20.7	26.9
Appledore	51 03	4 12	5 45	17.5	22.7

* A double tide occurs here.

TIDAL DATA.

ATLANTIC COAST OF EUROPE—Continued.

Place.	Lat. N.		Long. W.		High water interval.		Mean range.	Spring range.
	°	′	°	′	h.	m.	Feet.	Feet.
THE BRITISH ISLANDS—Continued.								
West Coast—Continued.								
Bideford	51	02	4	12	5	50	12.3	16.0
Barnstaple, Taw River	51	04	4	03	6	15	8.1	10.5
Ilfracombe, Bristol Channel	51	13	4	07	5	50	20.9	27.1
Lynmouth, Bristol Channel	51	14	3	50	5	50	23.4	30.4
Minehead, Bristol Channel	51	13	3	28	6	10	24.8	32.2
Bridgewater Bar, Bristol Channel	51	14	3	06	6	35	26.9	35.0
Bridgewater, Bristol Channel	51	08	3	00	7	45	13.8	17.9
Flatholm Island, Bristol Channel	51	22	3	07	6	40	29.0	37.6
Avonmouth	51	30	2	43	7	00	33.4	41.7
Bristol, Avon River	51	27	2	35	7	05	26.2	32.8
Chepstow, Severn River	51	39	2	40	7	15	29.1	37.8
Gloucester, Severn River	51	52	2	14	9	30	4.2	5.4
Newport, Severn River	51	34	2	59	7	00	29.0	37.7
Cardiff Bristol Channel	51	28	3	10	6	45	27.9	36.2
Nash Point, Bristol Channel	51	24	3	34	6	10	25.3	32.8
Port Talbot	51	35	3	47	5	50	23.2	29.0
Swansea, Bristol Channel	51	34	3	58	5	45	20.9	27.1
Worms Head, Bristol Channel	51	34	4	20	5	46	19.3	25.0
Carmarthen Bar, Towy River	51	42	4	27	5	30	19.9	25.8
Caldy Island	51	38	4	39	5	22	19.5	25.3
St. Anns Head, Milford Haven	51	41	5	10	5	51	17.3	21.7
Pembroke, Milford Haven	51	42	4	57	6	00	17.4	22.9
Smalls Lighthouse	51	43	5	40	5	45	16.1	20.9
Fishguard, Cardigan Bay	52	00	4	58	6	45	10.4	13.2
Cardigan, Cardigan Bay	52	07	4	42	6	46	9.1	11.8
New Quay, Cardigan Bay	52	13	4	21	7	15	9.9	12.9
Aberystwith, Cardigan Bay	52	24	4	05	7	25	10.9	14.2
Aberdovey, Cardigan Bay	52	32	4	03	7	40	10.9	14.1
Barmouth, Cardigan Bay	52	43	4	03	7	31	10.9	14.2
Pwllheli Bar, Cardigan Bay	52	53	4	22	7	35	11.4	14.8
Bardsey Island	52	46	4	47	7	24	11.5	14.9
Carnarvon, Menai Strait	53	08	4	16	9	15	12.0	15.6
Beaumaris, Menai Strait	53	16	4	05	10	15	17.9	23.2
Holyhead	53	19	4	37	10	00	12.2	15.8
Trwyn-Du Point	53	19	4	02	10	13	17.1	21.9
Air Point, Dee River	53	20	3	19	10	40	19.3	24.8
Chester, Dee River	53	12	2	54	0	00	7.6	9.8
Helbre Island, Mersey River	53	23	3	13	10	37	20.7	26.2
Liverpool, Mersey River	53	25	3	00	10	56	21.3	26.7
Northwest Light Vessel	53	31	3	30	10	50	19.3	25.0
Formby Point	53	34	3	17	10	20	19.6	25.5
Stanner Point, Ribble River	53	44	3	01	10	40	19.6	25.4
Preston, Ribble River	53	45	2	43	11	05	13.0	16.9
Fleetwood, Morecambe Bay	53	57	3	02	11	00	21.1	27.4
Lancaster, Lune River	54	03	2	48	11	05	6.6	8.5
Barrow, Piel Harbor	54	04	3	10	10	55	21.4	27.8
Whitehaven, Solway Firth	54	33	3	36	11	00	19.9	25.9
Workington, Solway Firth	54	39	3	34	10	50	19.8	25.7
Maryport, Solway Firth	54	43	3	30	11	10	19.1	24.8
Silloth, Solway Firth	54	52	3	24	11	25	19.8	25.7
Port Carlisle, Solway Firth	54	57	3	10	0	00	15.3	19.8
Ayre Point	54	25	4	22	10	55	15.2	19.7
Ramsey	54	19	4	22	11	00	15.8	20.5
Douglas	54	09	4	28	11	00	15.8	20.5
Castletown	54	04	4	39	10	58	15.2	19.7
Peel	54	14	4	42	10	56	12.4	16.1
Scotland, West Coast.								
Barnkirk or Annan Foot	54	58	3	16	11	55	23.1	28.5
Dumfries, Nith River, Solway Firth	55	04	3	36	11	50	4.9	6.0
Kirkcudbright	54	50	4	04	11	00	18.6	22.9
Wigton	54	52	4	26	11	20	11.4	14.0
Newton Stewart	54	57	4	30	11	50	9.6	11.8
Port William	54	45	4	35	11	00	14.5	17.9
Mull of Galloway	54	38	4	51	11	05	12.0	14.8
Port Patrick	54	50	5	07	11	00	11.9	14.7
Loch Ryan, Stranraer	55	00	5	03	11	32	7.5	9.5
Lamlash, Firth of Clyde	55	32	5	07	11	35	8.0	9.8
Ayr, Firth of Clyde	55	28	4	39	11	40	7.1	8.7
Ardrossan, Firth of Clyde	55	38	4	50	11	35	8.2	9.8
Greenock, Firth of Clyde	55	57	4	45	11	44	9.1	11.2
Dumbarton, Clyde River	55	56	4	34	0	05	8.2	10.1
Renfrew, Clyde River	55	53	4	23	0	35	8.8	10.8
Glasgow, Clyde River	55	51	4	17	0	55	9.1	11.2
Inverary, Loch Fyne	56	14	5	04	11	50	7.9	9.7
Campbelton	55	25	5	36	11	30	7.0	8.6
Mull of Cantyre	55	18	5	48	10	20	3.2	4.0
Port Ellen, Islay Island	55	37	6	12	4	50	3.9	4.8
Crinan	56	05	5	33	4	35	4.7	5.8
Colonsay Island	56	04	6	10	5	05	8.9	10.9
Oban, Firth of Lorne	56	25	5	28	5	10	10.4	12.8
Tobermory, Isle of Mull	56	37	6	05	5	20	10.5	12.9
Heynish, Tiree Island	56	29	6	54	5	15	9.6	11.8
Loch Moidart	56	47	5	53	5	30	11.0	13.5
Loch Nevis	57	00	5	31	5	35	11.7	14.4
Kyle Rgea, Isle of Skye	57	13	5	39	5	50	12.2	15.0

TIDAL DATA.

ATLANTIC COAST OF EUROPE—Continued.

Place.	Lat. N.		Long. W.		High water interval.		Mean range.	Spring range.
	°	′	°	′	h.	m.	Feet.	Feet.

THE BRITISH ISLANDS—Continued.

Scotland, West Coast—Continued.

Place.	Lat. N.		Long. W.		High water interval.		Mean range.	Spring range.
Kyle Akin, Loch Alsh	57	16	5	42	6	05	12.6	15.5
Portree, Isle of Skye	57	24	6	11	6	10	12.0	14.8
Loch Torridon	57	32	5	32	6	10	12.1	14.9
Loch Ewe, Inverasdale	57	46	5	36	6	20	12.1	14.8
Ullapool, Loch Broom	57	53	5	10	6	27	11.6	14.3
Loch Inver	58	09	5	18	6	30	11.4	14.0
Loch Laxford	58	25	5	07	6	35	10.7	13.5

Scotland, North Coast.

Cape Wrath	58	37	5	00	7	20	12.5	15.4
Loch Eriboll, Rispond	58	34	4	37	7	30	12.0	14.7
Loch Tongue	58	32	4	22	7	40	12.1	14.9
Thurso	58	36	3	33	8	15	11.0	13.5
Stroma Island, south side	58	40	3	08	9	35	7.3	9.0

Ireland, East Coast.

Red Bay Pier	55	04	6	03	10	15	3.2	3.8
Maiden Rocks	54	56	5	44	10	30	5.6	6.7
Belfast	54	36	5	55	10	42	7.9	9.3
Donaghadee	54	38	5	32	11	00	10.1	11.9
Killard Point, Lough Strangford	54	19	5	31	10	40	11.7	13.9
Strangford	54	22	5	33	0	15	8.7	10.4
Newcastle, Dundrum Bay	54	12	5	53	10	50	11.7	14.6
Cranfield Point, Carlingford Lough	54	01	6	03	10	45	12.6	15.8
Victoria Lock, Carlingford Lough	54	08	6	18	11	30	10.5	13.1
Dundalk	54	00	6	24	10	40	11.9	14.9
Drogheda, Boyne River	53	44	6	15	10	45	9.3	11.6
Balbriggan	53	37	6	11	10	25	10.2	12.8
Howth	53	23	6	04	10	55	10.2	12.7
Dublin, Poolbeg Light	53	20	6	09	11	00	10.5	12.8
Kingstown, Dublin Bay	53	18	6	08	10	52	8.8	10.9
Bray Head	53	10	6	04	10	30	9.4	11.8
Wicklow	52	59	6	02	10	15	7.0	8.7
Arklow	52	47	6	08	7	45	3.0	3.8
Wexford	52	20	6	27	7	05	3.9	4.9
Tuskar	52	12	6	12	5	30	7.0	8.8

South Coast.

Carnsore	52	10	6	22	5	45	6.9	8.9
Coninbeg Rock, Saltee Islands	52	07	6	36	5	25	9.9	8.9
Waterford, Duncannon Fort	52	13	6	56	5	05	9.5	12.3
Dungarvan Light, Ballinacourty	52	05	7	36	5	00	9.6	12.4
Youghal	51	57	7	50	4	50	9.7	12.6
Ballycottin	51	50	8	01	4	40	9.1	11.8
Queenstown	51	51	8	17	4	33	9.5	11.9
Kinsale	51	42	8	31	4	30	8.8	11.4
Courtmacsberry	51	38	8	41	4	20	8.2	10.7
Clonakilty Bay	51	35	8	50	4	15	8.4	10.9
Castletownsend	51	32	9	10	4	10	8.2	10.6
Baltimore	51	29	9	23	4	12	7.8	10.1
Cape Clear	51	25	9	31	3	50	6.8	8.8
Crookhaven	51	28	9	43	3	54	7.5	9.7

West Coast.

Dunmanus Harbor	51	32	9	40	3	40	7.0	9.4
Castletown, Bearhaven	51	39	9	54	4	00	7.1	9.6
Valencia Harbor	51	54	10	20	3	30	8.0	10.8
Castlemaine Harbor	52	06	9	55	4	15	10.6	14.3
Dingle	52	07	10	15	3	40	7.9	10.7
Smerwick Harbor	52	12	10	24	3	40	8.4	11.4
Tralee Bay, Fenit	51	18	9	52	3	50	9.1	12.3
Carrigaholt, Shannon River	52	36	9	42	4	30	10.2	13.8
Tarbert, Shannon River	52	35	9	21	4	42	10.6	14.3
Limerick, Shannon River	52	38	8	38	6	00	13.8	18.7
Liscanor Bay	52	56	9	24	4	10	10.1	13.7
Killeany, Arran Islands	53	07	9	39	4	15	9.9	13.4
Galway	53	16	9	03	4	19	10.7	14.7
Kilkieran Cove	53	17	9	41	4	20	11.2	15.1
Slyne Head	53	24	10	14	4	16	9.8	13.2
Inishbofin	53	37	10	15	4	20	9.0	12.1
Clare Island, Clew Bay	53	48	10	00	4	25	9.0	12.2
Westport, Clew Bay	53	48	9	32	4	40	9.4	12.7
Broadhaven Harbor	54	16	9	53	4	50	7.7	10.4
Killala Bay	54	15	9	08	5	10	7.6	10.2
Sligo Harbor, Oyster Island	54	18	8	34	5	10	8.4	11.4
Mullagmore, Sligo Bay	54	28	8	28	5	05	8.3	11.2
Donegal	54	37	8	13	5	05	8.4	11.4
Killybegs	54	38	8	26	5	03	8.3	11.2
Lough Rossmore	54	47	8	30	5	07	8.1	10.9

North Coast.

Ballyness Bar	55	10	8	07	5	10	8.6	11.4
Sheephaven	55	12	7	54	5	20	8.8	11.7
Mulroy Bay Bar	55	14	7	46	5	28	8.7	11.6

TIDAL DATA.
ATLANTIC COAST OF EUROPE—Continued.

Place.	Lat. N.		Long. W.		High water interval.		Mean range.	Spring range.
	°	′	°	′	h.	m.	Feet.	Feet.
THE BRITISH ISLANDS—Continued.								
North Coast—Continued.								
Rathmullan, Lough Swilly	55	05	7	31	5	30	9.3	12.4
Culdaff Bay	55	18	7	00	5	40	6.5	8.7
Moville, Lough Foyle	55	11	7	03	6	55	5.6	7.5
Londonderry, Lough Foyle	54	59	7	19	7	48	6.0	8.0
Coleraine	55	08	6	40	6	12	4.7	6.2
Port Rush	55	12	6	40	5	55	3.8	5.1
Ballycastle Bay	55	12	6	14	6	10	2.1	2.8
Hebrides.								
St. Kilda Island	57	48	8	34	5	25	6.8	10.0
Barra Head, Bernera Island	56	47	7	39	5	35	8.2	11.1
Loch Skiport, S. Uist	57	20	7	12	5	42	9.1	12.3
Loch Boisdale, S. Uist	57	09	7	06	5	35	9.4	12.7
Loch Maddy, N. Uist	57	36	7	06	5	55	9.3	12.5
Monach Island Light	57	31	7	39	5	34	9.0	12.2
East Loch Tarbert, Harris Island	57	51	6	42	5	56	10.0	13.5
West Loch Tarbert, Harris Island	57	55	6	55	5	50	8.7	11.7
Stornoway, Lewis Island	58	12	6	23	6	35	8.9	13.4
East Loch Roag, Lewis Island	58	13	6	45	6	10	8.9	11.8
Orkney Islands.								
Stromness, Mainland, or Pomona Island	58	57	3	18	8	45	7.3	9.9
Kirkwall, Mainland, or Pomona Island	58	59	2	58	9	05	6.0	8.5
Otterswick, Sanday Island	59	17	2	30	9	00	8.1	11.0
Shetland Islands.								
Scaddon, Fair Isle	59	33	1	38	10	50	3.7	5.0
Sumburgh Head, Mainland Island	59	51	1	17	9	35	3.8	5.2
Lerwick, Mainland Island	60	09	1	08	10	55	4.1	5.7
Balta, Unst Island	60	45	0	47	10	00	4.7	6.4
FAROE ISLANDS.								
Fugloe Fiord	62	19	6	18	11	05	4.8	6.5
Lervig Fiord	62	13	6	42	0	20	4.7	6.4
Myggenaes Fiord	62	06	7	30	8	50	6.8	9.3
Vaag Fiord	61	28	6	48	6	10	2.9	4.0
BELGIUM.			Long. E.					
Nieuport	51	10	2	44	0	05	12.3	15.7
Ostende	51	14	2	55	0	07	12.6	16.1
Blankenberghe	51	18	3	07	0	05	10.2	12.9
Antwerp, Scheldt River	51	14	4	25	3	35	13.5	14.8
Liefkenshoek, Scheldt River	51	18	4	17	3	15	12.7	16.3
NETHERLANDS.								
Vlissingen or Flushing, Schelde River	51	26	3	34	0	57	12.5	14.8
Terneuse or Neuzen, Schelde River	51	21	3	50	1	25	13.3	15.5
Hansweert, Schelde River	51	26	4	00	2	14	14.1	16.1
Wemeldinge	51	31	3	59	2	43	11.0	12.4
Zierikzee	51	38	3	54	2	19	9.5	10.8
Brouwershaven	51	44	3	56	1	58	8.1	9.2
*Hellevoetsluis	51	49	4	08	2	43	6.1	6.8
Willemstad	51	42	4	26	3	40	7.0	7.7
Dordrecht, Oude-Maas River	51	48	4	40	5	04	5.8	6.2
Gorinchem or Gorkum, Rhine River	51	50	5	00	5	49	3.1	3.4
Rotterdam, Nieuwe-Maas River	51	55	4	29	3	59	5.0	5.4
*Hoek van Holland	51	59	4	08	2	00	5.5	6.2
Ymuiden	52	28	4	34	2	51	5.5	6.4
*Helder	52	58	4	46	5	28	3.8	4.3
Vlieland	53	18	4	04	8	29	5.4	6.2
Harlingen, Zuider Zee	53	11	5	25	9	07	4.2	4.8
Durgerdam, Zuider Zee	52	23	4	59	0	37	1.1	1.2
West Terschelling Light	53	21	5	13	8	30	4.6	5.2
Ameland Island Light	53	27	5	37	9	10	4.8	5.4
Schiermonnikoog Island Light	53	29	6	09	9	30	4.4	5.0
Delfzyl, Ems River	53	20	6	56	11	19	9.4	10.7
GERMANY.								
North Sea.								
Borkum	53	36	6	39	11	02	8.0	8.8
Knock	53	20	7	03	12	13	8.8	9.8
Emden	53	22	7	13	0	16	9.8	10.8
Oldersum	53	20	7	21	0	56	8.8	9.8
Leer	53	12	7	25	1	35	8.5	9.5
Juist	53	41	7	00	11	09	7.5	8.5
Norddeich	53	37	7	10	11	37	7.4	8.2
Nordeney	53	43	7	10	11	56	7.5	8.7
Baltrum	53	44	7	22	11	44	7.7	8.5
Westeraccumersiel	53	40	7	30	12	03	7.0	7.9

* A double tide occurs here.

101890°—36——27

149

TIDAL DATA.

ATLANTIC COAST OF EUROPE—Continued.

Place.	Lat. N.	Long. E.	High water interval.	Mean range.	Spring range.
	° ′	° ′	h. m.	Feet.	Feet.
GERMANY—Continued.					
North Sea—Continued.					
Langeoog	53 44	7 28	11 48	8.0	8.8
Neuharlingersiel	53 42	7 42	12 07	6.5	7.2
Spiekeroog	53 46	7 40	11 44	8.4	9.2
Wangeroog west	53 46	7 51	11 48	8.7	9.8
Heligoland Island	54 11	7 52	11 48	7.2	8.5
Wangeroog east	53 48	8 00	12 04	9.3	10.5
Schillighorn	53 43	8 02	0 03	9.8	11.1
Hooksiel	53 38	8 03	0 20	10.2	11.5
Genius Bank	53 36	8 09	0 34	10.5	11.8
Wilhelmshaven	53 31	8 09	0 53	11.6	13.0
Schweiburger tief	53 27	8 13	1 00	12.0	13.4
Roter Sand Light	53 51	8 05	12 07	8.8	10.2
Hoheweg Light	53 43	8 15	0 18	10.0	11.1
Bremerhaven	53 33	8 34	1 10	10.7	11.9
Nordenham	53 29	8 29	1 20	10.6	12.1
Sanstedt	53 22	8 31	1 51	10.3	11.6
Braake	53 20	8 29	2 08	10.0	11.1
Elsfleth	53 14	8 28	2 31	9.0	9.5
Farge	53 12	8 31	2 50	7.5	8.3
Vegesack	53 10	8 38	3 28	6.5	7.1
Oslebhausen	53 07	8 43	3 47	5.4	6.0
Bremen	53 05	8 48	3 58	4.5	5.0
Scharhorn	53 58	8 26	12 20	9.2	10.5
Cuxhaven	53 54	8 40	0 49	9.0	10.4
Brunsbuttel	53 53	9 05	2 02	8.7	10.0
Gluckstadt	53 47	9 24	2 47	9.2	10.5
Brunshausen	53 38	9 31	3 42	8.3	9.4
Luhe	53 29	9 37	3 58	8.3	9.5
Schulau	53 34	9 42	4 11	7.8	8.8
Blankenese	53 34	9 49	4 26	7.8	8.8
Hamburg	53 33	9 58	5 14	6.6	7.1
Meldorf	54 05	9 00	1 33	9.0	10.2
Busum	54 08	8 51	0 44	9.8	11.1
Blauort Sand	54 11	8 40	0 40	9.8	11.1
Vollerwick	54 17	8 47	0 51	9.5	10.8
Tonning	54 19	8 57	1 23	8.4	9.7
Sudfall	54 28	8 43	1 21	9.7	10.8
Nordstrand	54 28	8 55	1 51	9.8	11.1
Husum	54 29	9 04	2 04	9.9	11.7
Pellworm	54 31	8 42	1 51	9.7	10.8
Hooge, Suder Aue	54 35	8 33	1 31	8.7	9.8
Wyk, Norder Aue	54 41	8 35	1 51	8.8	9.2
Dagebull, Norder Aue	54 43	8 41	2 05	8.7	9.8
Kniephafen	54 40	8 18	0 31	7.2	8.2
Hornum Odde	54 45	8 18	1 07	7.2	8.5
Munkmarsch	54 55	8 22	2 26	5.4	6.2
Hoyer	54 58	8 41	2 34	6.5	7.5
Rom I, South Point	55 05	8 34	2 11	5.6	6.5
East List Road Light	55 03	8 27	1 55	5.4	6.2
DENMARK.					
North Sea.					
Sonderho, Fano Island	55 25	8 28	1 40	3.6	4.5
Nordby	55 27	8 25	2 34	3.8	4.7
Hjerting	55 31	8 21	2 00	3.6	4.5
Blaavand Point	55 33	8 05	1 00	4.0	5.0
Horn Reefs	55 33	7 33	11 50	3.8	4.8
Nymindegab	55 48	8 11	2 35	1.7	2.1
Thybo Ron	56 43	8 14	4 00	1.4	1.8
Hirtshals	57 35	9 57	4 18	1.0	1.2
Skagen or the Skaw	57 44	10 38	5 46	0.8	1.0
Copenhagen, Baltic Sea	55 42	12 36	9 33	0.5	0.6
NORWAY.					
Frederickstad	59 12	10 57	5 02	1.5	1.8
Oscarsborg	59 40	10 37	5 09	1.1	1.3
Christiania	59 55	10 44	5 26	1.0	1.2
Frederiksvaern	59 01	10 05	4 34	1.1	1.3
Oster-Risoer	58 43	9 15	4 08	1.0	1.2
Arendal	58 28	8 46	4 08	0.8	1.0
Christiansand	58 08	8 00	4 16	0.8	1.1
Tananger	58 55	5 34	9 36	1.2	1.6
Stavanger	58 59	5 44	9 33	1.4	1.9
Skudesnaes	59 08	5 18	10 13	1.6	2.1
Bergen	60 24	5 18	10 17	3.2	4.1
Romsdals Islands	62 45	6 00	10 35	4.3	5.7
Christiansund	63 08	8 00	11 00	4.6	6.0
Trondhjem or Munkholm	63 27	10 24	11 12	6.4	8.4
Traen Islands	66 31	12 02	11 35	5.2	6.9
Vaero, Lofoten Islands	67 38	12 37	11 50	6.7	8.8
Andenaes, Lofoten Islands	69 12	16 11	0 42	5.6	7.0
Tromsoe	69 40	19 00	1 35	6.2	7.8
Hammerfest	70 40	23 40	2 20	6.6	8.3
Vardo	70 20	31 06	5 41	7.2	9.0

TIDAL DATA.

ATLANTIC COAST OF EUROPE—Continued.

Place.	Lat. N.	Long. E.	High water interval.	Mean range.	Spring range.
	° ′	° ′	h. m.	Feet.	Feet.
RUSSIA					
Petshenga Bay	69 41	31 25	6 00	5.8	7.3
Kola Road	68 53	33 00	7 04	5.4	6.7
Teriberskoi Bay	69 16	35 08	7 10	10.1	12.6
Sem or Seven Islands	68 49	37 21	8 10	9.2	11.5
Sviatoi Nos	68 10	39 48	9 15	11.1	13.9
Cape Orlov	67 11	41 25	10 38	15.6	19.5
Morjovets Island	66 46	42 30	11 10	13.5	16.8
Mezen, Mezen River	65 47	44 20	1 58	14.4	18.0
Sosnovetz Island	66 29	40 43	11 34	14.2	17.7
Tetrina	66 04	38 21	3 07	5.2	6.5
Kandalaksha	67 08	32 26	3 00	5.0	6.2
Jiginsk Island	65 12	36 49	5 05	3.0	3.8
Onega	63 56	38 00	9 02	7.3	9.1
Karetski Nos	65 38	39 40	4 20	4.2	5.3
Archangel, Dwina River	64 32	40 33	7 18	1.8	2.2
Cape Kanin	68 39	43 30	10 20	5.6	7.0
Bolvanskaya Bay	68 20	55 00	6 45	2.4	3.0
Khabarova, Yugorski Strait	69 39	60 26	5 30	2.3	2.9
Gulf of Ob, Cape Yamsale	66 55	71 40	0 50	1.6	2.0
Golchikka, Yenisei River	71 43	83 45	11 45	1.2	1.5
Port Dickson	73 32	80 50	1 50	1.1	1.4
NOVA ZEMBLA					
Cape Menshikova	70 43	57 43	4 18	1.8	2.2
Matochkin Shar	73 18	53 57	9 15	2.8	3.5
FRANZ JOSEPH LAND					
Cape Flora	79 57	49 59	9 44	1.0	1.2
Teplitz Bay	81 47	57 59	6 14	1.1	1.5
SPITZBERGEN					
Danes Island	79 41	11 02	0 14	4.2	5.3
Recherche Bay	77 30	14 44	0 56	5.3	6.6
JAN MAYEN ISLAND		Long. W.			
Mary Muss Bay	71 00	8 28	11 21	2.9	3.7
ICELAND					
Reykjavik	64 08	21 50	5 14	10.0	13.0
Akreyri, Eyia Fiord	65 40	18 00	5 19	4.2	5.4
ATLANTIC OCEAN ISLANDS					
Azores					
Horta Bay, Fayal Island	38 32	28 38	11 30	2.9	3.9
Angra Bay, Terceira Island	38 38	27 14	0 20	3.3	4.4
Arnel Point, San Miguel Island	37 49	25 08	0 15	4.3	5.7
Madeira Islands					
Funchal Bay, Madeira Island	32 28	16 55	0 35	5.0	6.6
Porto Santo Bay	33 05	16 22	0 40	5.0	6.6
Canary Islands					
Santa Cruz, Palma Island	28 40	17 45	0 20	6.5	8.6
Santa Cruz, Teneriffe Island	28 28	16 15	1 15	5.9	7.8
Puerto de la Luz, Gran Canaria Island	28 09	15 25	0 40	7.0	9.3
Port Naos, Lanzarote Island	28 57	13 33	0 50	6.4	8.5
Cape Verde Islands					
Porto Praya, St. Jago Island	14 53	23 31	5 50	3.6	4.8
Do Sino Point, Sal Island	16 34	22 56	7 30	3.3	4.4
Porto Grande, St. Vincent Island	16 53	25 00	5 50	2.5	3.3
Detached Islands	Lat. S.				
Ascension Island	7 55	14 25	5 20	1.5	2.0
St. Helena Island	15 54	5 44	3 00	2.1	2.8
Tristan da Cunha Island	37 10	12 15	11 50	3.9	5.2

Table 9.5

Schedule of new and full moons, 1981–2003

1981	New	Full	1982	New	Full
Jan.	6	20	Jan.	25	9
Feb.	4	18	Feb.	23	8
Mar.	6	20	Mar.	25	9
Apr.	4	19	Apr.	23	8
May	4	19	May	23	8
June	2	17	June	21	6
July	1, 31	17	July	20	6
Aug.	29	15	Aug.	19	4
Sept.	28	14	Sept.	17	3
Oct.	27	13	Oct.	17	3
Nov.	26	11	Nov.	15	1
Dec.	26	11	Dec.	15	1, 30

1983	New	Full	1984	New	Full	1985	New	Full
Jan.	14	28	Jan.	3	18	Jan.	21	7
Feb.	13	27	Feb.	1	17	Feb.	19	5
Mar.	14	28	Mar.	2	17	Mar.	21	7
Apr.	13	27	Apr.	1	15	Apr.	20	5
May	12	26	May	1, 30	15	May	19	4
June	11	25	June	29	13	June	18	3
July	10	24	July	28	13	July	17	2, 31
Aug.	8	23	Aug.	26	11	Aug.	16	30
Sept.	7	22	Sept.	25	10	Sept.	14	29
Oct.	6	21	Oct.	24	9	Oct.	14	28
Nov.	4	20	Nov.	22	8	Nov.	12	27
Dec.	4	20	Dec.	22	8	Dec.	12	27

1986	New	Full	1987	New	Full	1988	New	Full
Jan.	10	26	Jan.	29	15	Jan.	19	4
Feb.	9	24	Feb.	28	13	Feb.	17	2
Mar.	10	26	Mar.	29	15	Mar.	18	3
Apr.	9	24	Apr.	28	14	Apr.	16	2
May	8	23	May	27	13	May	15	1, 31
June	7	22	June	26	11	June	14	29
July	7	21	July	25	11	July	13	29
Aug.	5	19	Aug.	24	9	Aug.	12	27
Sept.	4	18	Sept.	23	7	Sept.	11	25
Oct.	3	17	Oct.	22	7	Oct.	10	25
Nov.	2	16	Nov.	21	5	Nov.	9	23
Dec.	1, 31	16	Dec.	20	5	Dec.	9	23

1989	New	Full	1990	New	Full	1991	New	Full
Jan.	7	21	Jan.	26	11	Jan.	15	30
Feb.	6	20	Feb.	25	9	Feb.	14	28
Mar.	7	22	Mar.	26	11	Mar.	16	30
Apr.	6	21	Apr.	25	10	Apr.	14	28
May	5	20	May	24	9	May	14	28
June	3	19	June	22	8	June	12	27
July	3	18	July	22	8	July	11	26
Aug.	1, 31	17	Aug.	20	6	Aug.	10	25
Sept.	29	15	Sept.	19	5	Sept.	8	23
Oct.	29	14	Oct.	18	4	Oct.	7	23
Nov.	28	13	Nov.	17	2	Nov.	6	21
Dec.	28	12	Dec.	17	2, 31	Dec.	6	21

1992	New	Full	1993	New	Full	1994	New	Full
Jan.	4	19	Jan.	22	8	Jan.	11	27
Feb.	3	18	Feb.	21	6	Feb.	10	26
Mar.	4	18	Mar.	23	8	Mar.	12	27
Apr.	3	17	Apr.	21	6	Apr.	11	25
May	2	16	May	21	6	May	10	25
June	1, 30	15	June	20	4	June	9	23
July	29	14	July	19	3	July	8	22
Aug.	28	13	Aug.	17	2	Aug.	7	21
Sept.	26	12	Sept.	16	1, 30	Sept.	5	19
Oct.	25	11	Oct.	15	30	Oct.	5	19
Nov.	24	10	Nov.	13	29	Nov.	3	18
Dec.	24	9	Dec.	13	28	Dec.	2	18

1995	New	Full	1996	New	Full	1997	New	Full
Jan.	1, 30	16	Jan.	20	5	Jan.	9	23
Feb.	—	15	Feb.	18	4	Feb.	7	22
Mar.	1, 31	17	Mar.	19	5	Mar.	9	24
Apr.	29	15	Apr.	17	4	Apr.	7	22
May	29	14	May	17	3	May	6	22
June	28	13	June	16	1	June	5	20
July	27	12	July	15	1, 30	July	4	20
Aug.	26	10	Aug.	14	28	Aug.	3	18
Sept.	24	9	Sept.	12	27	Sept.	1	16
Oct.	24	8	Oct.	12	26	Oct.	1, 31	16
Nov.	22	7	Nov.	11	25	Nov.	30	14
Dec.	22	7	Dec.	10	24	Dec.	29	14

1998	New	Full	1999	New	Full	2000	New	Full
Jan.	28	12	Jan.	17	2, 31	Jan.	6	21
Feb.	26	11	Feb.	16	—	Feb.	5	19
Mar.	28	13	Mar.	17	2, 31	Mar.	6	20
Apr.	26	11	Apr.	16	30	Apr.	4	18
May	25	11	May	15	30	May	4	18
June	24	10	June	13	28	June	2	16
July	23	9	July	13	28	July	1, 31	16
Aug.	22	8	Aug.	11	26	Aug.	29	15
Sept.	20	6	Sept.	9	25	Sept.	27	13
Oct.	20	5	Oct.	9	24	Oct.	27	13
Nov.	19	4	Nov.	8	23	Nov.	25	11
Dec.	18	3	Dec.	7	22	Dec.	25	11

2001	New	Full	2002	New	Full	2003	New	Full
Jan.	24	9	Jan.	13	28	Jan.	2	18
Feb.	23	8	Feb.	12	27	Feb.	1	16
Mar.	25	9	Mar.	14	28	Mar.	3	18
Apr.	23	8	Apr.	12	27	Apr.	1	16
May	23	7	May	12	26	May	1, 31	16
June	21	6	June	10	24	June	29	14
July	20	5	July	10	24	July	29	13
Aug.	19	4	Aug.	8	22	Aug.	27	12
Sept.	17	2	Sept.	7	21	Sept.	26	10
Oct.	16	2	Oct.	6	21	Oct.	25	10
Nov.	15	1, 30	Nov.	4	20	Nov.	23	9
Dec.	14	30	Dec.	4	19	Dec.	23	8

Currents

In addition to knowing the time of high and low tide it is useful to know what the associated current is doing. There is an annual government publication which gives these predictions, but I have rarely used it. I prefer to keep in mind some simple rules-of-thumb and to rely on direct observation of the current. After all, the tables are based on averages of readings taken over a period of years and so many things affect the current on any particular day that the tables provide really more of a guide than an answer.

The first thing to keep in mind about tide is that it is a vertical motion of the water. The moon "lifts" the water rather than moving it sideways. At sea, therefore, there is very little tidal current. Near shore, however, this lifting of the waters translates into a lateral motion as the water moves in to fill areas that are lower lying. Generally the greater the range of the tide, the stronger the current—i.e., the higher the water is lifted, the faster it tends to flow onto the lower-lying shore. If you are out cruising and want to gauge the speed of the current, the simplest thing is to look at the flow past a buoy or pot marker. After you have done this a few times, you will be able to judge the velocity of the current very well and, more importantly, you will be able to gauge its effect on you by your motion (or lack of it) relative to the buoy.

If you are preparing to set out and would like to know about when to expect the maximum and/or minimum current, there is a very simple one-two-three rule, which you can use: the tide rises (and the current flows) in semidiurnal areas one-twelfth full height, and speed of current, the first hour; two-twelfths the second hour; three-twelfths the third hour; etc. Diagrammed, it looks like this:

Hour	1	2	3	4	5	6
Tide and Current	$\frac{1}{12}$	$\frac{2}{12}$	$\frac{3}{12}$	$\frac{3}{12}$	$\frac{2}{12}$	$\frac{1}{12}$

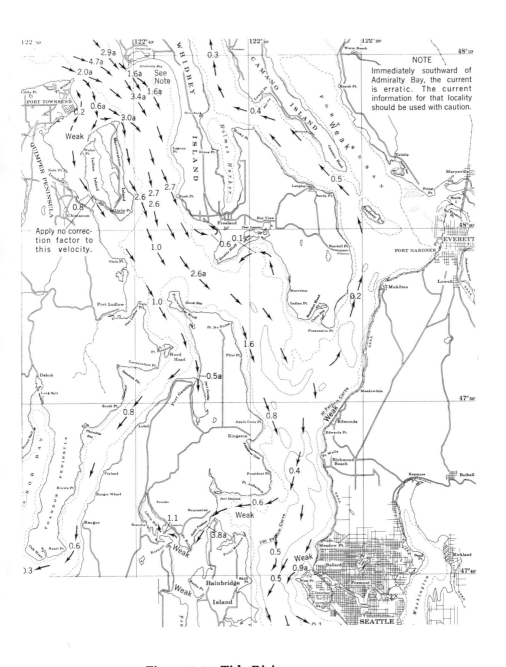

Figure 9.1 Tide Rising
Maximum flood currents in the vicinity of Seattle, Washington.
The velocities shown are for times of new and full moon. The
cautionary note in upper left is ample reminder that tide and current data are *predictions*.

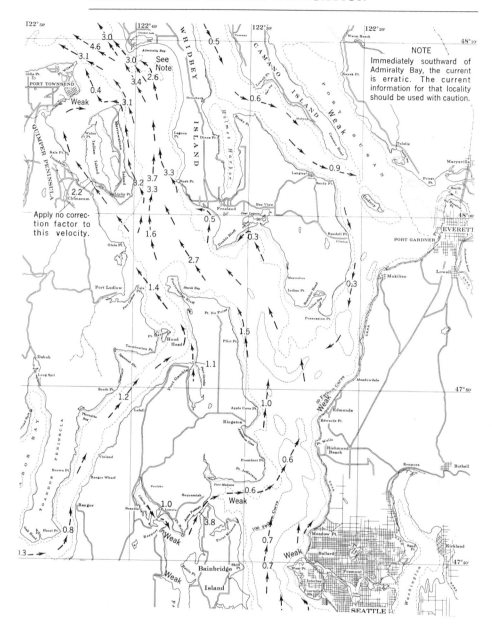

Figure 9.2   **Tide Falling**
Maximum ebb currents near Seattle, Washington.

Generally the greatest rise of tide and the strongest current occur during the third and fourth hours of the six-hour cycle.

Now we all know that it is desirable to have a following current and a nuisance to have the current against us. Navigationally, current ahead or behind causes few problems. It doesn't affect our course; it just speeds us up or slows us down. There are times, though, when you have to sail across the current; and since in this situation the current affects the course, you have to compensate so that you make good the desired course. The boat must be given a heading at which the combined motion of the boat moving forward and the current carrying it sideways causes the boat to make good the desired compass course over the bottom.

For any given current speed and boat speed it is possible to figure out mathematically or geometrically the proper number of degrees to point the boat into the current. The problem is that the speed of the current is probably not known to us within 20 percent or so and, if tidal, is changing with time anyway. If the boat is a sailboat, its speed is probably varying also.

This situation often occurs in racing: you round a mark and are going to be heading across the current to the next mark. The skipper asks the navigator for the course to steer for the next mark and the navigator has to come up with a number.

What I do in this situation is to look at the mark we are rounding and guess at the current speed as revealed by the flow past the buoy. Then I look at the knotmeter and make a fraction of current speed/boat speed and multiply 60° by this fraction to come up with the number of degrees needed to correct for the current. If the current is abeam, or nearly so, I apply this number of degrees to the course; if the current is on the bow or quarter, I reduce the number by one-third and apply that. To illustrate: the boat is going six knots and I judge the current to be one knot directly across the desired course:

$$\frac{\text{current speed}}{\text{boat speed}} = \frac{1}{6} \times \frac{60°}{1} = 10°$$

Head the boat 10° into the current. This would mean adding 10° to the compass course if the current was coming from the right (starboard) and subtracting 10° if the current was coming from the left (port).

You can "fine tune" this by looking back at the turning-mark and either watching the shore behind the buoy or taking bearings on the buoy. If the buoy appears to be moving against the background, you are not fully compensating for the current; adjust the heading until the buoy appears to remain stationary (and bears a reciprocal of the course you wish to make good). To check the course or if there is not land behind the buoy to serve as a reference, make several checks with the handbearing compass to see whether the bearing is steady on the reciprocal of the course (course plus 180°).

If the leg between the turning buoy and the next mark is a long one, you are going to lose sight of the turning buoy before you can see the next mark, so you will have to figure out to which side of the course the current and heading are going to have put you when you reach the mark. This will depend upon whether the current is increasing or decreasing as you continue to sail on the heading established at the turn. Here, the one-two-three rule can help. Say the tide is in its second hour and coming from the left as you turned the mark. It is eighteen miles to the next buoy; that means it is going to take you three hours to reach it. In the next three hours the tide will go through the period of maximum flow and then start to slow down. If you continue to hold your heading, the net effect will be that you will most probably end up to the right of the mark. Knowing this, you can swing left at the proper time and use, say, a depthfinder to sail along the contour line on which the buoy is located, since they are generally located on specific depth curves (figure 9.3). Alternatively, you might determine from the

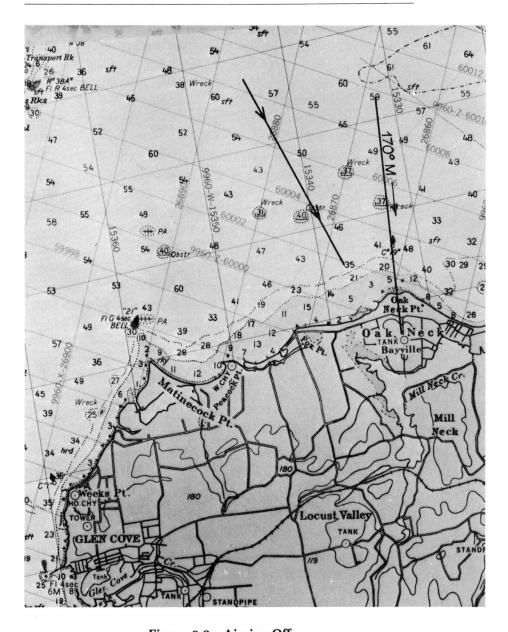

Figure 9.3 **Aiming Off**
Plan to strike five-fathom curve to right of buoy (can "19"). Turn left and follow depth to buoy. Alternatively pick up watertank on Oak Neck and run in on bearing through mark (can "19").

chart that the buoy lies on a specific bearing from a shore object which might be visible before the buoy, sail to that bearing and then along it to the mark (figure 9.3).

The above is an instance of the piloting technique known as *aiming off*. Since it is difficult to set a course that will surely bring you to the mark, you can overcorrect to one side or another to make sure you know which side of the mark you will be at by the end of the run. That way you know which way to turn to find it and can then use other means as aids. Of course in a sailboat you would want to arrange to be to the windward side of the mark so that you would bear off to run down on it and not have to beat to windward. In the example this might mean that you would head the boat another 10° into the current to compensate for the fact that it is increasing during your run; in this way you would make sure of ending up to the left of the mark.

PART II

NAVIGATING
AT NIGHT

10

Sailing at Night— Running Lights

O ver the years I have formed the impression that the reasons so few yachtsmen go boating at night are (1) they think that they will not be able to see anything, and (2) they feel that their judgment of distances will be impaired because it is difficult to tell whether any given light is a bright one at a distance or a dim one close by. This second consideration is far more valid than the first. You can, in fact, see quite well at night in all but the most overcast conditions.

After about an hour out on the water at night the pupils of your eyes open sufficiently to see remarkably well. Except in fog or storm there is a surprising amount of light in the night sky. Also, starlight and reflected light from the binnacle and running lights will enable you to move around the boat with confidence and to handle sheets, halyards, and other gear without needing a flashlight. If you acquire the ability to go out in your boat at night, you will not only add a new dimension to your boating, you will greatly expand your cruising range since with one other person aboard who can manage the boat at night, you can make passages to more distant cruising grounds. Too, the water world at night can be a magic place of moonlight, gem-hung bridges, and cities and towns like stretches of fire on the shore, not to mention the red, white, and green of lighted buoys, beacons, and lighthouses.

If you don't have any romance in you, you probably wouldn't be messing around with boats, so what I suggest you do as a first step toward acquiring the confidence to go boating at night is go aboard your boat some evening and just sit there until your eyes are fully dark adapted. Notice how much you can, in fact, see and become familiar with the look of your harbor at night. Next take your boat out some clear moonlit night and just putter around in the immediate vicinity of your harbor. Do this a few times until you get the hang of how your port looks at night and can relate what is shown on the chart to the lights around you. After a while you will get to know all the winking lights in your immediate area and can begin to extend your range. The trick is to begin gradually so that you don't get overwhelmed. Generally in United States coastal waters there are so many lighted aids to navigation winking and flashing around you that there is a real danger of getting confused. Slow and easy is the best way to get into night sailing.

One of the most important new things you must learn in order to sail safely at night is to identify other vessels by their running lights, tell at once in what direction they are moving, whether or not they are approaching, and who has the right-of-way. The basic principle underlying the system of red, green, and white lights carried by your boat and every other vessel is that the other guy carries your traffic signal. The lights are arranged on your boat and the other guy's boat in accordance with this principle. Thus, in an overtaking or crossing situation at night, the first thing you do is check to see that *your* lights are working.

As a way of becoming familiar with running lights in general, start with those on your own boat. Some evening take the dinghy out to your boat and snap on the switches marked *navigation lights* if you own a power boat or *navigation lights* and *bow light* (sometimes marked *masthead* on newer boats) if you own a sailboat. These are the lights required from sunset to sunrise when operating under power.

Row away from your boat about a hundred feet and, starting from directly ahead, row slowly around your boat. From dead ahead you will see a green light on your left, a red light on your right, and a white light between and some distance above them. This, then, is what you would see at night if a power boat were heading directly at you.

Row around to your right. Once you are off the direct line to your boat you will no longer be able to see the green light. You will see only the red light and the white light. This is what you would see if a boat under power were coming at you from the right. If it were a daylight crossing situation, he would have the right-of-way. At night in accordance with the basic principle you see the nautical equivalent of a stop light to remind you that you are the burdened vessel and must keep clear.

Keep rowing in your one hundred-foot circle. As you row, you will notice that you will continue to see the red light and the white light until you are well abaft the beam of your boat. Then these two will blot out and you will pick up the white light in the stern. The situation at this point is that the boat is ahead of you. At night on the water, therefore, if you saw a steady white light only, you must assume that you may be overtaking another vessel. As in daytime, the overtaking boat must keep clear.

As you row across the stern of your boat and start up the other side, you will see only the white stern light until you are about two points (22½°) abaft the beam on the starboard side, at which point you will pick up the green light and the white bow light and lose the stern light. At night on the water this is what you would see if a power boat were coming across your course from the left. His green light indicates you have the right of way and, if you think about it a bit, you will see that in this situation he would be seeing your red light.

If your boat is a sailboat and you want to see what a sailboat looks like at night, turn off the bow light. That's the difference; a sailboat does not show the white bow light unless she's under power.

This white light is also sometimes confused with the anchor light, so to help you identify it on your auxiliary sailboat, remember it is the light about fifteen feet up on the forward side of the mast, not the light that may be at the very top of the mast. That's the anchor light.

Figure 10.1 shows an overhead view of the lights on a typical power or auxiliary sail yacht.

The rule that the other guy carries your traffic light is not always true for sailboats under sail at night. Consideration of figures 10.2–10.9 in which the crossing of two sailboats is shown as the wind shifts progressively clockwise, will indicate the conditions in which the burdened vessel sees a green light and the right-of-way boat a red light. When under sail at night, you use your knowledge of the wind direction to figure out the other fellow's point of sail (tack). The prescribed arcs through which the lights are supposed to show are given in degrees, but it must be pointed out that there is most always some overlap (which you no doubt noticed on your row around your boat). Presently new rules are being implemented which will add new lights to the pattern to positively distinguish a stern light and to cut down on overlapping of the arcs.

As you know, I feel it is good sense to stay away from commercial vessels. To do this at night you need know only one additional thing. Vessels up through 150 feet in overall length are lighted like power boats—that is, they have red and green side lights, a bow light, and a stern light. They

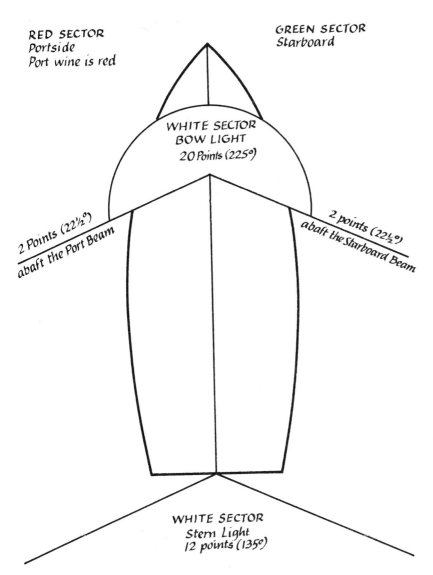

WHITE BOW LIGHT
Now officially called masthead lite
Overlaps red and green sectors

RED SECTOR
Portside
Port wine is red

GREEN SECTOR
Starboard

WHITE SECTOR
BOW LIGHT
20 Points (225°)

2 Points (22½°)
abaft the Port Beam

2 points (22½°)
abaft the Starboard Beam

WHITE SECTOR
Stern Light
12 points (135°)

Figure 10.1 Location of lights on a typical power or auxiliary sail yacht.

may, however, carry an additional white light, called a *range light*, aft of and higher than the bow light. Vessels over 150 feet must carry the range light. This light has the same arc as the bow light and its purpose is to provide a range to enable another vessel to judge relative angles more easily. Seen from directly ahead, a vessel with a range light would show red and green; between them in a vertical line, the white bow light; and above the bow light, the white range light. Seen from the side, there would be the low bow light and aft, the higher range light and either the red or green side light. The fact that the range light is higher than the bow light makes it easy to figure out which way the vessel is headed. The main point is if you see a pattern of lights like this, it is most likely a commercial vessel whose maneuverability is a great deal less than yours, so in a crossing situation give them the benefit of any doubt.

In most coastal waters tug boats are a common sight either towing or pushing empty or loaded barges. At night these tugs will display from two to three masthead lights, depending upon whether they are towing or pushing and how long the tow is. It seems to me that the best rule of thumb is to give these vessels extra room and to look carefully for the barges, which will carry red and green side lights like all other vessels underway after sunset.

Now, of course, there are other types of commercial craft. If you normally sail in an area where fishing is carried on at night or where dredging is usually being done, you will see these vessels around during the day and should take that as your cue to inquire about their nighttime light signals. Similarly, if you sail in the area of a naval base, you should find out the special lights used by minesweepers when they are streaming paravanes and you should know that a submarine shows a yellow light that gives either ninety flashes per minute, or one flash per second for three seconds followed by three seconds of darkness.

Basically at night on the water you are going to see

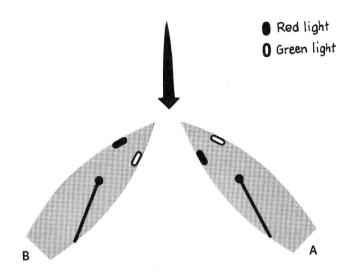

Red light

Green light

Figure 10.2

A—Starboard tack, close hauled
B—Port tack, close hauled

Starboard tack will always be to right of port and lights show correctly. Burdened boat B sees red light and privileged vessel sees green.

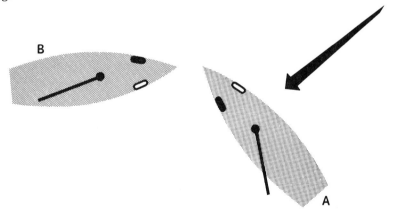

Figure 10.3

A—Starboard tack, beam reach
B—Port tack, close hauled

Lights show correctly. Burdened B sees red of right-of-way boat A. A sees B's green running light.

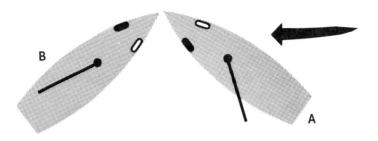

Figure 10.4

A—Starboard tack, broad reach
B—Starboard tack, close hauled

Lights reversed, Here A is burdened because he is sailing freer than B (i.e. is defined as being more manuverable). But A sees the green light of the right-of-way vessel B.

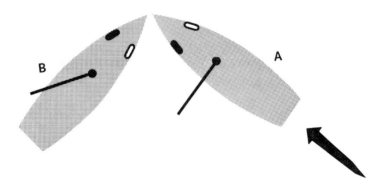

Figure 10.5

A—Starboard tack, running free
B—Starboard tack, beam reach

Essentially the same situation as 10.4. A is still sailing freer than B and the light colors are still the reverse of convention. A could push her main boom to starboard and resolve the ambiguity since she would then be on port tack. Tack is officially termed from the side opposite that on which the main boom is carried.

170

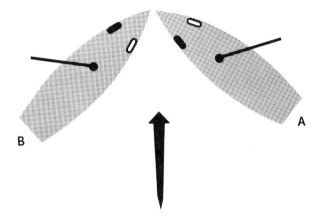

Figure 10.6

A—Port tack, broad reach
B—Starboard tack, broad reach

Light convention still reversed. Right-of-way (privileged) B sees red light and burdened A sees green.

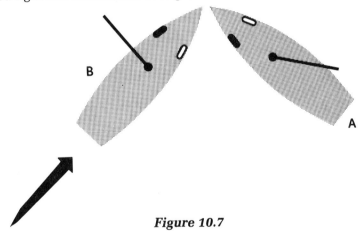

Figure 10.7

A—Port tack, beam reach
B—Starboard tack, running free

Here B has given herself right of way by opting to carry boom on port side. Light signals are still reversed. If B were to jibe boom to starboard side, she would become burdened vessel because she'd be on a freer point of sail with the same tack as A and light signals would conform to basic convention.

171

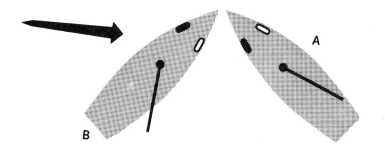

Figure 10.8

A—Port tack, close hauled
B—Port tack, broad reach

B is burdened and the light pattern is conventional.

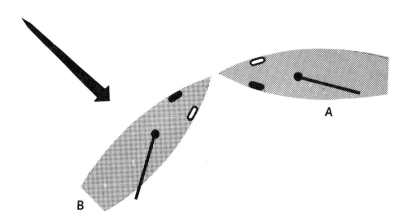

Figure 10.9

A—Starboard tack, close hauled
B—Port tack, beam reach

B is burdened and the light pattern conforms to the basic convention.

mostly commercial vessels and if my experience is any guide, not very many of those. Even when cruising most yachtsmen anchor by sunset and commercial traffic drops off. This is one of the reasons that boating at night can be so enjoyable. You have a cool, beautiful world practically to yourself.

CHAPTER

11

Lights

One way to get an idea of the system of lights used in coastal waters is to imagine that you are making a landfall at night after an offshore passage and are going to proceed from landfall into your usual harbor.

As you approach the shore but are still out of sight of land the first lights you might see would be on either a lightship or lighttower stationed out in deep water. These days they often show a bright xenon flash which looks like lightning when seen from over the horizon. The color of the light and what it does is given on the chart with very straightforward abbreviations:

F	Fixed light
Occ	Occulting light
Fl	Flashing light
Iso E Int	Isophase light (equal interval)
Qk Fl	Quick-flashing (scintillating) light

Int Qk Fl I Qk Fl	Interrupted quick-flashing light
S Fl	Short flashing light
Alt	Alternating light
Gp Occ	Group occulting light
Gp Fl	Group flashing light
S-L Fl	Short-long flashing light
Gp S Fl	Groups short flashing light
F Fl	Fixed and flashing light
F Gp FL	Fixed and group flashing light
Mo	Morse code light
Rot	Revolving or rotating light

These lights are set up to flash at certain intervals and the patterns are generally arranged so that lights in the same area do not have the same pattern. There are many patterns, but the main ones are *fixed* (abbreviated F), which means a steady light; *flashing* (Fl), which indicates a light pattern where the period of dark following the flash is longer than the flash; *occulting* (occ), which is the opposite—more light than dark; and *quick flashing,* which is a continuous series of fast blips tumbling on the heels of one another. The basic pattern of flashes are most often varied by the interval between flashes, such as one flash every four seconds, ten seconds, etc. They can also be grouped, such as three flashes every six seconds (abbreviated on the chart as *Gp Fl 6 sec*), etc. All of these can occur on lighthouses and buoys, as well as towers and ships, although the lights on ships and towers are generally white, while buoys and lighthouses can show colors. For timing lights it is a good idea to have a stopwatch, since the intervals are often quite short (four to ten seconds) and difficult to count accurately.

Anyway, to continue our hypothetical inbound trip, the next light you are likely to pick up is one on a lighthouse situated on the shore. Then there usually will be a lighted buoy at the start of the channel and lights every so often along the channel, frequently at the turns in the channel. A look at the chart will indicate these along with their colors and characteristics of their pattern of flashes. The main thing to remember is that the overall system marks important points, such as the entrances to major harbors, with large, high-powered lights visible for great distances. The power of the lights steadily diminishes depending upon the size of the harbor and the amount and type of traffic using the harbor. Thus New York and San Francisco are marked by lights visible from far at sea and the channel looks like a freeway, whereas my home port (Larchmont, New York), which has no commercial traffic, is marked by a single flashing white light visible for about three miles on a clear night.

About the only other basic thing you need to know about the lights on the smaller structures, such as buoys, is that red lights are only on red buoys and green lights are only on black buoys. White lights can appear on either and are normally used for lights at the entrances to harbors, because, for the same wattage, white is visible at a greater distance. The way to get started with lights on buoys, etc., is to take chart in hand and get to know the ones in your harbor and the ones you will see on an average evening's sail. In order not to destroy your night vision, you should look at the chart under a very dim white light by, for example, holding your fingers over the flashlight. Some people advocate using only red light, but this washes out any red on the chart, so a dim white light is more practical on balance for chart work. Anyway, once you know the lighted buoys well you can really thrill your non-night-sailing friends by taking them out for a view of their hometown they have never imagined.

12

Passagemaking at Night

I suggested earlier that one of the reasons to sail at night is that you can extend your cruising range. This, of course, requires that there be at least one other person on board who can manage the boat so that you can take it in shifts and each one can rest. Like anything else, night passagemaking is best learned in gradual steps. Make your first ventures short and to harbors with which you are familiar and keep in mind that it is much easier to make the passage between ports after sunset than it is to enter an unfamiliar harbor at night.

With the coming of night a very important element of daytime crosschecking is lost—the ready perception of depth that we have in daylight. At night it is hard to tell whether you are a few hundred feet, a few hundred yards, or even a mile from something. What this means is that the DR is of even greater importance at night than during the day. Also, it is important to check the DR with more fre-

quent fixes than you might during the day. In taking bearings, take several and average them.

Before going into the various ways of checking the DR
at night, I want to make a point of the importance of *preplanning* in making a night passage. Before you start get out
the chart, lay out the course on it, and with the starting time
and probable speed in mind write down on a piece of paper
the times at which you should see the *major* lights along
your route and make a note of their color and flash patterns.

The range at which major lights are visible is given
with the rest of the data on the chart as a number followed
by a capital M for miles. Prior to 1973 this range was figured
for an observer whose eye was fifteen feet above the water
and therefore needs to be reduced somewhat for small
boats. A useful rule of thumb is to take the visibility range
of the light given on the chart, subtract four miles and then
add, in miles, the square root of your height above the
water. On an average boat between, say, twenty-six and
forty feet this would net out to a reduction in the visible
range of the light of about one mile. The reason for this is
that the distance a light is visible (assuming it is powerful
enough) is, roughly, the straight-line distance from it to the
horizon, plus the straight-line distance from you to the
horizon. This distance is approximately the square root of
the sum of the respective heights of the light and your eye
above the water. You should also know that the range of
any given light shown on the chart is for clear weather and
you should not expect to see it at that distance if the atmosphere is hazy or worse.

Many foreign charts still use the above method, but on
United States charts published after June, 1973, the power
of the light itself is taken into account and the charts give
the actual distance that the light will penetrate clear air.
Thus, the range at which you can see a light will be either
the sum of the two straight-line distances to the horizon or

the range shown on the chart, whichever is the least.

If your course happens to pass close to any lighted buoys, make a note of the approximate time you should see them and on which side of the boat, since these will be a very good check on the DR.

You should also note the approximate times when major lights will be at appropriate bearings to give fixes to check the track of the vessel.

As the skipper of a boat navigating at night or in fog, it is important to keep in mind the need to anticipate the times in the passage when you must be on deck so that you will be able to rest during those times when the running of the boat can be left to the crew. This, of course, depends upon the composition and competence of your crew. If there is no one who can manage the straightforward routine of keeping the boat on course and maintaining a good lookout, your ability to make passages at night is going to be determined solely by your endurance. But if you do have one person who can at least steer and stay alert, you can get some rest and conserve your energies for the times when you have to take command. These times are usually at the end of the trip when you enter the harbor or when you have to get by some potential hazard, such as a narrow strait, a point of land, or a shoal.

Before you leave the deck to rest you should leave with the man on deck the list of times at which the various checkpoints should be spotted, with the instructions to call you if they are not seen at the expected times and at the expected bearings. Depending upon the abilities of the person left on deck, you should also issue instructions to rouse you should a vessel be seen, should the wind or speed change, and whatever else is appropriate to the situation.

On ships the above procedure is formalized and written out in what is called the *Night Order Book* and, if the number of things that would require a call amounts to more than three, it might be a good idea for you to write them out for the reference of the person left in charge of the boat while you rest.

Having said this much about preplanning and watch-keeping, let's go on to methods of checking the DR during a night passage.

13

Distance Off
at Night

At night you will normally pick up what is called the *loom* of a large light before you can see the actual flash of the light itself. At the moment when you see the light itself, you can figure your distance away from it as being roughly equal to the visible range given on the chart. As I mentioned in the previous chapter, however, the range on United States charts published after June, 1973, is the actual distance that the particular wattage of the light will penetrate clear atmosphere.

The range at which you will actually see a light is calculated by taking the square root of its height and adding the square root of the observer's height of eye plus 14 percent. Thus, for a 60-foot light, the square root of 60 plus 14 percent is 8.9. In the average cruising boat your height of eye will be between 6 and 12 feet. The square root for this range of numbers is about 3; so for you, a 60-foot-high light in clear weather would be visible at about 12 miles, that is $8.9 + 3 = 11.9$.

If the chart showed this light on, say, *60 ft 20 M,* you would still not pick it up until you were about 12 miles off, because at any greater distance than 12 miles, the curvature of the earth (horizon) would be between you and the light.

Likewise, if the chart showed the light as *60 ft 7 M* you would not see it sooner than 7 miles off because the bulb in the tower would not have the power to penetrate any farther into average clear weather.

If, when you first see the light, you also take a bearing on it, you can get a check on your position. If you can also get a depth sounding, this will add confirmation to the check, and you will have a rough fix.

Another way to get a rough fix from one light is to take two bearings at an interval of about two miles run along your track. Plot the two bearings and then see where in the V formed by the two bearings your distance run fits (figure 13.1).

As I mentioned in the chapter called "The Magic Number—Sixty", if you want to pass a certain distance away from the light, you divide sixty by your distance away from the light when you first pick it up dead ahead, then multiply the result by the number of miles off you want to be. The result is the degrees to change course.

Another way is to use the method of bow and beam bearings to determine how far you are away from a given light when you have it abeam.

If you want to know how far off you will be by the time you have a light abeam, take two bearings at a reasonable interval (at least ten minutes, preferably more, if you have time) and use table 13.1. Go to table 13.1 with the difference between the course and the first and second bearings. Your distance from the light at the time of the second bearing is your distance run multiplied by the number in the first column. The distance you will be off the mark when you have it abeam is found by multiplying the distance run between the two bearings by the number in the second column.

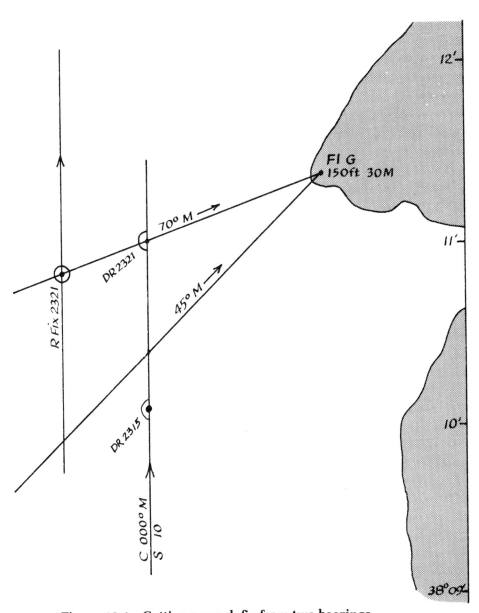

Figure 13.1 Getting a rough fix from two bearings
Boat is bound north in an area of zero variation, going 10 knots.
At 2315 hours, navigator gets bearing on lighthouse on point and
plots point where DR and bearing meet. Six minutes later—i.e.,
after running one mile—navigator takes another bearing and finds
point where one-mile distance fits between V of bearings on line
parallel to course. This point is called a running fix. From this
point the track is marked and a new DR begun.

Example: you are sailing east at six knots and spot your next checkpoint. Your course is 90° and it bears 130°. Twenty minutes later it bears 150°. The difference between first bearing and course is 40°; between second bearing and course is 60°. At six knots you have gone two miles in twenty minutes. From the table, your distance off at the time of the second bearing is 2 × 1.9, or a little under four miles. When the light is abeam, it will be 2 × 1.6, or a little over three miles away on your starboard side.

Difference between the course & second bearing	Difference between the course & first bearing												
	20°		30°		40°		50°		60°		70°		80°
	A	B	A	B	A	B	A	B	A	B	A	B	A	B
30°	2.0	1.0	—	—	—	—	—	—	—	—	—	—	—	—
40°	1.0	.6	2.9	1.9	—	—	—	—	—	—	—	—	—	—
50°	.7	.5	1.5	1.1	3.7	2.8	—	—	—	—	—	—	—	—
60°	.5	.5	1.0	.9	1.9	1.6	4.4	3.8	—	—	—	—	—	—
70°	.5	.4	.8	.7	1.3	1.2	2.2	2.1	5.0	4.7	—	—	—	—
80°	.4	.4	.7	.6	1.0	1.0	1.5	1.5	2.5	2.5	5.4	5.3	—	—
90°	.4	.4	.6	.6	.8	.8	1.2	1.2	1.7	1.7	2.8	2.8	5.7	5.7

Table 13.1   **Distance Off by Two Bearings**
Distance off at second bearing = distance run *times* A
Distance off when abeam = distance run *times* B

Most harbors in populated areas have a lighted buoy at the entrance to the harbor, so if you get within three miles of the harbor, you will normally pick up this buoy, although you may have to look carefully to spot it against the clutter of lights ashore. In some places, however, the first buoy marking the channel is an unlighted can or nun. There are two basic techniques to use to find an unlighted mark and both involve aiming off.

Set your course so that you will come into the area of the mark definitely to one side or the other. Prior to starting, pick out a light on shore or somewhere around the buoy and

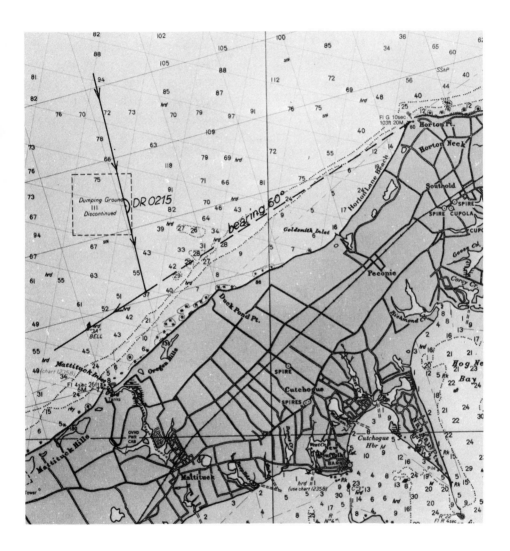

Figure 13.2 Aim off to come in to left of buoy and turn right when on the bearing from Bell "3A" to major green light on Horton Point.

draw a bearing line from it through the buoy. When you come onto the bearing, turn either left or right and run down to the buoy (figure 13.2).

If there is no light you can use, run to the depth contour on which the buoy is located, turn onto it and sound your way to the mark.

As a closing comment I would like to mention that you will often notice as you are coming in at a lighted buoy that the light will seem to vary in intensity. This is due to the fact that the lights have Fresnel lenses which aim the light in a narrow, horizontal beam and, as the buoy rocks, you are not always in the direct path of the beam. So if you have identified the light by its characteristics and it squares with your DR, carry on.

14

A Note about Safety at Night

Over the years a few people have been lost when they went overboard at night. Usually these incidents occurred in strong winds and rough water. Even in fairly calm conditions, it is difficult to see a person in the water at night. Every boat on the water at night should be equipped with a horseshoe life ring or a man-overboard pole with an attached xenon flasher and a drogue to prevent the wind from blowing it away. It should be ready for instant use.

When sailing with people who are not sailors, I have found that it is best not to let them move around on the boat. Keep them in the cockpit; let them steer a little. Don't take novices out at night if it is rough.

If you happen to be alone at the helm at night, don't go out on deck by yourself. When something needs doing, get someone up to do it or to keep watch while you do. If it's at all rough, have the person going onto the deck wear a safety harness and see that he clips it to something *inboard* and *solid*, *not* to the lifelines. Remember, we're boating for fun, not to prove we're hot-shot daredevils or stuntmen.

15

DR Navigation—Night

Let's say it is summer and you are on your way south. The weather reports are good and you decide to leave Ocean City, New Jersey, for Norfolk, Virginia, where you will pick up the Intracoastal Waterway.

The first thing is to calculate the ranges of the lights for your height of eye at the steering position in your boat. Let's say this is 10 feet. The square root of $10 = 3.16$, and multiplying by 1.14 gives the distance for you to the horizon as 3.6 nautical miles. This is the number you add to the range calculated from the heights of the lights.

Example: The *Gp Fl (2) 5 sec 154 ft* light at Assateague Island. Square root of $154 = 12.41$. Multiplied by 1.14, this is 14.14 nautical miles for light to horizon. Plus 3.6 for your height of eye $= 17.7$ nautical miles. This is the range at which you will see it. Even though the light has the power to penetrate 22 nautical miles of clear air, it can't penetrate the curvature of the earth.

Similar figuring gives the following ranges:

Ocean City	9.6 nautical miles
Hog Island	8 nautical miles
Smith Island	18.9 nautical miles
Chesapeake Light Tower	15.9 nautical miles

Note that by calculation from the height of the tower, the Hog Island light is theoretically visible at 9.8 miles. Since the light is not that powerful, though, the 8 miles stated on the chart is the range to use.

The proposed course line is now marked on the chart and the visible ranges of the lights swung with a compass. With the time of departure and planned speed mark off the expected DR positions for every hour and make up a table showing the time of appearance and disappearance of each light and its bearing.

Date	Time	Light	Appears	Bearing	Disappears	Bearing
7/22	2000	E Int 6 sec	X	—	—	—
"	2100	"	—	—	X	10°
"	2120	Gp Fl (2) 5 sec	X	235°	—	—
"	2140	Fl Bell	X	Abeam Port of Course		
"	2220	Fl Bell	X	Ahead on Course		
"	2300	Fl Whistle	X	Abeam Starboard of Course		
7/23	0030	Gp Fl (2) 5 sec	—	—	X	000° (N)
"	0320	Fl 5 sec	X	265°	—	—
"	0340	Gp Fl (2) 5 sec	X	220° (Dead Ahead)	—	

Since you expect to see the three major lights—Assateague, Smith, and Chesapeake—at distances of about 15 miles, a discrepancy in the bearing of 10° (by rule of sixty) would mean a distance off course of about 3 miles. Therefore, you should leave word to be called in the event of such

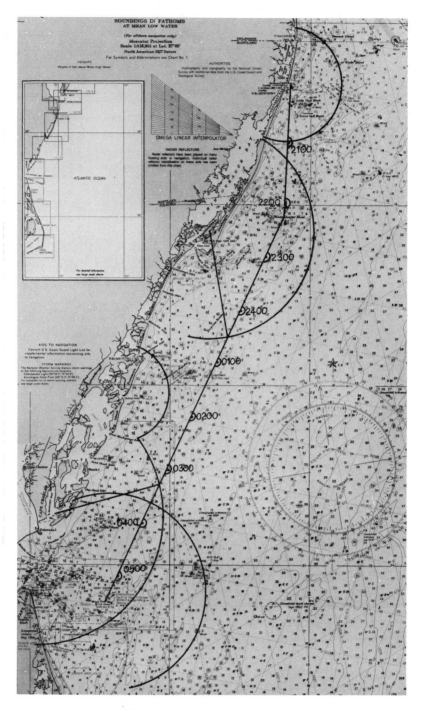

Figure 15.1 Expected lights.

an occurance. At ten knots you cover one mile in 6 minutes, so you should also ask to be told if lights are not spotted within 20 minutes of expected times. Since there is a three-hour stretch between the arcs of Assateague and Smith lights, this might be a good time for you to take the watch to ensure careful steering. Your warning signal that you are to the right of your planned course is the four-second flasher on Hog Island.

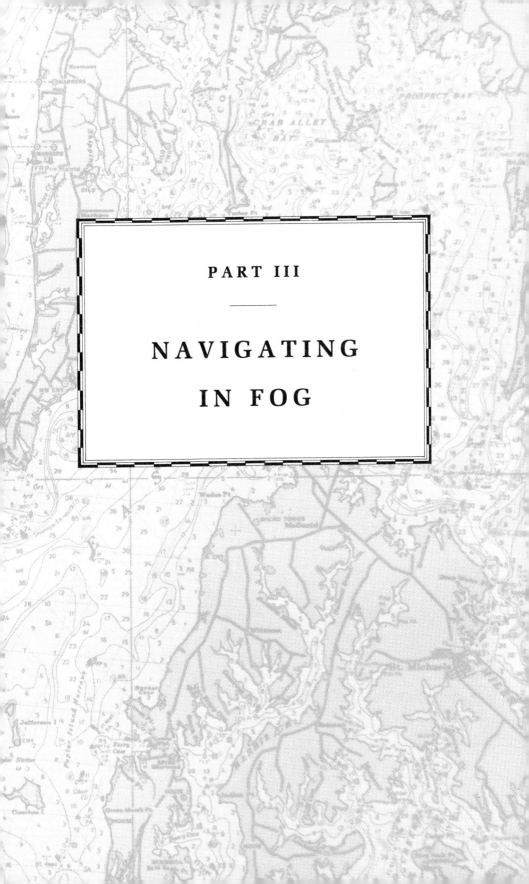

PART III

———

NAVIGATING

IN FOG

16

The Depthfinder

In several places earlier in this book I have mentioned the use of the depthfinder as an aid to navigation. In fog the depthfinder comes into its own.

Before the advent of the electronic depthfinder sailing ship skippers used to heave-to periodically in fog to sound the bottom with a lead weight attached to a line marked in fathoms. This lead had a cup-shaped hollow on its bottom surface and tallow was put into this hollow. That way when it hit the bottom, bits of sand or mud would adhere to the tallow and when the lead was raised, the skipper knew not only the depth of water, but also the character of the bottom.

The charts of those days would give the color of the mud or the type of sand or pebbles in the bottom and with this information and his DR, the skipper of a ship could make his way slowly into harbor.

Unless you are an experienced navigator fog is to be avoided like the plague—when possible. However, with as little equipment as a reliable compass, an electronic depth-

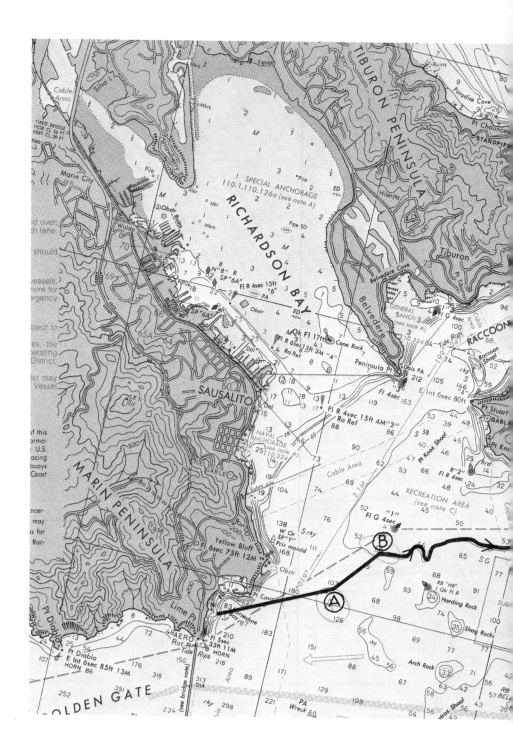

196

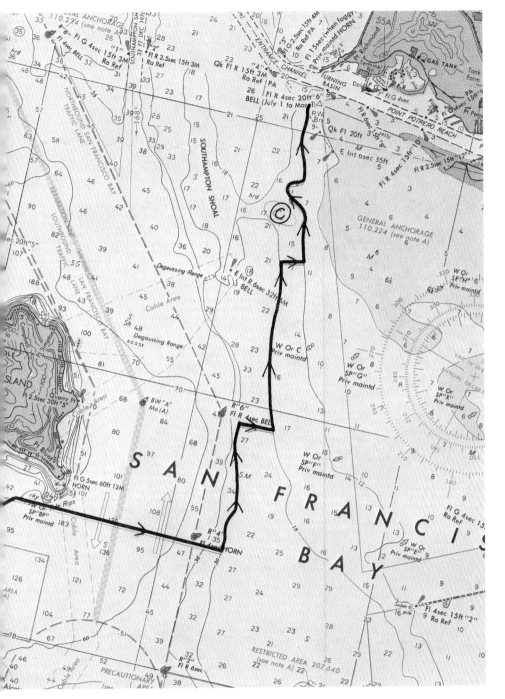

Figure 16.1 Contour line navigation.

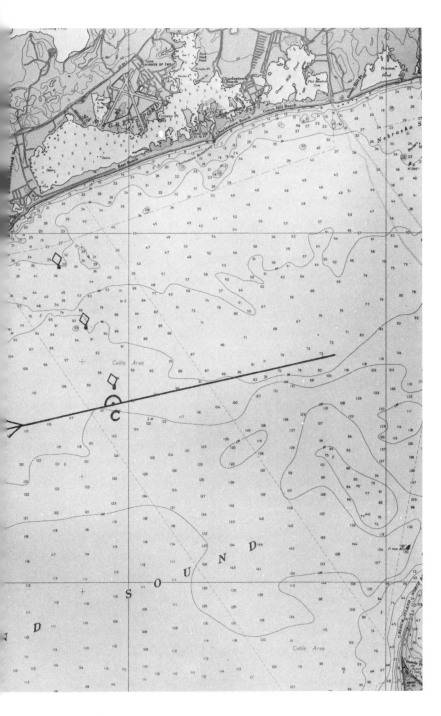

Figure 16.2 Running checks with depthfinder.

finder, or a hand lead, navigating in a fog can be accomplished safely. With an electronic depthfinder you will be able to move faster than if you only have a hand lead, but either will do.

There are two basic techniques of navigating by depthfinder: *contour line* and *running checks*. Examples are probably the most efficient way to describe these techniques. Look at figure 16.1.

Suppose you had set out from Horseshoe Bay in San Francisco to go to Richmond Yacht Harbor and the fog rolled in when you were at point A. You would aim to strike the ten-fathom (sixty-foot) curve (marked by a solid line on the chart) at B; follow the contour line northeast until you pick up the horn on Pt. Blunt; cross the ship channel as fast as possible, allowing for current; and aim for buoy # 4, which has a horn. Pick up the five-fathom (thirty-foot) curve and follow it north until you hear the bell on red buoy # 6. Now cross to the three-fathom (eighteen-foot) curve and your next check would be the bell on the tower (E Int R 6 sec 32ft 6M) on your left. At this point, you could go on north and cross the slight bar at C, then pick up the three-fathom curve again and follow it until the depthfinder indicated you were in the entrance channel or you could cross to the two-fathom (twelve-foot) curve and follow it to the channel.

Before going on, a few notes about handling the boat in fog. First, go slow. Second, if possible, have a man at the bow as lookout and give him the horn so that he can sound the correct signal (discussed in the next chapter).

Now for the other method: *running checks*. This method requires a more continuous monitoring of the chart, since it is basically a method of confirming the DR track at short intervals. Here is an example, figure 16.2.

Suppose your last checkpoint was at the whistle buoy at A. The fog rolls over you at B and several hours later when your DR has you at C, you pick up a white and orange buoy on your left but are not able to get its letter. On the chart these are shown as private buoys and there are three of them in a row out from shore. By the DR the buoy should have been the third one. The depthfinder checks out pretty well with this, reading 114 feet. You continue to watch the depthfinder and when you have run about one-quarter mile it reads 95 feet, then shoals to 90 feet in the next mile. It is very obvious that you are running along on course and you can continue to monitor the chart and depthfinder and coordinate with the DR to keep yourself on the desired course.

If you do your boating in an area where fog can be expected, try these techniques in fair weather. Have a crew member sit below, call out the depthfinder readings to him, and let him navigate while you check visually. It's an interesting game and a confidence builder.

CHAPTER

17

Fog Signals

The rules of the road still apply in fog and so before the advent of radar a system of sound signals was devised to let one boat know what another was doing. Although fog can sometimes do funny things to sounds, it is normally possible to determine the direction from which the signal is coming and so take appropriate action, depending upon which vessel is privileged and which burdened. In this signal system, a prolonged blast means a blast of four to six seconds. The signals are:

> A motor vessel under way: at intervals of no more than two minutes, prolonged blast.

> A motor vessel under way, but stopped and having no way upon her: two prolonged blasts with about two seconds between them.

> A sailing vessel under way: at intervals of not

more than one minute, one long blast followed
by two short blasts.

A vessel at anchor rings a bell rapidly for about
five seconds at intervals of not more than a minute.

A motor vessel towing: every minute a prolonged
blast followed by two short blasts (a vessel being
towed may also use this signal).

Fishing vessels when trawling: same as a sailing
vessel underway or a motor vessel towing.

Since most commercial vessels now have radar, it is a
good idea for yachts to deploy a radar reflector. Sailboats
should not rely on radar picking up an aluminum mast and
no yachtsman should rely on being picked up by radar
alone; sound your proper signal and keep your speed mod-
erate.

The fundamental rule in fog is that before you make a
maneuver, be sure where the other fellow is. If in doubt,
slow down or stop. Collision in fog is avoided by *stopping*,
not by *dodging*.

There are also sound signals on buoys and lighthouses
to help you find your way when you are unable to identify
them visually. These sound signals come in a great variety
and are marked on the chart alongside the symbol for the
buoy or lighthouse. Most are unambiguous, but you might
not know the difference between a gong and a bell unless it
was pointed out: *a bell sounds one tone, a gong more than
one.* To me a gong sounds like a fight in a scrap yard. A bell
sounds like a bell. Take note of these differences whenever
you pass by a buoy during the day in clear weather.

18

—————

The Radio
Direction Finder
(RDF)

Fog navigation is where the many electronic aids come into their own, and something like an automatic Loran C, which can produce continuous fixes, is a great comfort to navigators when used properly—i.e., as another check on the DR in addition to checks with the depthfinder, the skipper's bunions, or whatever. Omega, Loran C, Omni, and automatic direction finders are all very expensive, however, and really outside the scope of this book, which has sought to keep things simple and cheap. Suffice it to say that although these more sophisticated electronic aids are often miraculous, they are far from infallible and should never be relied upon alone. A continuous DR track is essential under all circumstances.

A small, relatively inexpensive RDF can be a useful tool in fog. If you were standing in sight of the transmission tower of a radio station and had a transistor radio in your hand tuned to the station, you would notice that the music would be loudest when the back or front of the radio faced the tower and least audible when the edge of the radio was aimed at the tower. If there were a shielded compass attached to the top of the radio, you could read the bearing to the station when the radio is rotated so that the sound was loudest or least. Such an RDF bearing provides one line of position on the chart, just as though the fog-bound radio tower were a lighthouse.

Several types of RDF sets are exactly like this—a radio with a compass on top. You aim the radio and sweep it about until you pick up the signal. Then you find the bearing at which the sound is least (you try for the least because this is easier to discern). Other RDF sets have a rotating antenna on top of the set with a movable compass rose underneath. You set the rose to agree with your course and then rotate the antenna until you have the area of least sound (called the *null*) and note the bearing.

You may have noticed that I said the *area* of the null and not the point. The reason is that most RDFs are not good enough to let you distinguish the null to better than five degrees or so (some manufacturers claim better) unless you are very close to the transmitter. So, the way to use an RDF is to find the null area and take the bearing as the point halfway between the edges, or take five or more bearings and average them.

RDF stations are identified on the chart by "R Bn" for radio beacon and the frequency and signal transmitted are shown. Usually this is a Morse code signal repeated for fifty seconds followed by a ten-second continuous signal.

Most people learn to use an RDF quickly and the only thing that seems to trouble anyone at first is getting used to the sound of Morse code. Although the code signal might be written · — · — — ·, etc., it sounds like di dah, di dah dah, dit.

The techniques applicable to the use of a handbearing compass can be used with an RDF: bearing checked by depthfinder, two bearings at intervals, etc., although it must

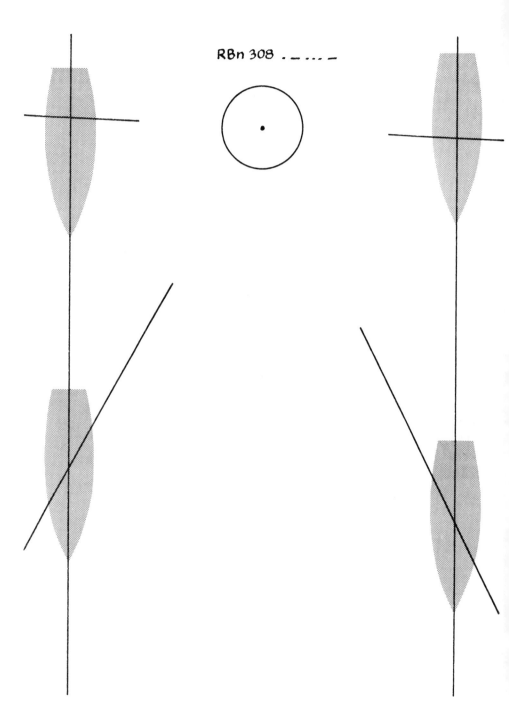

RBn 308 . _ ... _

Figure 18.1 Resolving 180° ambiguity.

be remembered that the accuracy of RDF bearings is not as great as that of visual bearings.

If you keep a DR, you should not run into the problem of 180° ambiguity—i.e., not know on which side of you an RDF beacon lies. Should this happen, however, the thing to do is alter course so that you have the bearing abeam. Continue this new course and pretty soon the bearings will begin coming over the after quarter on which the beacon lies (figure 18.1). Put another way, whatever side draws the bearing aft is the side toward the beacon.

Once again, practicing this stuff during clear weather is the way to learn it.

Postscript

It boils down to this: the navigator's job consists of two parts—(1) keeping the DR and (2) checking up on the DR.

A little further thought indicates that much of what are commonly considered to be "navigation" devices and methods properly belong to the second category, because the DR requires only methods or devices that give course and speed. In the context of Western civilization, this generally means chart, magnetic compass, and knotmeter. Radar, Loran, sextant, bearings, etc., belong to the other half of navigation.

As you practice navigation, think and read about it. It may help to keep things straight if you have an outline something like the following in your head:

A. Keeping the DR
   —Methods and instruments for determining direction
   —Methods and instruments for determining speed

B. Checking the DR
   —Seaman's eye
   —Bearings
   —Depthfinder
   —Radio Direction Finder
   —Celestial LOP's
   —Loran
   —Radar
   —Omega
   —Omni
   —Satellites

Fair weather navigation of small craft often entails little more than keeping the DR and verifying it by simply looking around to determine one's position relative to obvious landmarks and making small adjustments as appropriate. Restricted visibility reduces the ease with which the DR can be verified and it is in these conditions that special equipment can be very helpful. Never forget, though, that its function is to aid you in checking the DR, not to be a sole means of navigation. A navigator always proceeds in this order: plot the DR, check the DR, make sure any differences make sense.

Bibliography

American Practical Navigator (NVPUB9), two volumes, Defense Mapping Agency Hydrographic Center, Washington, D.C., 1977. Begun in 1802 by Nathaniel Bowditch, a Salem, Massachusettts, shipmaster, the copyright was purchased by the United States Navy in 1868. Now written in a style that can charitably be described as opaque, it is a fine example of what happens to a good thing once it gets out of the hands of an individual and into the hands of a committee. Nonetheless, it is a gold mine. Just be prepared to dig.

Dutton's Navigation & Piloting, edited by Elbert S. Maloney, Naval Institute Press, Annapolis, Maryland, 1978. This is the text for the United States Naval Academy. The language and illustrations are generally clearer than Bowditch, but it is not the delightful treasure trove of tables, methods, history, and odd bits of lore.

Index